CORTE SUPREMA

SPANISH-
ENGLISH

DICTIONARY
OF
LAW
AND
BUSINESS

THOMAS L. WEST III

J.D., UNIVERSITY OF VIRGINIA SCHOOL OF LAW

Para Jennifer
Amor de mi vida

Spanish - English Dictonary of Law and Business
Thomas L. West III.
1999
Published by Protea Publishing
ISBN 1-883707-37-4

to order:

kaolink@msn.com email
(404) 814 0220
(404) 84 20798 fax
(888) 287 9212 toll free in US

creditcards accepted worldwide:
VISA, MASTERCARD, AMERICAN EXPRESS, DISCOVER

Protea Publishing
2855 Piedmont Road NE
Atlanta
Georgia 30305-2767
USA

PREFACE

This new dictionary is different from the other Spanish legal dictionaries on the market[1] in three significant ways. First, it contains a wealth of terms that are not to be found in any of them. These terms include standard ones that are used throughout the Spanish-speaking world (e.g. *caución de no ofender*), Latin words and phrases[2] that commonly appear in Spanish-language court opinions and legal briefs (e.g. *in dubio pro reo*), abbreviations common in legal and commercial documents (see Appendix 1), and most importantly, standard legal terminology that is unique to a certain Spanish-speaking country. Indeed, my primary goal in writing this dictionary has been to give lawyers and translators access to the meaning of legal and commercial terms that are not used in the two countries (Spain and Argentina) where most of the legal dictionaries available in the United States are produced. Thus, for example, I have included all of the terminology used in a Mexican *amparo* proceeding. This dictionary is also particularly rich in the legal vocabulary of Colombia, Peru, and Venezuela. To collect these country-specific words, I first sorted legal documents by country. I then reviewed them for recurring terminology. I also studied the commercial codes from various countries in order to determine what words were used in each country to refer to a certain concept. After identifying these terms, I acquired as many monolingual legal dictionaries from the various Spanish-speaking countries as I could, and compared their definitions with those in American legal dictionaries.[3] In other words, my goal has been to be as terminologically correct as possible. That points to the second difference between this dictionary and the others on the market. To the extent possible, I have endeavored to translate terms by terms rather than by explanations. For example, the entry for "attorney-client privilege" in the Butterworths dictionary reads as follows: "relación de confidencialidad entre el abogado y su cliente, que da origen a la obligación de no divulgar la información obtenida como consecuencia del

---

[1] Among these are Cabanellas and Hoague's *Butterworths Spanish/English Legal Dictionary*, Alcaraz and Hughes' *Diccionario de términos jurídicos inglés-español, Spanish-English*, Robb's *Diccionario de términos legales*, Ramos and Gleeson's *Diccionario de términos jurídicos, inglés-español, Spanish-English*, Solís and Gasteazoro's *West's Spanish-English/English-Spanish Law Dictionary*, and Kaplan's *Wiley's English-Spanish and Spanish-English Legal Dictionary*.

[2] It is important to note that the set of Latin phrases used in civil-law countries is completely different from that used in common-law countries (with a few exceptions such as "habeas corpus"). Therefore, Latin phrases appearing in a legal document must be translated along with the rest of the document.

[3] A list of monolingual dictionaries consulted can be found in Appendix 3.

vínculo entre esas partes, y al derecho de no revelar tal información, cuando sea solicitada por terceros." Although that is a fine explanation of this legal concept, it certainly would not fit neatly into a translation, nor does it have to, because there is a functional equivalent in Spanish: el secreto profesional entre el abogado y su cliente. On the Spanish-to-English side of the same dictionary, we find the following under "obligación de medios": "obligation related to the means used to achieve a given end." Again, the authors have given us an explanation when what we need is a term. Lawyers would call this concept a "best efforts obligation."

The final major difference between this and other bilingual legal dictionaries is that I have attempted to include as much phraseology as possible. For example, a translator faced with translating the phrase "habilitar el tiempo" will find only the term "habilitar" in the Alcaraz/Hughes dictionary, which translates it as "authorize, enable, qualify," none of which collocates with "time" in English. The term "habilitar" by itself is also included in Robb's dictionary, again with translations that do not seem to fit in the phrase "habilitar el tiempo": to equip, fit out; to validate; to enable, qualify; to finance; to provide, furnish. The Ramos/Gleeson is no more helpful; it, too, contains only the word by itself, translating it as "to authorize; to validate; to enable; to make legally competent." Finally, the Butterworths dictionary does not include the phrase, but provides the following entry for "habilitar":

> to authorize, make competent (to do something not otherwise permitted); to validate; to enable, qualify; to grant legal emancipation of a minor; to authorize the carrying out of legal acts on non-juridical days; to hand over the administration of an estate of bankrupt to him; to share corporate or business profits with employees thereof; to equip, fit out; to give a share in the profits of a business

Buried in the midst of that entry is the correct meaning of "habilitar el tiempo": "to authorize the carrying out of legal acts on non-juridical days," or in perhaps better English: to allow judicial acts to be performed on a court holiday. In other words, "habilitar" in this phrase means deeming a day that is "inhábil" to be "hábil." It is my hope that by including not only individual words, but also words in context, this dictionary will greatly facilitate the work of the translator.

I initially set out to write a law dictionary, but soon came to realize the day-to-day work of a legal translator goes well beyond the scope of purely legal language. Accordingly, this dictionary covers the following fields: accounting, banking, contracts, corporate law, economics, intellectual property, labor law, political science, procedural law, real property, securities law, taxation, and torts. It also includes some terms from the field of criminal law, but probably not as many as an interpreter would like. My intention has been not to include any "filler" words whatsoever, but I did include a few technical terms that might appear in a lease agreement (see e.g. "chapa," "serenazgo," "terma") or in a collective bargaining agreement (see e.g. "gafete," "casco"). I would appreciate suggestions from readers as to words that should be included in the next edition, and can be reached via e-mail at translation@mindspring.com.

<u>A word about the English-to-Spanish section.</u> Writing a law dictionary is more complicated than writing other types of dictionaries because the corpus of words used in one legal system differs so greatly from the corpus used in the other. As a result, the dictionary cannot be "flipped"; instead, the English-to-Spanish section involves new research as to how to translate uniquely U.S. legal terms into Spanish. Because my research focused on Spanish-language materials, my original intent had been not to include an English-to-Spanish section at all. However, in the end I have decided to provide translations of four types of terms from English into Spanish: (1) terms that are missing from other law dictionaries (e.g., certificate of incumbency, risk-based capital, Y2K compliance); (2) terms for which other dictionaries include only an explanation and not a translation (e.g., attorney-client privilege); (3) terms that vary from country to country so that the into-Spanish translator can know what term to use for a certain country (e.g., gross domestic product, shareholders' meeting, value-added tax, board of directors);[4] (4) terms for which there is an official translation (e.g. the United Nations Convention on Contracts for the International Sale of Goods). It is my hope that in future editions of this dictionary the English-to-Spanish section will be expanded to cover the full range of U.S. law.

---

[4] Appendix 4 offers guidance on how to write numbers when translating into Spanish.

Acknowledgments

Special thanks are due to the following people, without whose assistance this dictionary would never have seen the light of day: Madeline Newman Ríos of Los Angeles, for her help with Mexican terminology in general and the terminology of amparo in particular; Lucila Llausás and Richard Cadena of Mexico City for sharing their personal glossaries with me; Leticia Leduc of the Centro de Estudios de Lingüística Aplicada in Mexico City for her assistance with some of the translations into Spanish; Ricardo Hearne of the law firm of Allende & Brea in Buenos Aires for explaining Argentine terminology to me; Scott Brennan of Washington, DC for discussing terminology and purchasing law books in Peru for me; Catherine McCabe of Atlanta for sharing her list of elusive terminology with me; Barbara Cohen of Miami for her help in procuring the Commercial Codes from Central American countries, and Holly Mikkelson and Mike Stacy for reviewing the Spanish-to-English portion of the manuscript. Any remaining mistakes and omissions are my own.

CORTE SUPREMA

SPANISH-
ENGLISH

Abbreviations

Arg	Argentina
Bol	Bolivia
Chi	Chile
Col	Colombia
Cos	Costa Rica
Cub	Cuba
Dom	Dominican Republic
Ecu	Ecuador
Gua	Guatemala
Hon	Honduras
Lat	Latin word or phrase
Mex	Mexico
Nic	Nicaragua
Pan	Panama
Per	Peru
Pue	Puerto Rico
Sal	El Salvador
Spa	Spain
Uru	Uruguay
Ven	Venezuela

a cargo de cierto banco drawn on a certain bank

a ese fin for that purpose, to that end

a fondo perdido non-reimbursable

a granel in bulk

a instancia de parte at the request of one of the parties [*as opposed to "de oficio"*]

a instancias de at the request of, on the petition of

a la brevedad as soon as possible

a la letra verbatim

a mayor abundamiento to further illustrate this point, furthermore, in addition

a medio plazo in the medium term

a menos que aquí se especifique otra cosa unless otherwise specified herein

a menos que se estipule lo contrario por escrito unless otherwise provided in writing

a mi cargo over which I preside

a mi leal saber y entender to the best of my knowledge and belief

a partir de as of, starting

a petición de parte at the request of one of the parties [*synonym of "a instancia de parte"*]

a plazos in installments

a quien corresponda to whom it may concern

a quien pueda interesar to whom it may concern

a quo the trial court judge, the judge below [*short for "el juez a quo"*]

a razón del 3% anual at the rate of 3% per annum

a requerimiento de at the request of

a saber namely, to wit, viz.

a sabiendas knowingly

a satisfacción de acceptable to

a solicitud de at the request of

a su entero juicio in its sole discretion, at its sole discretion

a su solo criterio in its sole discretion, at its sole discretion

a sus autos el ocurso (Mex) The petition/pleading is ordered to be added to the file.

a título consultivo in an advisory capacity

a título de donación as a gift

a título gratuito as a gift, for free, free of charge

a título oneroso for valuable consideration, against payment

a título particular [*inheritance*] of one or more specific items of property

a título precario for temporary use and enjoyment, merely as a loan

a título universal [*inheritance*] of all or part of an estate

a un valor reducido at a nominal price

a un solo efecto both (all) equally authentic

a virtud de by virtue of

ab intestato (Lat) intestate [*without leaving a will*]

abajo firmante (el) the undersigned
abandono abandonment, desertion
    abandono de apelación abandonment of the appeal
    abandono de atropellado (Mex) hit and run
    abandono de familia desertion of family
    abandono de la acción abandonment of the action [*also called "desistimiento de la acción"*]
    abandono de la instancia abandonment of the action
    abandono de recurso abandonment of the appeal
    abandono del hogar desertion
abarcar to cover
    los bienes abarcados por el contrato the goods covered by the contract
abigeato theft of livestock
abocarse a algo to address oneself to something, to direct one's efforts toward something [*This verb is a synonym of "dedicarse a algo." It should not be confused with "avocar," which means "to take over a case from a lower court."*]
abogacía the practice of law
    ejercer la abogacía to practice law
abogado lawyer, attorney
    abogado acusador plaintiff's attorney
    abogado colegiado attorney admitted to the bar
    abogado constituido appointed attorney, designated attorney
    abogado consultor legal advisor
    abogado de empresa in-house lawyer
    abogado de familia family lawyer [*meaning "a lawyer who specializes in family law"*]
    abogado de oficio court-appointed attorney
    abogado de pobres court-appointed attorney
    abogado de secano shyster, incompetent lawyer
    abogado defensor defense attorney, defense counsel
    abogado en ejercicio a practicing attorney
    abogado fiscal prosecutor
    abogado igualado attorney on retainer
    abogado interno in-house lawyer
    abogado laboralista labor lawyer [*meaning "one who specializes in labor law"*]
    abogado litigante trial lawyer, litigator
    abogado patrocinante (Arg) attorney who advises clients [*as opposed to "abogado apoderado," who has a power-of-attorney to represent them in court. One person can perform both functions.*]
    abogado penalista criminal lawyer, criminal attorney
    abogado que consta attorney of record
    abogado querellante plaintiff's attorney
    abogado tributarista tax lawyer, tax attorney

recibirse de abogado to get a law degree, to graduate from law
school
abolengo ancestry
abonar 1. to pay, to make partial payments 2. to credit to someone's
account
abonar en cuenta to credit to someone's account
abono 1. payment 2. installment 3. crediting money to an account
abono a cuenta payment on account
abono de horas extras overtime pay
abono parcial payment on account
abrir to open
abrir el juicio a pruebas to bring the case to trial, to proceed to
the trial of the case
abrir una carta de crédito to open a letter of credit
abrir una sesión to call a meeting to order
Se abre la sesión. 1. The meeting will come to order. 2. Court is
now in session. 3. We're on the record.
abrogación de una ley repeal of a law
abrogar to repeal [a *law*], to revoke [*regulations*]
absentismo failure to vote [*which is a crime in some Latin American
countries—also called "abstencionismo electoral"*]
absolución 1. [*in the criminal context*] acquittal 2. [*in the civil
context*] dismissal of the case
absolución con reserva dismissal without prejudice [*i.e., the
plaintiff can file the suit again*]
absolución de la demanda dismissal of the complaint, finding
for the defendant
absolución de la instancia dismissal of the case, acquittal
absolución de posiciones answering of interrogatories
absolución perentoria summary dismissal of a criminal action
absolver
absolver consultas to provide the information requested
absolver de la instancia to acquit for lack of evidence
absolver en la demanda finding in favor of the defendant
si el demandado fuere absuelto en la demanda if the court
finds in favor of the defendant
absolver posiciones to answer interrogatories [*In Spanish-
speaking countries, written interrogatories are drafted by one
party and then asked orally of the other party in open court,
whereas in the US, interrogatories are always written
questions, never oral ones.*]
abstencionismo electoral failure to vote [*which is a crime in some
Latin American countries*]
abuso abuse
abuso de autoridad abuse of authority [*such as police brutality*]
abuso de confianza breach of trust, betrayal of confidence
[*such as embezzlement*]

abuso de derecho malicious prosecution, abuse of process

abuso de firma en blanco fraudulent misuse of a document signed in blank

abuso de menores taking advantage of minors [*e.g., forcing them to sign a document that they don't understand*]

abuso de poder abuse of authority, misfeasance [*e.g., government official or police officer inflicts punishment on or insults or unjustly humiliates a person*]

abuso deshonesto (Arg, Mex, Per) sexual assault [*taking indecent liberties (such as fondling without consent) with a person of the opposite sex—also referred to as "indecent assault" in English and as "atentado al pudor" in Spanish*]

acaparamiento cornering the market, hoarding something, buying up all of something

acápite section, paragraph

acatar

  acatar a una decisión judicial to comply with a judicial decision

  acatar órdenes to obey orders

accidente

  accidente de trabajo occupational injury

  accidente de tránsito traffic accident

  accidente in itinere accident on the way to or from work [*This is considered an "on-the-job injury" in Spanish-speaking countries, but in the United States, under the "going-and-coming" rule, a person is not covered by workers' compensation for accidents on the way to or from work.*]

acción 1. action 2. share of stock [*see "acciones"*]

  acción accesoria subsidiary action, collateral action

  acción ad exhibendum action for production of personal property that is the subject of the *acción real* that the petitioner wishes to file [*also called "acción exhibitoria"*]

  acción alternativa action for relief either in rem or in personam

  acción aquiliana tort action

  acción cambiaria collection action based on a negotiable instrument

  acción cambiaria directa collection action brought against the acceptor of a negotiable instrument or his guarantor [*avalista*]

  acción cambiaria de regreso collection action brought against any obligor of the negotiable instrument other than the acceptor or his guarantor

  acción causal the underlying action [*i.e., action based on the underlying relationship between obligor and obligee of a promissory note rather than suing to enforce the promissory note on its face, because that type of enforcement action has lapsed or is barred by the statute of limitations*]

  acción cautelar action for interim equitable relief [*such as a temporary restraining order or an attachment*]

acción civil civil action

acción coactiva action to enforce

acción confesoria action for the recognition and enforcement of an easement ejectment action

acción conjunta joint action

acción constitutiva test action [*action that attempts to establish, modify or abolish a legal right*]

acción de apremio action for collection of a debt, foreclosure

acción de condena criminal prosecution

acción de cumplimiento (Per) compliance action [*action brought pursuant to Article 200(5) of Peruvian Constitution seeking to have public officials comply with the law*]

acción de desahucio eviction action, unlawful detainer action

acción de desalojo eviction action

acción de deslinde action to define a property line

acción de despojo eviction action

acción de filiación paternity suit

acción de hábeas corpus (Per) habeas corpus action [*see Article 200(1) of Peruvian Constitution*]

acción de hábeas data (Per) action seeking access to information

acción de inconstitucionalidad (Per) unconstitutionality action [*The Constitutional Court decides whether acts with the status of law are unconstitutional in substance or form.*]

acción de jactancia action to force someone who publicly claims a right to prove his title or remain silent [*similar to an "action to quiet title" in the common law*]

acción de nulidad action to have a contract declared null and void [*also called an "acción de anulación"*]

acción de petición de herencia type of probate proceeding brought to divide an estate, by heirs or legatees/devisees or certain relatives of the heirs

acción de preterición lawsuit by a pretermitted heir [*i.e., a descendant of the testator who would be an heir under the laws of intestate succession, but who is not named in the will. The omission is presumed to be unintentional.*]

acción de reclamación de paternidad paternity action

acción de regreso collection action brought against any obligor of the negotiable instrument other than the acceptor or his guarantor

acción de reivindicación replevin [*action to recover possession of personal property that is unlawfully detained and to recover damages for the unlawful retention*]

acción declarativa action for a declaratory judgment

acción ejecutiva executive action [*summary action to collect on a negotiable instrument*]

acción estimatoria action by buyer against seller for a price reduction because of defects in what was sold [*also referred to as "quanti minoris"*]

acción exhibitoria action for production of personal property that is the subject of the *acción real* that the petitioner wishes to file [*also called "acción ad exhibendum"*]

acción hipotecaria foreclosure action

acción incidental accessory action

acción judicial lawsuit, legal action

acción mancomunada joint action

acción militar military intervention

acción mixta action based on a right that is both in personam and in rem

acción negatoria action to quiet title [*action by a property owner who disclaims an alleged easement*]

acción oblicua (Mex) action for subrogation [*action brought by a creditor to allow him to exercise the rights of his debtor*]

acción pauliana action by which creditors move to void all acts by which a debtor defrauded them [*also called an "acción revocatoria"*]

acción penal criminal action

acción personal personal action, action in personam [*seeks to enforce an obligation imposed on the defendant by contract or tort law, as opposed to an acción real*]

acción petitoria petitory action [*action to establish title to land, as opposed to a lawsuit to gain physical possession of the land*]

acción popular (Per) "people's action" [*action filed to challenge rules, administrative regulations, and general resolutions and decrees that violate the Constitution—somewhat analogous to a taxpayer's suit in the United States*]

acción posesoria possessory action [*to acquire or recover something that is not in plaintiff's possession or to keep something that is in his possession*]

acción precautoria action for a provisional remedy

acción privada private action

acción procedente action that lies, action that the plaintiff is entitled to file

acción pública criminal action

acción publiciana (Mex) action to acquire property by prescription

acción real action in rem [*examples include acción reivindicatoria, acción confesoria, acción negatoria*]

acción redhibitoria action for rescission against the seller of defective goods

acción regresiva *see "acción cambiaria de regreso"*

acción reivindicatoria replevin [*action to recover possession of personal property that is unlawfully detained and to recover damages for the unlawful retention*]

acción rescisoria action for rescission

acción revocatoria action by which creditors move to void all acts by which a debtor defrauded them [*synonym of "acción pauliana"*]

accionada defendant [*short for "parte accionada"*]

accionante plaintiff

accionar to sue

accionariado obrero employee stock-sharing plan

acciones shares, shares of stock, stock

    acciones al portador bearer shares

    acciones amortizables redeemable shares

    acciones amortizadas redeemed shares [*i.e., shares that the company can buy back from shareholders*]

    acciones cartulares (Arg) certificated shares, shares represented by certificates [*opposite of "acciones escriturales"*]

    acciones comunes (Mex) common stock, shares of common stock

    acciones con derecho a voto voting shares, voting stock

    acciones de aportes (Arg) shares issued for property turned in

    acciones de capital inflado watered stock [*stock issued with a par value greater than the value of the underlying asset*]

    acciones de cartera treasury shares [*synonym of "autocartera"*]

    acciones de crecimiento growth stock [*as opposed to income stock*]

    acciones de disfrute dividend right shares, retired share benefits [*no equivalent in the U.S.*]

    acciones de favor (Arg) stock issued for services

    acciones de goce (Col, Mex) dividend right shares, retired share benefits

    acciones de industria (Chi, Mex) stock issued for services [*also called "acciones industriales"*]

    acciones de la misma categoría shares of the same class

    acciones de preferencia preferred stock, preferred shares

    acciones de premio (Arg) stock issued for services

    acciones de rendimiento income stock [*as opposed to growth stock*]

    acciones de tesorería treasury shares [*also called "acciones rescatadas" and "acciones propias"*]

    acciones de trabajo (Mex, Per) stock issued for services

    acciones desembolsadas (Spa) fully paid-up shares, non-assessable shares [*referred to as "acciones liberadas" in Mex*]

    acciones desertas shares for which payment is in default

acciones doradas preferred shares with voting rights

acciones en circulación outstanding shares

acciones en especie (Mex) shares issued for property turned in

acciones escriturales (Arg) book-entry shares [*i.e. uncertificated shares*]

acciones exhibidas (Mex) fully paid-up shares, non-assessable shares [*referred to as "acciones desembolsadas" in Spain*]

acciones fraccionadas fractional shares

acciones gratuitas bonus shares

acciones impropias shares that do not represent the capital stock

acciones industriales (Mex) stock issued for services

acciones integradas (Arg, Par) fully paid-up shares, non-assessable shares

acciones laborales stock issued for services

acciones liberadas 1. (Arg, Chi, Per, Spa) bonus shares [*issue of additional free shares to existing shareholders in proportion to their holdings when a company has built up considerable capital reserves in relation to the size of its capital (synonym of "acciones gratuitas"). Note that the term "acciones liberadas" has a different meaning in Mexico.*] **2. (Mex)** fully paid-up shares, non-assessable shares

acciones neutras non-voting shares

acciones nominativas registered shares

acciones ordinarias common stock, shares of common stock

acciones pagadoras called-up capital stock, partly-paid shares, assessable shares

acciones preferenciales (Col) preferred stock, preferred shares

acciones preferentes preferred stock, preferred shares

acciones preferidas preferred stock, preferred shares

acciones privilegiadas preferred stock, preferred shares

acciones propias 1. (Mex) shares that represent the capital stock [*as opposed to "acciones impropias"*] **2. (Arg, Spa)** treasury shares [*shares reacquired by the company – also called "acciones de tesorería" and "acciones rescatadas"*]

acciones provisionales temporary share certificates, scrip

acciones redimibles callable shares

acciones rescatadas (Arg, Cos, Spa) treasury shares [*shares reacquired by the company*]

acciones sin derecho a voto non-voting shares

acciones sin valor a la par no-par value shares

acciones sin valor nominal no-par value shares

acciones y aportaciones capitales stock investments and capital contributions

accionista shareholder, stockholder [*Both terms are used in the US; only "shareholder" is used in the UK.*]

accionista industrial holder of stock issued for services
accionista mayoritario majority shareholder
accionista minoritario minority shareholder
accionista registrado shareholder of record
que pueden ser o no accionistas who may but need not be
shareholders
acefalía lack of a leader [*term used when the Presidency is vacant
due to death or resignation*]
aceptación acceptance
aceptación bancaria bankers' acceptance [*bank will pay if
drawer does not*], due from customers on acceptances [*as
an asset on a balance sheet*], acceptances outstanding [*as a
liability on a balance sheet*]
aceptación pura y simple unconditional acceptance
aceptar
aceptar el cargo y protestar desempeñarlo fielmente to
accept the position and affirm that he will perform his duties
faithfully
aceptar un cheque to honor a check
acervo undivided assets of an estate or business ———
acervo comunitario the corpus of EU law [*including the Treaty
of Rome and the decisions of the Court of Justice of the
European Union*]
acervo cultural cultural heritage ———
acervo familiar the family fortune
acervo hereditario assets of an estate
aclaración de sentencia petition to have the judge clarify part of the
judgment
acompañar
acompañar las copias pertinentes to attach the relevant
copies
los documentos acompañados a la solicitud the documents
attached to the petition
acordado resolved ———
acordar
acordar un dividendo to declare a dividend
acordar un plazo to give someone a set amount of time, to set
a deadline for someone
acoso sexual sexual harassment [*also called "hostigamiento
sexual"*]
acrecencia accretion [*right of heirs to a proportional increase of their
inheritance if another heir's portion is not claimed or is expressly
waived*]
acrecimiento accretion [*right of heirs to a proportional increase of
their inheritance if another heir's portion is not claimed or is
expressly waived*]
acreditado borrower

acreditante lender
acreditar to evidence
    acreditar su personalidad to evidence one's authority to represent another person
    acreditar su personería to evidence one's authority to represent another person
    acreditar su representación to evidence one's authority to represent another person
acreedor creditor
    acreedor alimentario person entitled to maintenance
    acreedor anticresista mortgagee in possession [*see explanation under "anticresis"*]
    acreedor cambiario holder of a bill of exchange
    acreedor común unsecured creditor
    acreedor de cosa cierta creditor entitled to a specific asset
    acreedor de dominio creditor by right of ownership
    acreedor ejecutante judgment creditor [*creditor who has a money judgment entered against the debtor and may enforce the judgment*]
    acreedor escriturado creditor whose security interest was recorded by a notary [*therefore, a "secured creditor"*]
    acreedor garantizado secured creditor
    acreedor hipotecario mortgagee [*i.e., the bank making the mortgage loan*]
    acreedor inferior junior creditor
    acreedor mancomunado joint creditor
    acreedor pignoraticio creditor in possession [*of a pledged asset*]
    acreedor por fallo judgment creditor [*creditor who has a money judgment entered against the debtor and may enforce the judgment*]
    acreedor postergado unpaid creditor
    acreedor preferente preferred creditor
    acreedor prendario pledgee [*chattel mortgage creditor*]
    acreedor privilegiado secured creditor
    acreedor quirografario unsecured creditor
    acreedor refaccionario lender of working capital
    acreedor secundario junior creditor
    acreedor superior senior creditor
    acreedor testamentario devisee, legatee
    acreedores a entregar por reporto securities payable under repurchase agreement [*as an item on a balance sheet*]
    acreedores diversos other payables, other liabilities
acta certificate
    acta circunstanciada detailed certificate
    acta constitutiva articles of incorporation, charter

acta de asamblea general ordinaria minutes of an ordinary shareholders' meeting
acta de audiencia record of a hearing taken by the court clerk
acta de constitución articles of incorporation
acta de defunción death certificate
acta de deslinde certificate of boundary lines
acta de emisión bond indenture
acta de fallo de adjudicación official award of a contract
acta de matrimonio marriage certificate
acta de nacimiento birth certificate
acta de notoriedad notary's recording of facts that are common knowledge [*and therefore need not be proven*]
acta de protocolización notary public's certificate that the document was recorded in the notarial record book
acta legalizada notarial instrument
acta notarial notarial certificate
actas del registro civil vital records
activación de gastos capitalization of expenses
activo assets
activo agotable wasting assets
activo amortizable depreciable assets
activo circulante (Chi, Ecu, Gua, Hon, Mex, Spa, Ven) current assets [*called "activo corriente" in other countries*]
activo circulante neto (Mex, Spa) net current assets
activo consumible (Mex) wasting assets
activo contable book assets
activo corriente (Arg, Bol, Col, Pan, Per) current assets [*called "activo circulante" in other countries*]
activo de fácil realización liquid assets, quick assets
activo devengado accrued assets
activo disponible liquid assets [*cash on hand and in banks*]
activo eventual contingent assets
activo ficticio intangible assets
activo fijo fixed assets
activo financiero financial assets [*either cash or an investment that can be converted into cash, e.g. bonds, shares, and certificates of deposit*]
activo físico tangible assets
activo improductivo non-performing assets
activo inmaterial (Spa) intangible assets [*called "bienes intangibles" in other countries*]
activo inmovilizado (Spa) fixed assets
activo intangible intangible assets
activo nominal intangible assets
activo oculto concealed assets
activo pignorado pledged assets
activo real tangible assets

activo realizable quick assets, liquid assets
activo rentable income-earning assets
activo subyacente underlying asset
activos assets
activos con superávit surplus assets
acto act
    acto administrativo act of a governmental authority
    acto continuo thereupon [*synonym of "acto seguido"*]
    acto dañoso tort
    acto de constitución organizational meeting [*i.e., meeting to organize a company*]
    acto de dominio act of ownership, act to acquire or sell property
    acto de riguroso dominio act to acquire property in fee simple
    acto de última voluntad last will and testament
    acto ilícito civil tort
    acto ilícito civil doloso intentional tort
    acto jurídico an act with legal consequences, an act having legal effect [*an act by which the party or parties declare their intent to make changes in legal relations and to which the law attaches the power of producing such changes. An "acto jurídico" is wider than the term "contract" or even "agreement." It includes, e.g., a notice to a tenant, a declaration by which one party avoids a contract on the ground of fraud, the grant of authority to an agent, the making of a will, etc.*]
    acto mixto transaction that is commercial for one of the parties and civil for the other
    acto prejudicial pre-filing act, act before a lawsuit is filed
    acto procesal procedural step, step in judicial proceedings [*act in the course of a court proceeding that creates, modifies or extinguishes procedural rights*]
    acto público de la apertura de los sobres public ceremony of opening the envelopes [*in a public tender*]
    acto reclamado (Mex) act being challenged [*in an amparo case*]
    acto seguido thereupon, immediately thereafter [*synonym of "acto continuo"*]
    actos concatenados joint acts
    actos conciliatorios conciliation acts
    actos de administración acts of administration, day-to-day management functions
    actos de comercio commercial transactions
    actos de conciliación conciliatory acts
    actos de disposición acts to dispose of property
    actos de dominio acts to dispose of property

actos de gestión acts of administration, day-to-day management functions
actos electorales political rallies
actos entre vivos inter vivos transactions
actor plaintiff
   actor civil plaintiff claiming damages in a criminal case
   actor criminal prosecutor
actuación order
   actuación de pruebas (Per) production of evidence
   actuaciones judiciales judicial proceedings
   actuaciones policiales police investigations
   actuaciones sumariales preliminary investigations [*i.e., investigations during the "sumario" (q.v.)*]
actualización adjustment for inflation, restatement of amounts based on changes in the National Consumer Price Index
   actualización de costo de ventas restatement of cost of sales
   actualización patrimonial restatement of shareholders' equity
actualizar to restate [*for purposes of inflation only*]
   actualizar su libreta (Spa) to obtain one's bank balance
actuar to act
   actuar de buena fe to act in good faith
   actuar de mala fe to act in bad faith
actuaría office of the clerk of the court
actuario clerk of the court [*also performs functions of process server and is also referred to as "secretario de actas." Note that an "actuary" in English is a "perito en estadísticas de seguros."*]
acuchillador stabber [*person who stabs someone*]
acudir to apply to
   Toda persona deseosa de contraer matrimonio acudirá a cualquiera de las personas autorizadas para celebrarlo. Any person who desires to get married shall apply to any of the persons authorized to perform a marriage ceremony.
   acudir a la vía judicial to bring a lawsuit, to go to court
   acudir a las urnas to go to the polls
   acudir al arbitraje to resort to arbitration
acuerdo 1. agreement 2. decision, ruling [*of a court*] 3. resolution [*adopted by shareholders or board of directors*]
   acuerdo arancelario tariff agreement
   Acuerdo de Cartagena Cartagena Agreement [*established the Andean Pact*]
   acuerdo de pleno decision handed down by the full court
   acuerdo de voluntades meeting of the minds
   acuerdo plenario decision handed down by the full court
   acuerdo preliminar memorandum of understanding (MOU)
   acuerdo preventivo (Arg) agreement with creditors to avoid bankruptcy [*also called "concordato preventivo"*]
   acuerdo provisional interlocutory order

acuerdo resolutorio (Arg) agreement offered to creditors after the debtor is declared bankrupt

acuerdo verbal oral agreement [not "verbal agreement"]

acumulable 1. taxable, subject to taxation 2. recognizable (and thus taxable) [as in "income recognized in the preceding tax year"] 3. capable of being joined in a lawsuit

acumulación

acumulación de acciones joinder (of parties or causes of action)

acumulación de autos consolidation of cases

acumulación de existencias stockpiling

acumulación de ingresos (Mex) recognition of income

acumulación fiscal taxation

acusación privada any party other than the State who prosecutes another person criminally

acusado criminal defendant, the accused

acusador

acusador particular (Spa) private prosecutor [victim who prosecutes a crime that can only be prosecuted at the request of the victim]

acusador popular (Spa) "people's prosecutor" [person other than the victim who prosecutes a crime that can only be prosecuted at the request of the victim]

acusar

acusar rebeldía to give notice of default

acusar recibo to acknowledge receipt

acusar una ganancia to show a profit

acusar una pérdida to show a loss

Todas las pruebas la acusan. All the evidence points to her.

acuse de recibo acknowledgment of receipt

ad honorem (Lat) pro bono, free of charge

ad quem the appellate court judge [the judge "ad quem" i.e. to whom the appeal is made]

adeco (Ven) member of the Acción Democrática

adeudar to owe

adeudo indebtedness

adherir to become a member, to join

adherir a la apelación to concur in the appeal [party who won the lawsuit being appealed joins in the losing party's appeal because he disagrees with certain aspects of the judgment being appealed]

adherir a un tratado to accede to a treaty

adhesión

adhesión a la apelación concurrence in the appeal [party who won the lawsuit being appealed joins in the losing party's appeal because he disagrees with certain aspects of the judgment being appealed]

adhesión al tratado accession to the treaty
adición de la herencia acceptance of an inheritance
adicionar to make an addition to
adir la herencia to accept an inheritance
adjudicación
    adjudicación al mejor postor award to the highest bidder
    adjudicación de quiebra adjudication in bankruptcy
    adjudicación de una herencia distribution of an estate
    adjudicación en pago accord and satisfaction [*synonym of*
    "dación en pago" (q.v.)]
adjudicar 1. to award 2. to adjudicate
    adjudicar un contrato to award a contract
adjudicatario successful bidder, winning bidder
adjunción type of accession uniting two pieces of properties of
    different owners such that they form one, but may be separated
    later
adminicular to provide additional evidence, to corroborate
adminículo corroboration
administración irregular gross mismanagement
administrador (Gua, Hon, Mex, Spa) board member, director [*i.e.,*
    one who sits on the board of directors. Note that in these
    countries, the Spanish word "director" means "manager," not
    "director" in the sense of "board member."]
    administrador judicial receiver [*in bankruptcy*]
    administrador único sole director and C.E.O. [*The person acts*
    as both the company's board and as its highest officer.]
admisibilidad admissibility
admisión
    admisión a cotización en bolsa listing on the exchange
    admisión a cotización oficial listing on the exchange
    admisión temporal temporary admission [*a system of admitting*
    goods to a country for later export, and under specified
    conditions no duty is applied—also called "internación
    temporal"]
admitir
    admitir el recurso en el efecto devolutivo to allow an appeal
    of a lower court's decision to proceed without staying the
    execution of that decision
    admitir valor a cotización to list a security on the exchange
    admitida la demanda the plaintiff having been granted leave to
    proceed
    Esta ley admite varias lecturas. There are several ways to
    interpret this law. This law is open to various interpretations.
adopción adoption
    adopción plena (Arg) full adoption [*All adoptions in the US are*
    equivalent to "adopción plena" in Argentina. In this type of
    adoption, all relationship with the birth parents is severed.]

adopción simple (Arg) simple adoption [*No equivalent in the US. This type of adoption can be revoked and does not extinguish the ties between the adopted child and his birth parents. It creates a relationship solely between the adoptive parent and the adopted child. No relationship is created between the adopted child and the adoptive parent's family.*]

adoptado adopted child, adoptee

adoptante adoptive parent

adoptar

    adoptar medidas adecuadas to take appropriate action

    adoptar un acuerdo to adopt a resolution [*at a meeting*]

adquirente acquiror, purchaser

    adquirente a título gratuito recipient of a gift

    adquirente a título oneroso purchaser for value

    adquirente de buena fe good faith purchaser

adquirir en propiedad to acquire ownership of

adquisición

    adquisición hostil hostile takeover

    adquisición procesal (Mex) benefits to third parties as a result of a judicial decision

adscrito assigned

    adscrito a in the service of [*an office or corporation*]

aduana customs

aduanero customs official

aducir to argue, allege

    aducir pruebas to produce evidence

adulteración de documentos falsification of documents

advertencia 1. remark 2. admonishment, warning

afectable capable of being encumbered (property)

afectar to earmark, to allocate

    afectar en fideicomiso to place in trust

    afectar en garantía to furnish as collateral

afecto a subject to

affectio societatis (Lat) mutual trust among the partners

afianzado bonded, guaranteed

afianzadora bonding company

afianzar to guarantee

afincar to own real estate, to become landed

afloramientos de activos (Arg) accounting recognition of assets that were previously hidden in order to avoid taxes

aforado person entitled to a privilege

Afore (Mex) Pension Fund Administrator [*short for "administradoras de fondos para el retiro"*]

aforar to appraise for customs purposes

aforo valuation of goods for customs purposes

afrontar los cargos to face the charges

agencia de calificación rating agency

agenciar to promote, to negotiate
agente agent
    agente de aduana customs officer
    agente de bolsa stockbroker
    agente de despacho forwarding agent
    agente de población (Mex) immigration officer
    agente de policía police officer, law enforcement officer
    agente de traspaso transfer agent
    agente del mercado abierto (Arg) over-the-counter dealer
    agente del ministerio público public prosecutor
    agente económico economic agent [*person who plays a role in the economy of a country*]
    agente fiscal public prosecutor
    agente inmobiliario real estate agent
    agente procesal agent for service of process
agio 1. speculative profit on exchange of money or other paper 2. usury
agiotista profiteer, usurer
agotamiento depletion, exhaustion
    agotamiento de la vía administrativa exhaustion of administrative remedies
    agotamiento previo de recursos prior exhaustion of remedies
agraviado (Mex) petitioner in an amparo proceeding [*also called the "quejoso"*]
agraviarse de algo (Mex) to include something among one's causes of action
agravio 1. exception [*written objection to a judge's ruling*] 2. (Mex) cause of action [*in amparo*]
agregación
    Se ordena la agregación de los documentos acompañados. The documents attached hereto are ordered to be added to the file, to be entered in the record.
agregado 1. aggregate 2. attaché
    agregado cultural cultural attaché
    agregado militar military attaché
    agregados monetarios monetary aggregates
agregar los documentos acompañados to enter the documents filed herewith in the record
agremiación 1. labor union 2. unionization
agremiado union worker
agremiarse to form a labor union, to unionize
agrimensor surveyor
agrupación
    agrupación financiera (Mex) financial group [*An "agrupación financiera" is composed of a "sociedad controladora" (holding company) and at least two of the following entities: institución de banca múltiple (full-service bank), casa de bolsa*]

(brokerage firm), and institución de seguros (insurance company).]

agrupación sectorial trade association
aguantador (Ven) fence [*person who receives stolen goods*]
aguinaldo Christmas bonus
AJUSTABONOS (Mex) Federal Government Adjustable Bonds
ajustar
    ajustar su conducta al derecho to conform one's conduct to the law
    ajustarse a derecho to conform to law
    la negativa a contestar se ajusta a derecho cuando ... refusal to answer is legally proper when ...
ajuste adjustment
    ajuste de cuentas getting even, settling scores with someone
    ajuste por apalancamiento (Arg) financing adjustment [*adjustment that reflects the extent to which the equity shareholders' investment in an enterprise is shielded from the effects of changing prices due to the existence of borrowings—called "gearing adjustment" in the UK*]
    ajuste por endeudamiento (Spa) financing adjustment [*see previous entry*]
    ajustes por periodifiación (Spa) 1. prepayments [*as an asset on the balance sheet*] 2. accruals [*as a liability on the balance sheet*]
ajusticiado criminal who has been executed
ajusticiamiento execution, death by capital punishment
ajusticiar to implement the death penalty, to put to death, to execute
al amparo de under, in reliance on
    No tiene derecho de dar por terminado el contrato al amparo del artículo 8. He has no right to terminate the contract in reliance on Article 8.
al calce at the foot, at the bottom [*of a document*]
al crédito on credit
al efecto to that effect, for that purpose
al margen in the margin
    al margen de la partida citada recorded in the margin of the above entry
    al margen de las reglamentaciones pertinentes (Arg) in violation of the relevant regulations
al pie de la letra literally, verbatim, exactly as indicated
al por mayor wholesale
al por menor retail
al portador bearer
al tenor de las siguientes declaraciones y cláusulas pursuant to the following recitals and sections
alarde periodic review by a court of its docket

albacea
> **albacea dativo** administrator of an estate [*appointed by the court when a person dies intestate*]
> **albacea judicial** administrator of an estate [*synonym of "albacea dativo"*]
> **albacea testamentario** executor of an estate [*named by testator in the will*]

albarán (Spa) delivery note [*called a "remito" in Argentina*]
albedrío free will
alcabala 1. (Ecu, Per) transfer tax [*on purchase and sale of real property, ships and airplanes*] **2. (Ven)** police roadblock
alcahuete pimp
alcaide prison warden, jailer
alcaidía 1. office of the prison warden 2. (Cos) small claims court
alcalde mayor
alcance scope
alcanzar
> **alcanzar la mayoría** to reach the age of majority
> **hasta donde alcance** until it runs out
> **si el dinero no alcanza para cubrir todos los gastos** if the money is insufficient to cover all the expenses

aleatorio random, uncertain, contingent
alegar to argue, to put forward, to assert [*"allege" in English is "pretender" in Spanish*]
> **alegar de bien probado** to make one's closing arguments
> **alegar de conclusión (Col)** to make one's final arguments [*Once the evidentiary period is over, the judge orders the file to be delivered to the plaintiff and then to the defendant, so that they can review the entire file and make their final arguments. The delivery of the file to the parties is called the "traslado."*]

alegato argument
> **alegato de bien probado** closing argument
> **alegatos** oral argument (if oral), brief (if written) [*after the evidence is presented, the lawyers have the chance to make a final argument. This is similar to our oral argument in jury trials and proposed findings in bench trials.*]

alevosía 1. specific intent, malice aforethought, aggravating circumstances 2. (Mex) killing a defenseless victim by surprise
alevoso person who commits crime under aggravating circumstances
alguacil marshal, bailiff, process server
alguno o varios one or more
alícuota de amortización depreciation rate
alimentante provider of support [*such as a divorced parent*]
alimentista recipient of support
allanamiento search of a house by order of a judge

allanamiento a la demanda acceptance of the claim, acquiescence to the claim [*by the defendant*]

allanamiento de domicilio trespass, unlawful entry, breaking and entering

allanamiento de morada trespass, unlawful entry, breaking and entering

allanar to enter a house by court order

almacén warehouse

> **almacén afianzado** bonded warehouse
>
> **almacén general de depósito** bonded warehouse

almoneda pública public auction [*also called "subasta pública"*]

alta gerencia upper management

altas y bajas en el ejercicio fixed assets added or retired during the fiscal year

alteración del orden público breach of the peace, disturbing the peace

alzable appealable

alzado debtor who conceals assets from his creditors

alzamiento

> **alzamiento de bienes** concealment of assets by a debtor
>
> **alzamiento de una garantía** release from a guarantee

amanuenses del notario notary's associates and staff members

ámbito

> **ámbito de aplicación de la ley** the scope of the law
>
> **ámbito espacial de validez de la ley** territorial prescriptive jurisdiction, spatial applicability of the law
>
> **ámbito personal de validez de la ley** prescriptive jurisdiction over the parties
>
> **ámbito temporal de validez de la ley** period of time during which a law is in effect, usually from publication to repeal, except where retroactive
>
> **su ámbito de competencia** his area of responsibility
>
> **una empresa de ámbito nacional** a company with offices nationwide

amigable componedor amiable compositeur [*English uses the French term—see explanation under "árbitro arbitrador"*]

amonestación 1. warning, reprimand 2. publication of marriage banns

> **amonestaciones matrimoniales** banns of matrimony

amortización 1. repayment of a loan 2. redemption of shares 3. amortization 4. depreciation [*Note that in English, tangible assets are depreciated, and intangible assets are amortized.*]

> **amortización acelerada** acclerated depreciation
>
> **amortización anticipada** early repayment
>
> **amortización constante** straight-line depreciation
>
> **amortización de acciones** redemption of shares
>
> **amortización de cuota fija** straight-line depreciation

amortización de pérdidas loss carryforward
amortización decreciente declining balance depreciation
amortización degresiva declining balance depreciation
amortización en proporción simple straight-line depreciation
amortización financiera provision for a sinking fund
amortización fiscal tax write-off
amortización lineal straight-line depreciation
amortizacion porcentual declining balance depreciation
amortización sobre el saldo declining balance depreciation
amortización única bullet payment [*of a bond*]
amortizar 1. to amortize 2. to pay back [*a loan*] 3. to redeem [*shares*]
amovible subject to removal from his position [*e.g., a public official*]
ampararse to rely on
    la cláusula en la cual se amparan los apelantes the clause on
        which the appellants are relying
amparista (Mex) the petitioner in an amparo proceeding
amparo 1. (Mex) amparo [*appeal for relief under the Constitution in
    a case of violation of civil rights. This is a constitutional remedy
    aimed at preserving the rights and freedoms established by the
    Federal Constitution from legislative acts, acts of authority and
    court decisions, as well as preserving local and federal
    sovereignty in interstate and federal-state disputes.*] **2. (Arg)**
    amparo [*Argentine amparo is a judicially created remedy,
    whereas Mexican amparo is a constitutionally created remedy.
    Unlike Mexican amparo, Argentine amparo cannot be used as a
    substitute for habeas corpus or appeal, and whereas Mexican
    amparo can be used only to challenge state action, Argentine
    amparo will lie against actions of private groups such as unions.*]
amparo administrativo (Mex) amparo proceeding against acts
    of administrative officials, when it is not possible to resort to
    an administrative tribunal
amparo bi-instancial (Mex) *see "amparo indirecto"*
amparo contra leyes (Mex) amparo proceeding to challenge
    the constitutionality of laws, regulations or decrees
amparo directo (Mex) direct amparo, "one-step amparo" [*The
    appeal is filed directly with the Circuit Panel Courts or the
    Supreme Court. Direct amparo is used when the
    administrative act being challenged is final and binding.*]
amparo indirecto (Mex) indirect amparo, "two-step amparo"
    [*The appeal is filed first with a federal district court judge,
    whose decision may be appealed to the Supreme Court.
    Indirect amparo is used when the administrative act being
    challenged is not final and binding.*]
amparo judicial (Mex) amparo proceeding against final judicial
    decisions for which no legal remedy or recourse exists
    because the violation occurred during the proceedings or in
    the decision itself

amparo uni-instancial (Mex) see "amparo directo"

ampliación supplemental pleading

    ampliación de capital capital increase [by issuing new shares]

    ampliación de la demanda amendment of the complaint to include additional claims

    ampliación de la hipoteca making the mortgage extend to other assets of the debtor

    ampliación de los antecedentes provision of additional evidence for something

    ampliación de un plazo extension of a term

    ampliación de operaciones expansion of operations

    ampliación del embargo extension of the attachment to additional property [also called "mejora del embargo"]

ampliar

    ampliar el plazo to extend the stipulated term

    ampliar un auto to expand upon a ruling

anales digest, compilation

análisis analysis

    análisis bursátil stock market analysis [There are 2 basic types: fundamental analysis and technical analysis.]

    análisis de costos-beneficios cost-benefit analysis

    análisis de gestión management's discussion and analysis ("MD&A")

    análisis financiero financial analysis

    análisis fundamental fundamental analysis [analysis based on a company's financial statistics]

    análisis técnico technical analysis [relies on price and volume movements of stocks and does not concern itself with financial statistics.]

anatocismo compound interest

anexo 1. exhibit, schedule, attachment 2. enclosure [with a letter]

    anexo A del presente contrato Exhibit A to this agreement [note that we say "exhibit to an agreement" in English, but "anexo de un contrato" in Spanish]

animus domini the intent to be the owner

anotación

    anotación contable accounting entry

    anotación marginal note in the margin

    anotación preventiva annotation in the Land Register of a dispute over the rights to the property

anotar e inscribir en un registro to enter and record in a registry

ante los oficios del notario before the notary

antecedentes [in a contract] recitals

    antecedentes de hecho factual background

    antecedentes penales criminal record, arrest record

antecontrato preliminary contract

antefirma title before a signature

antejuicio preliminary hearing to ensure that there is probable cause to bring criminal charges against a judge or officer of the court

anteproyecto de ley preliminary draft of a bill

anterior (lo) the foregoing

anteriormente 1. heretofore 2. above [*in a text*]

anticipo advance payment, prepayment, down payment
  anticipo de herencia inter vivos gift
  anticipo de honorarios retainer
  anticipo en efectivo cash advance
  anticipo laboral (Per) advance payment of benefits for purposes of constructing housing
anticipos prepayments, advances
  anticipos a proveedores advances to suppliers
  anticipos de clientes advance payments from customers
anticresis antichresis [*a contract whereby the debtor consents to have his creditor enjoy the fruits and produce or rental of the estate he delivers until the obligation is canceled. Specifically, any contract whereby the debtor encumbers a property in favor of his creditor to enable the creditor to collect rent in lieu of payment of the debt*]

antigüedad seniority
  antigüedad de ingreso en el trabajo age at entry into the labor force
  antigüedad de saldos accounts receivable aging

anuencia consent, acceptance

anulable voidable

anulación cancellation
  anulación de la factura cancellation of an invoice [*cancelación de la factura means "paying the invoice"*]
  anulación de matrimonio annulment of marriage

anular to declare null and void
  anular el testamento de alguien to defeat someone's will
  anular la expedición de la citación to vacate the subpoena
  anular un contrato to rescind a contract
  anular un proyecto de ley to veto a bill
  anular una sentencia to reverse a judgment, to set aside a judgment, to vacate a judgment

año
  año bisiesto leap year
  año calendario calendar year
  año civil calendar year
  año contributivo (Pue) tax year
  año emergente twelve-month period [*that does not begin on January 1*]
  año fiscal fiscal year

año legal statutory year [*to simplify calculations, the year is deemed to have 12 months of 30 days*]

año móvil twelve-month period [*that does not begin on January 1*]

año natural calendar year

año social accounting year [*which may be more or less than 12 months*]

Años 186 y 137 (Ven) 186th Year of Independence and 137th Year of the Federation [*sometimes the numbers appear alone, e.g. 186 y 137*]

apalancamiento leverage

apalancamiento de capital capital ratio

aparejada ejecución: el documento trae aparejada ejecución the document is enforceable on its face [*see "título ejecutivo"*]

apelación appeal

apelación accesoria appeal in which the winning party joins in the losing party's appeal of the case

apelación adhesiva appeal in which the winning party joins in the losing party's appeal of the case

apelación desierta withdrawn appeal

apelación en relación (Arg, Uru) appeal in which no additional evidence may be produced [*abbreviated form of appeal of an interlocutory order that is filed with and argued before the judge who issued the interlocutory order. The appellate court only reviews the lower court's file. The appellant does not have the right to argue the appeal before the appellate court.*]

apelación extraordinaria appeal on a question of procedure

apelación libre (Arg, Uru) appeal in which additional evidence may be produced [*appeal of a final judgment that is made to a higher court. The appellant can argue the case before the appellate court in the form of "agravios" (exceptions).*]

apelación ordinaria appeal on the merits

apelación subsidiaria (Arg, Uru) appeal of an interlocutory order to a higher court that is made in the alternative when a motion for reconsideration is made to the court that issued the interlocutory order

apelado appellee

apelante appellant

apelar to appeal

apelar ante la Corte Suprema to appeal to the Supreme Court

apelar en subsidio to appeal in the alternative

apeo y deslinde description of boundaries [*survey and demarcation*]

apercibimiento warning

apersonamiento (Per) entry of appearance

apersonarse al proceso (Per) to enter an appearance in the case

apertura opening

aplicación supletoria (discretionary, non-mandatory)

apertura de una sucesión passing of the estate to the heirs [*This occurs upon the decedent's death.*]

apertura del testamento judge's opening of a "closed" will or holographic will

aplazamiento adjournment

aplazar to postpone, to adjourn, to defer [*A meeting is postponed before it starts, but adjourned after it starts.*]

aplicación
  aplicación de fondos application of funds
  aplicación de una ley enforcement of a law
  aplicación de utilidades appropriation of profits

aplicado consistentemente applied on a consistent basis

aplicar
  aplicar la ley to enforce the law
  aplicar una sanción to impose a sanction

apoderado attorney-in-fact, legal representative
  apoderado generalísimo (Cos) representative with unlimited authority
  apoderado judicial judicial representative, representative in court

apoderamiento seizure

aporía (Mex) problem that arises when there are contradictory precedents with respect to an issue

aportación contribution
  aportación dineraria cash contribution
  aportación en efectivo cash contribution
  aportación en numerario cash contribution

aporte contribution
  aporte de capital capital contribution
  aporte en dinero cash contribution
  aporte en especie contribution in kind

apostilla apostille [*a standard certification provided under the Hague Convention of 1961 for purposes of authenticating documents for use in foreign countries*]

apoyar una moción to second a motion [*in parliamentary procedure*]

apreciación de las pruebas weighing of the evidence [*The judge can evaluate evidence in one of two ways: in some cases he must assign it the weight given to it by statute ("prueba tasada"), and in other cases he is allowed to use his good judgment ("sana crítica") to determine how much probative value it has.*]

apreciar to evaluate, to assess, to estimate
  apreciar el riesgo to assess the risk
  apreciar las pruebas to evaluate, to weigh, to consider evidence

aprecio valuation, appraisal, estimate

apremiar 1. to pressure, to coerce 2. to present a final demand to 3. to obtain a court order against

    apremiar el pago to compel payment

apremio 1. court order 2. tax collection proceeding 3. pressure, coercion, duress 4. interrogation to obtain a confession 5. late charge, penalty for being late

    apremio de pago demand note

    apremio ilegal illegal pressure to force a confession

    apremio judicial foreclosure sale

    apremios físicos physical coercion

    apremios policiales police harassment [*to force a confession*]

aprisionar to imprison

aprista (Per) member of the Alianza Popular Revolucionaria Americana

apropiación appropriation

    apropiación ilícita misappropriation

    apropiación indebida misappropriation

aprovechamientos taxes for public services, public use taxes

aprovisionamiento procurement

arancel

    arancel aduanero tariff schedule

    arancel de importación import tariff

    arancel externo común common external tariff

    arancel financiero revenue tariff

    arancel fiscal revenue tariff

    arancel judicial schedule of court fees

    arancel notarial schedule of notary's fees

    arancel proteccionista protective tariff

arbitrable arbitrable

arbitraje 1. arbitration 2. arbitrage

    arbitraje comercial commercial arbitration

    arbitraje de conciencia equitable arbitration, arbitration ex aequo et bono [*arbitration where the arbitrator is not bound by legal principles - follows the rules agreed to by the parties with respect to procedure and decides the case as seems fair to him, without regard for the law*]

    arbitraje de derecho de jure arbitration [*arbitrator decides the case in accordance with the law*]

    arbitraje judicial arbitration decided pursuant to court rules

    arbitraje obligatorio binding arbitration

arbitrajista arbitrageur

arbitramento (Col, Ven) arbitration

arbitrio 1. discretion 2. tax

    arbitrio de plusvalía (Spa) local capital gains tax on land

    arbitrio judicial 1. judicial decision 2. judicial discretion

    arbitrio municipal (Per) tax for municipal services [*garbage collection, streetlamps, etc.*]

arbitrio rentístico means of generating revenue
arbitrios de aduana (Pue) customs duties
**Queda al arbitrio de su Señoría establecer el monto que
corresponda.** It is up to Your Honor's discretion to establish
the appropriate amount.
árbitro arbitrator
árbitro arbitrador (Chi) amiable compositeur, arbitrator ex
aequo et bono [*arbitrator not bound by legal principles -
follows the rules agreed to by the parties with respect to
procedure and follows equitable principles rather than the
law with respect to the merits*]
árbitro de conciencia (Per) amiable compositeur, arbitrator ex
aequo et bono [*synonym of "árbitro arbitrador" (q.v.)*]
árbitro de derecho de jure arbitrator [*follows the law with
respect to both substance and procedure*]
árbitro de equidad amiable compositeur, arbitrator ex aequo et
bono
árbitro dirimente umpire
árbitro mixto (Chi) arbitrator who follows the rules agreed to by
the parties with respect to procedure and follows the law with
respect to the merits
archivamiento filing away [*as opposed to the initial filing of the case
with the court*]
archivamiento final (Per) final dismissal of a case
archivamiento temporal (Per) temporary stay of proceedings
archivar to file away, to put a document in the proper file [*as
opposed to filing a document with the court, which is "entablar
ante el tribunal"*]
arma asesina murder weapon
armonización fiscal tax law harmonization
arqueo cash count [*counting the money on hand*]
arraigar to post bail
arraigo 1. (Arg) posting a bond to pay court costs and fees if the
party subsequently loses the lawsuit **2. (Mex)** ne exeat order
[*order not to leave the jurisdiction—also called "arraigo en juicio"*]
arras down payment, earnest money
arrastrar un saldo to carry a balance forward
arrebato (Per) purse snatching
arreglar extrajudicialmente to settle out of court
arreglo extrajudicial out-of-court settlement
arrendable rentable, leasable
arrendador (Chi, Mex, Per, Spa) lessor, landlord
arrendadora financiera financial leasing company
arrendajo (Mex) poor imitation, poor copy
arrendamiento lease, leasing
arrendamiento financiero financial lease
arrendante (Cos) lessor, landlord

arrendatario (Chi, Cos, Mex, Per, Spa) lessee, tenant
arrestar to arrest, to place under arrest
arresto arrest
    arresto domiciliario house arrest
    arresto preventivo preventive detention
arroba the @ symbol
articular y absolver posiciones to submit and answer
    interrogatories
artículo 1. article 2. product, good
    artículo único article one of one
    artículo 2 y demás relativos (el) Article 2 and other related
    articles
    artículos alimenticios foodstuffs
    artículos básicos basic commodities
    artículos de comercio commodities
    artículos de primera necesidad staple products
    artículos elaborados manufactured goods
    artículos en camino goods in transit
    artículos falsificados counterfeit goods
    artículos terminados finished goods
artífice author, designer, person responsible for something
asalariado wage earner, salaried employee
asalariar to employ
asalto robbery, hold-up
    asalto a mano armada armed robbery
asamblea
    asamblea celebrada en segunda convocatoria reconvened
    meeting
    asamblea constitutiva organizational meeting
    asamblea constituyente constitutional convention
    asamblea especial (Arg, Cos, Gua, Hon, Mex) meeting of
    shareholders of a certain series of shares
    Asamblea General (Uru) the Uruguayan Legislature [*made up
    of the Senado and the Cámara de Diputados*]
    **asamblea general extraordinaria (Arg, Col, Cos, Gua, Hon,
    Mex, Par, Uru, Ven)** extraordinary shareholders' meeting
    [called "junta general extraordinaria" in other countries]
    **asamblea general ordinaria (Arg, Col, Cos, Gua, Hon, Mex,
    Par, Uru, Ven)** ordinary shareholders' meeting [*called "junta
    general ordinaria" in other countries*]
    asamblea legislativa the Legislature
    asamblea mixta combined ordinary and extraordinary meeting
    of shareholders
    asamblea resolvió (la) the shareholders resolved [*In Spanish,
    one speaks of the "asamblea" doing something, while in
    English, one says that the "shareholders" did something at a
    meeting.*]

ascender a to amount to, to add up to
ascendiente (adj.) ascending
ascendiente (m/f) ancestor
asegurable insurable
asegurador insurer
asegurar bienes to insure assets
asentar to post [*on the books*]
    asentar en el expediente to place on the record, to have the record reflect
    asentar para constancia to place on the record, to have the record reflect
    asentar un nacimiento to record a birth
asesinar to kill, to murder
asesinato murder
    asesinato medio precio murder for hire
    asesinato por recompensa murder for hire
asesino murderer, killer
    asesino a sueldo hired assassin, hitman
    asesino en serie serial killer
    asesino múltiple serial killer
asesor advisor, consultant
    asesor de menores guardian ad litem
    asesor fiscal tax advisor
asesoramiento advice
asesorar a la administración to act in an advisory capacity to management
asesoría jurídica legal services, legal counsel
aseveración assertion
así las cosas given this situation
asiento
    asiento compensatorio offsetting entry
    asiento contable accounting entry
    asiento de abono credit entry
    asiento de cargo debit entry
    asiento de diario journal entry
    asiento de mayor ledger entry
    asiento de presentación initial recording of ownership in the Public Registries
    asiento de reversión reversing entry
asignación
    asignación de recursos allocation of resources
    asignación familiar (Arg) family allowance [*payment in addition to salary based on the number of an employee's dependents*]
asilo político political asylum
asistir 1. to attend 2. to assist 3. to have
    el derecho que asiste a mi representado the right to which my client is entitled

asistencia técnica technical assistance
asociación
    asociación civil business form used by charitable and non-profit organizations
    asociación delictiva conspiracy
    asociación delictuosa (Mex) conspiracy of three or more persons [*Art. 164 of the Criminal Code for the Federal District*]
    asociación de ingresos y costos matching costs and revenues
    asociación en participación (contractual) joint venture [*i.e., no joint venture entity is formed*]
    asociación mercantil trade association
    asociación para delinquir conspiracy
    asociación sindical labor union
asociado contributing partner [*in a joint venture*]
asociante managing partner [*in a joint venture*]
astreintes (Arg, Per) fine for failure to comply with a court order
atacar la jurisdicción to challenge the jurisdiction
atenerse a to comply with, to abide by
    sin atenerse a la ley without due process of law
atentado criminal attempt, attempted crime
    atentado al pudor (Mex, Pue) sexual assault [*taking indecent liberties (such as fondling without consent) with a persón of the opposite sex—also referred to as "indecent assault" in English and as "ultraje al pudor" in Spanish*]
    atentado a la autoridad crime of using force or intimidation to coerce a public official to do or not to do an official act
    atentado contra la seguridad del Estado threat to national security, treason
    atentado contra la vida de alguien attempt on someone's life
    atentado contra las buenas costumbres indecent behavior
    atentado contra libertad de comercio restraint of trade
atentar
    Atentaron contra su vida. They made an attempt on her life.
    una ley que atenta contra los derechos de los inmigrantes a law that violates the rights of immigrants
    actos que atentan contra la seguridad del Estado actions that threaten national security
atento a lo solicitado the court having considered the petition filed herein
atestado policial police report
atestiguar to witness, to attest
atrasado in arrears, past due, overdue
atraso cambiario overvaluation of the local currency
atribuciones power, authority, jurisdiction

audiatur et altera pars (Lat) the rule that both parties to a lawsuit must be heard [*The phrase literally means "let the other party be heard." This concept is also referred to as the "principio de contradicción."*]
audiencia hearing
  audiencia a puerta cerrada in camera hearing
  audiencia constitucional (Mex) the hearing in an amparo proceeding
  audiencia de conciliación settlement hearing
  audiencia incidental (Mex) hearing on a motion
  Audiencia Nacional (Spa) court based in Madrid with nationwide jurisdiction. In criminal matters it has jurisdiction over cases dealing with terrorism, drug trafficking, counterfeiting money, etc. In administrative matters it has jurisdiction over appeals from acts of administrative officials. In labor matters it has jurisdiction over any dispute involving a collective bargaining agreement that applies nationwide.
  audiencia previa a las partes pre-trial conference
  audiencia pública hearing in open court
  audiencia testimonial hearing at which the witnesses (rather than the parties) testify
auditor auditor
  auditor ambulante field auditor
  auditor externo external auditor
  auditor fiscal tax auditor
  auditor interno internal auditor
auditoría audit
  auditoría externa external audit
  auditoría interna internal audit
  auditoría limpia unqualified opinion
aumentar
  aumentar el salario mínimo to raise the minimum wage
aumento
  aumento de capital capital increase
  aumento de sueldo a pay raise
auto order [*that is interlocutory*]
  auto aclaratorio (Mex) order dismissing an amparo petition until the petitioner provides a more definite statement of his claim
  auto acordado order by a court sitting en banc, order by a full court
  auto admisorio order admitting a pleading
  auto apertorio (Per) order to commence investigation [*of a criminal case*]
  auto cabeza del proceso court order establishing jurisdiction
  auto de autorización de albacea letters testamentary
  auto de declaratoria de herederos ruling acknowledging the legal heirs to an intestate succession

auto de detención arrest warrant
auto de estar a derecho order requiring the defendant to enter
an appearance in court
auto de formal prisión (Mex) indictment and order to stand trial
auto de inicio (Mex) court order establishing jurisdiction and
opening case file
auto de libertad por falta de méritos (Mex) court order
dismissing charges for lack of evidence
auto de prisión incarceration order
auto de procesamiento official notice that the case is going to
trial
auto de radicación (Mex) court order establishing jurisdiction
auto de sobreseimiento acquittal of criminal charges
auto de vista a las partes order allowing the parties to review
the file
auto para mejor proveer order requiring parties to furnish
additional evidence
auto resolutorio final order, decision
autos court files, the entire record
autos caratulados case captioned [*Smith v. Jones*]
autos en estado de dictar sentencia a case that is ripe for
decision
autos y vistos it appearing to the court that…, in view of the
present proceedings…, having heard this case…
autoacusación voluntary confession of a crime
autoaplicativo self-executing
autocartera (Spa) treasury shares
autocomposición out-of-court settlement
autocontrato contract entered into by one party on his own behalf
and that same party on behalf of another
autodeterminación self-determination
autofinanciación internal financing
autonomía autonomy
autopsia de ley autopsy required by law
autónomo (Spa) self-employed person, freelancer [*short for*
"trabajador autónomo"]
autor
   autor intelectual (de un delito) mastermind (behind a crime)
   autor material (de un delito) perpetrator (of a crime)
autoridad
   autoridad competente the proper authorities
   autoridad responsable (Mex) the respondent authority [*the*
   authority against whom an amparo proceeding was filed]
   autoridades hacendarias (Mex) the tax authorities
autotutela self-help, taking the law into one's own hands [*For*
example, the Uniform Commercial Code allows a debtor to

repossess collateral without going to court if he does so without a breach of the peace.]

auxiliar
    auxiliar de cuentas por cobrar accounts receivable ledger
    auxiliar de cuentas por pagar accounts payable ledger
    auxiliar de la administración de justicia judicial adjunct
    auxiliar del mayor subsidiary ledger
    auxiliar junior junior clerk
    auxiliar senior senior clerk
    auxiliares subsidiary ledgers
auxilio judicial mutual judicial assistance [*one court helping another*]
aval guarantee by endorsement [*endorsement renders the guarantor jointly and severally liable with the principal debtor*]
avalar to guarantee by endorsement
avalista guarantor
avaluación anticipada de perjuicios liquidated damages
avalúo appraisal
    avalúo catastral assessed valuation
ave negra (Arg) shyster, unscrupulous lawyer
avenencia agreement to settle a lawsuit
averiguación previa (Mex) preliminary investigation, pretrial investigation
aviador (Mex) phantom employee [*fictitious employee on the payroll whose wages are collected illegally*]
avío working capital loan
aviso notice
    aviso de alta (Mex) notice of new hires [*given to the Mexican Social Security Administration*]
    aviso de baja (Mex) notice of terminated employees [*given to the Mexican Social Security Administration*]
    aviso de protesto notice of protest [*a sworn statement that a promissory note was presented to the maker for payment and the maker refused to pay*]
    aviso comercial commercial slogan
    hasta nuevo aviso until further notice
avocación reach-down jurisdiction [*assumption of jurisdiction by a higher court over a matter pending in a lower court—Note that this is not the same thing as "certiorari."*]
avocarse el conocimiento de una causa to exercise reach-down jurisdiction, to take over a case from a lower court [*This verb must not be confused with "abocarse."*]
ayllu (Bol) self-governing, land-owning peasant community in Bolivia's highlands
ayuntamiento 1. town council 2. city government, municipal government

baja 1. fall, drop 2. decline, downward trend 3. leave of absence 4. retirement of assets
    baja por enfermedad (Spa) sick leave
    baja por maternidad (Spa) maternity leave
bajo under
    bajo apercibimiento de ley under the penalties provided by law
    bajo cargo (Per) being liable for failure to do so
    bajo coacción under duress
    bajo falsas apariencias under false pretenses
    bajo fe de juramento under oath
    bajo juramento under oath
    bajo mi fe y sello (Pue) under my hand and seal
    bajo mi firma y sello (Pue) under my hand and seal
    bajo pena under penalty
    bajo protesta de decir verdad (Mex) under oath, under penalty of perjury
    bajo responsabilidad (Per) being liable for failure to do so
    Los Registros públicos procederán al levantamiento de los gravámenes, sin costo alguno, bajo responsabilidad. The public registries shall remove the liens at no cost, and shall be liable for failure to do so.
balance 1. balance sheet 2. (Pue) balance [*In Puerto Rico, the word is used to mean "saldo."*]
    balance de cierre closing balance sheet
    balance de comprobación trial balance
    balance de prueba trial balance
    balance de situación balance sheet
    balance fiscal balance sheet for tax purposes
    balance general balance sheet
    balance general consolidado consolidated balance sheet
    balance general dictaminado (Mex) audited balance sheet
    balance provisional interim balance sheet
    balance provisorio interim balance sheet
    balance regularizado restated balance sheet
balanza
    balanza comercial balance of trade [*difference over a period of time between the value of a country's imports and exports*]
    balanza de divisas balance of foreign exchange
    balanza de pagos balance of payments [*system of recording all of a country's economic transactions with the rest of the world during a particular time period*]
    balanza de poderes balance of powers
    balanza económica balance of payments
baldío uncultivated land, wasteland
balota (Per) ballot
    balota blanca (Per) a vote in favor of someone or something
    balota negra (Per) a vote against someone or something

balotear (Per) to blackball
banca 1. banking 2. the banking industry 3. seat in the legislature
    banca de inversión investment banking
    banca de menudeo retail banking
    banca de sucursales branch banking
    banca electrónica electronic banking services
    banca extraterritorial offshore banking
    banca múltiple universal banking, full-service banking [*also called "banca universal"—i.e., offering both commercial banking and investment banking services*]
    banca universal universal banking, full-service banking [*offering both commercial banking and investment banking services*]
bancada delegation [*members of the legislature from the same political party*]
bancarrota bankruptcy
banco bank
    banco corresponsal correspondent bank
    banco de ahorros savings bank
    banco de fomento development bank
    banco de primera categoría first-tier bank, leading bank
    banco de segundo piso wholesale bank [*a bank that caters to rich individuals, big business, and institutions and government*]
    banco emisor issuing bank
    Banco Mundial the World Bank
    bancos cash in banks [*as an item on a balance sheet*]
banquero banker
banquillo de los testigos witness stand
barandillero (Spa) scalper [*a trader on the stock exchange who attempts to profit on relatively small price changes*]
Barra Mexicana de Abogados (Mex) Mexican Bar Association
barrilete (Mex) junior attorney
base base, basis
    base acumulativa accrual basis
    base gravable tax base
    base semestral semi-annual basis
    bases de la acción grounds for the action
    bases de un concurso bid documents, request for proposal, terms of reference [*also called "pliego de condiciones"*]
bastantear to examine a power of attorney for sufficiency
bastanteo note written on a power of attorney declaring it sufficient for its purpose
bastantero person in charge of examining a power of attorney authorizing lawyers to represent individuals in a lawsuit
beneficiario beneficiary
    beneficiario de franquicia franchisee
    beneficiario de un cheque payee

beneficiario de un pagaré payee
beneficio 1. profit 2. benefit
beneficio bruto gross earnings
beneficio contributivo (Pue) tax shelter
beneficio de división guarantor's right to obtain a court order
that the proceedings be brought against all guarantors
beneficio de excusión guarantor's right to force a creditor to go
against the debtor before the creditor takes action against
the guarantor
beneficio de explotación (Spa) operating income
beneficio de inventario heir's right to accept inheritance on the
condition that he is not obligated to pay estate's creditors
more than the value of his inheritance
beneficio de justicia gratuita (Spa) entitlement to legal aid
beneficio de litigar sin gastos (Arg) right to proceed in forma
pauperis
beneficio de pobreza right to proceed in forma pauperis
beneficio extrasalarial fringe benefit
beneficio neto net income, net profit
beneficio por acción earnings per share (EPS)
beneficio privado private benefit [versus "social benefit"]
beneficio social social benefit [economic term meaning "benefit
that all persons get from a good"]
beneficios de los fundadores (Per) founders' shares,
founders' stock
beneficios por incapacidad disability benefits
beneficios por retiros de personal personnel retirement
pension benefits
Benemérita (Spa) another name for the Guardia Civil
beneplácito approval
bien de familia homestead [exempt pursuant to homestead laws
from seizure or sale for debt—also called "patrimonio de familia"]
bienes 1. assets 2. goods
bienes accesorios property permanently affixed to the land
bienes adventicios property of eldest son who is under
parental control, which property is acquired through his own
efforts or through gift or devise other than from his father.
The property belongs to the son, but the parents have the
right to use it.
bienes afectados en garantía collateral [assets furnished as
security]
bienes agotables wasting assets
bienes alodiales property free from liens and other
encumbrances
bienes antifernales property that a husband settles on his wife
bienes arrendados leased premises
bienes bajados retired assets

bienes castrenses military earnings, property acquired through military service
bienes comunes jointly owned assets
bienes corporales tangible assets
bienes dados de baja retired assets
bienes de abolengo assets inherited from one's grandparents
bienes de cambio (Arg) inventory
bienes de capital capital assets
bienes de consumo consumer goods
bienes de dominio del poder público property in the public domain
bienes de dominio público public property
bienes de equipo capital equipment, capital goods
bienes de producción capital goods
bienes de propiedad privada private property
bienes de uso (Arg) fixed assets (UK), property, plant and equipment (US)
bienes dotales dowry
bienes duraderos durable goods
bienes en arriendo (Chi) rental properties
bienes en consignación goods on consignment
bienes en custodia property in custody
bienes en dominio (Chi) properties owned [*as opposed to "bienes en arriendo"*]
bienes en fideicomiso trust assets, property held in trust
bienes en tránsito goods in transit
bienes falsificados counterfeit goods
bienes fideicomitidos trust assets, property held in trust
bienes físicos tangible assets
bienes futuros property to be acquired in the future
bienes gananciales community property [*acquired during marriage*]
bienes hereditarios inherited assets
bienes incorporales intangible assets
bienes inembargables nonattachable assets
bienes inmuebles real estate, real property [*also called "bienes raíces"*]
bienes intangibles intangible assets
bienes litigiosos property in dispute
bienes mancomunados joint property
bienes mostrencos unclaimed personal property
bienes muebles personal property, chattel
bienes no transables non-tradable goods
bienes parafernales wife's separate property brought into a marriage

bienes patrimoniales 1. a person's net worth, the entire assets and liabilities of a person 2. private property owned free and clear

bienes privativos separate property [*in a community property system*]

bienes profecticios property obtained by a son because of his father or using his father's assets

bienes propios private property owned free and clear

bienes raíces real estate, real property

bienes relictos inherited property, the estate of a deceased person

bienes semiduraderos semi-durable goods

bienes semovientes livestock

bienes sujetos a agotamiento (Chi) wasting assets

bienes terrenales worldly goods

bienes transables tradable goods, fungible goods

bienes vacantes parcels of land of unknown ownership

bienes y servicios goods and services

bienestar welfare

Bienestar Familiar (Col) Welfare Service [*short for "Instituto Colombiano de Bienestar Familiar"*]

bienestar público public welfare

bienestar social social welfare

bienhechurías improvements [*also called "mejoras"*]

billete de banco banknote

bines (Ven) BIN's [*bank identification numbers*]

binomio a pair of two persons, a team, running mates [*can be used to refer to the Presidential and Vice Presidential candidates, for example*]

blanquear dinero to launder money

blanqueo de capitales (Arg) tax amnesty [*government agreement to accept late tax payments without imposing any penalty*]

bloque bancario (Per) bank block [*annotation that a bank requests from the Public Registry such that the real property being furnished as collateral cannot be the subject of any other transaction at the same time*]

bloquear un cheque to stop payment on a check

boca de urna exit poll

boce (Arg) economic consolidation bond [*short for "bono de consolidación económica"*]

bocon (Arg) debt consolidation bond [*short for "bonos de consolidación de deudas"*]

bocre (Arg) export credit bond [*short for "bono de crédito a la exportación"*]

bodega 1. **(Chi, Col, Cos, Mex, Nic)** warehouse [*In other countries the terms "almacén" and "depósito" are used.*] 2. **(Cub, Per, Ven)** grocery store

bodega fiscal bonded warehouse
bodegaje (Chi) storage fees
boleta (Per) partial notarial copy of a notarial instrument, containing only the parts thereof that are of interest to the person requesting the copy
boleta bancaria (Chi) certificate of deposit
boleta de arancel judicial (Per) receipt showing that court fees have been paid
boleta de circulación routing slip
boleta de citación summons
boleta de contravención (Ecu, Ven) traffic ticket
boleta de depósito (Arg, Chi) deposit slip
boleta de empeño (Mex) pawn shop receipt
boleta de expedición (Mex) waybill
boleta de garantía (Chi) performance bond [*in the form of a certificate of deposit*]
boleta de impuestos tax receipt
boleta de inventario (Arg) inventory tag
boleta de pago (Per) pay stub [*evidencing that employee has received his salary*]
boleta de pago predial real estate tax receipt
boleta de presentación (Per) registration form [*used to file something with the public registry*]
boleta de ventas (Chi, Per) sales receipt
boleta electoral (Arg, Mex) ballot
boleta predial real estate tax receipt
boletear (Col) to extort
boleteo (Col) extortion
boletín
    Boletín Oficial (Arg) Official Gazette of Argentina
    Boletín Oficial del Estado (Spa) Official Gazette of Spain
boleto de compraventa (Arg) bilateral promise of sale or an agreement of sale [*the precursor or preliminary agreement to the sale of real property*]
bolsa
    Bolsa de Comercio de Buenos Aires (Arg) Buenos Aires Stock Exchange
    bolsa de contratación commodities exchange
    bolsa de valores securities exchange
bonde (Mex) government development bond [*short for "bono de desarrollo del Gobierno Federal"*]
bonex (Arg) external bond [*short for "bono externo"*]
bonificación 1. bonus 2. discount
    bonificación de fin de año (Ven) year-end bonus [*also called "aguinaldo"*]
    bonificación por consumo (Spa) volume discount [*also called a "rappel"*]

bonificación por no siniestralidad (Spa) reduction in insurance premium for not having filed any claims

bono bond

bono ajustable index-linked bond

bono al portador bearer bond

bono basura junk bond

bono clásico straight bond [*bond conforming to the standard description, i.e., unquestioned right to repayment of principal at specified future date—also called "bono ordinario"*]

bono con certificado warrant bond

bono con cupón coupon bond [*has interest coupons attached*]

bono con interés variable floating rate bond

bono convertible convertible bond

bono de consolidación de deudas (Arg) debt consolidation bond [*also called "bocon"*]

bono de consolidación económica (Arg) economic consolidation bond [*also called "boce"*]

bono de crédito a la exportación (Arg) export credit bond [*also called "bocre"*]

bono de estabilización monetaria monetary stabilization bond

bono de fundador (Cos, Gua, Hon, Mex) founders' shares, founders' stock

bono de goce (Arg) redemption bonds issued to holders of fully paid-up stock, entitling them to a share of company profits, and in the event of dissolution to a share of proceeds derived from liquidation

bono de participación (Arg) participation bonds for amounts which are not capital contributions and which entitle holders to a share of profits in the fiscal year. They may also be made available to employees in profit-sharing programs and in such case are non-transferable.

bono de prenda collateral certificate [*certificate issued by bonded warehouse as evidence of a lien on goods deposited therein as security for a loan; see also "certificado de depósito"*]

bono de reconocimiento (Per) statement of contributions to old security system that can be redeemed in the new system

bono de renta vitalicia annuity bond

bono de rentabilidad revenue bond [*principal and interest are paid solely from earnings*]

bono de transporte (Ven) supplement for transportation [*supplement to an employee's salary*]

bono de vencimiento escalonado serial bond [*a certain portion of the bond is retired at regular intervals*]

bono del Colegio Público de Abogados (Arg) contribution to the Bar Association [*contribution must be made to the bar every time a lawsuit is filed or answered*]

bono emitido con descuento original issue discount bond
bono externo (Arg) external bond [*also called "foreign bond"*]
bono nocturno (Ven) night differential [*extra pay for working the night shift*]
bono nominativo registered bond [*states the name of the owner*]
bono ordinario straight bond [*see "bono clásico"*]
bono público government bond
bono quirografario unsecured bond
bono redimible callable bond [*all or part can be redeemed before maturity*]
bono referencial benchmark bond
bono sin cupón zero coupon bond
bono sin garantía específica debenture
bono verde green bond [*used to finance agriculture*]
bonos bancarios bank bonds
bonos bancarios de desarrollo (BBD) (Mex) development bank bonds
bonos de desarrollo del Gobierno Federal (bondes) (Mex) Federal Government Development Bonds
bonos de la Tesorería de la Federación (tesobonos) (Mex) Treasury Bonds
bonos de renovación urbana (bores) (Mex) urban renewal bonds
bores (Mex) urban renewal bonds [*short for "bonos de renovación urbana*]
borrador draft [*of a document before the final version*]
bote (Arg) treasury bond [*short for "bono del tesoro"*]
brevete (Per) driver's license, pilot's license
buen padre de familia reasonable man
buena fe good faith
buena pro the awarding of the bid
  obtener la buena pro to be awarded the bid
buenos oficios good offices [*a dispute settlement procedure in which a respected third party or a neutral State acting on request or at its own discretion seeks through diplomatic means to persuade the disputing parties to meet and resume direct negotiation—Good offices is not synonymous with mediation, but is essentially confined to the initiation by a disinterested third party of direct negotiations without any further participation by that third party.*]
bufete (Mex, Per, Spa) law firm [*term not used in Argentina, where the correct term is "estudio de abogados"*]
burlar la ley to find a loophole in a rule, to find a way around a rule
bursatilidad marketability
bursatilización securitization
buzón nocturno night depository [*at a bank*]

C. Juez (Mex) Honorable Judge [*The "C" stands for "ciudadano," but it is not customary to refer to a judge as "Citizen Judge" in English.*]

    A usted C. Juez, atentamente pido se sirva (Mex) Wherefore, plaintiff/defendant prays that this Honorable Court [*depending on whether the document is filed by the plaintiff or the defendant. Note that documents are addressed to the* judge *in Mexico and to the* court *in the United States.*]

caballero blanco white knight

cabecera 1. (Pan) capital city of one of the nine provinces **2. (Mex)** county seat [*main city in a "municipio"*] **3. (Hon, Nic)** capital city of one of the "departamentos"

caber

    cabe afirmar que it is important to note, importantly, significantly

    cabe destacar que it is important to note, importantly, significantly

    cabe señalar que it is important to note, importantly, significantly

cabeza de familia head of household

cachear to frisk

cacheo frisk, body search

cada vez que sea necesario as often as necessary

cadena perpetua life imprisonment

caducar to lapse, to expire

caducidad lapse, expiration, loss of validity

    caducidad de la acción termination of action by lapse of time

    caducidad de la instancia constructive abandonment of lawsuit for failure to prosecute [*roughly equivalent to the U.S. doctrine of laches*]

    caducidad de un derecho forfeiture of a right

caduco lapsed, expired, no longer valid

caja 1. cash on hand **2.** cash register

    caja chica petty cash

    caja de ahorro savings and loan, savings bank

    caja de resistencia strike fund [*union funds for allocation during a strike to cover costs of benefits, legal fees, publicity, etc.*]

    caja de seguridad safe deposit box

    caja de valores central securities depository

    caja fuerte bank vault, safe

    caja mutual de crédito (Arg) credit union

    caja nocturna night depository [*at a bank*]

    caja permanente automated teller machine (ATM)

    caja social corporate treasury

    caja y bancos cash on hand and in banks

    caja y bancos de clientes client cash balances

cajero 1. teller [*in a bank*] **2.** cashier [*in a store*]

cajero automático automated teller machine (ATM)
cajero mixto (Mex) unit teller [*a teller who accepts deposits and cashes checks*]
cajero múltiple (Mex) full-service teller
cajero pagador payroll clerk
cajero principal head teller
calidad 1. quality 2. capacity
calidad de venta merchantable quality
en su calidad de in his capacity as
calificación
calificación crediticia credit rating
calificación de la quiebra determination of the bankrupt's degree of fault [*whether it is "culpable," "casual" or "fraudulente"*]
calificación del delito classification of the crime
calificadora de valores rating agency
calumnia wrongfully accusing someone of a criminal act
calumniar to accuse falsely of a criminal act
cámara chamber
cámara alta the upper house
cámara baja the lower house
cámara de apelaciones (Arg) court of appeals
cámara compensadora clearing house
cámara de comercio chamber of commerce
Cámara de Comercio Internacional International Chamber of Commerce (ICC)
cámara de compensación clearing house
cámara de diputados House of Representatives
cámara de senadores Senate
cámara joven the lower house [*i.e., the Cámara de Diputados*]
camarista (Arg) appellate court judge
cambio 1. change 2. exchange 3. share price
cambio exterior foreign exchange
cambios de cierre closing prices
cambios patrimoniales changes in equity
cambista money changer
camino road
camino vecinal secondary highway
Caminos y Puentes Federales de Ingresos y Servicios Conexos (Mex) Federal Toll-Road and Toll-Bridge Authority
campaña electoral election campaign
cancelación
cancelación de cuentas incobrables bad debts written off
cancelación de la factura payment of the invoice
cancelación en libros to write off
cancelar 1. to pay 2. to cancel 3. to write off
cancelar el impuesto to pay the tax

cancelar el monto principal de la obligación to repay the principal amount of the obligation
cancelar la radicación de un documento to pay the filing fees [*with respect to a document*]
cancelar una cuenta to close an account
cancelar una deuda incobrable to write off a bad debt
cancelar una multa to pay a fine
Canciller (Arg, Per) Minister of Foreign Affairs [*similar to U.S. Secretary of State*]
Cancillería (Arg, Per) Ministry of Foreign Affairs [*similar to U.S. Department of State*]
canje barter, exchange
canje de cheques clearing of checks
canon 1. (Spa) royalty [*called "regalía" in other countries*] **2. (Per)** tax paid for acquiring or using a public asset [*The most common "canon" is the "canon de minería" (oil contribution), which must be paid for exploration and production.*]
canon de alquiler rent, rental payment
canon de arrendamiento rent, rental payment
cantidad de dinero sum of money
cantón (Ecu) canton [*The provinces are divided into cantones (which are called "municipios" in other countries).*]
capacidad capacity, ability
  capacidad adquisitiva purchasing power [*the ability of a certain currency at a certain point in time to purchase goods and services. Inflation results in lost purchasing power.*]
  capacidad crediticia borrowing power, creditworthiness
  capacidad de actuar capacity to act
  capacidad de derecho legal personality [*All natural persons and legal entities have this type of "capacity," which is best translated as "personality" in order to avoid confusion with the capacity of persons who have reached the age of majority, which is capacity to contract.*]
  capacidad de ejercicio capacity to contract [*also called "capacidad de hecho"*]
  capacidad de goce (Mex) legal personality [*also called "capacidad de derecho"*]
  capacidad de hecho capacity to contract [*legal capacity of a person to exercise his rights independent of other persons*]
  capacidad empresarial entrepreneurship
  capacidad financiera financial standing
  capacidad jurídica legal personality
  capacidad legal legal personality
  capacidad legal para contratar y obligarse capacity to contract and to comply with obligations assumed
  capacidad ociosa idle capacity
  capacidad para testar testamentary capacity

capacidad procesal capacity to be a party to an action, capacity to sue and be sued

capacidad sancionatoria enforcement authority

capital 1. capital 2. principal [*of a loan*]

  capital adicional additional paid-in capital [*as an item on a balance sheet*]

  capital ajeno borrowings, borrowed capital, long-term debt

  capital autorizado authorized capital

  capital circulante (Spa) net current assets

  capital contable (Mex) shareholders' equity [*Also called "capital en giro." This is called "patrimonio neto" in Latin America and "fondos propios" in Spain.*]

  capital contable de subsidiarias equity in subsidiaries

  capital corriente (Arg) net current assets [*current assets minus current liabilities*]

  capital de explotación working capital

  capital de riesgo venture capital

  capital de trabajo working capital

  capital desembolsado paid-in capital

  capital e intereses principal and interest

  capital económico trading capital

  capital en giro (Mex) shareholders' equity [*also called "capital contable"*]

  capital escriturado (Spa) authorized capital stock

  capital exhibido (Mex) paid-in capital

  capital fijo owner's equity invested in fixed assets

  capital flotante floating capital [*net working capital or that part of capital that is invested in current assets (net of current liabilities) as opposed to fixed or other capital assets*]

  capital golondrina hot money [*short-term capital that moves between countries because of uncertainty regarding the stability of exchange rates or security of capital. Note that the term "hot money" is also used to mean "stolen money," but that is not what is meant here.*]

  capital humano human capital

  capital integrado paid-in capital

  capital más intereses principal plus interest

  capital pagado paid-in capital

  capital riesgoso venture capital

  capital social capital stock

  capital suscrito subscribed capital

  capital variable variable capital

capitalismo capitalism

capitalización capital structure

  capitalización bursátil market capitalization

capitalización de beneficios plow back of earnings [*i.e.,* *reinvesting them in the business rather than distributing them as dividends*]
capitalización de intereses compounding of interest
capitalización de la deuda debt-equity conversion
con capitalización anual compounded annually
capitulaciones matrimoniales prenuptial agreement
captación collection
   captación de capital raising capital
   captación de fondos 1. raising funds, funding 2. attracting deposits
   captación de recursos raising funds by borrowing
   captación de ventanilla over-the-counter deposits
   captación de votos winning of votes
carácter capacity
   carácter de los árbitros capacity of the arbitrators [*i.e., whether they will be "árbitros de derecho" or "árbitros de equidad" (q.v.). Note that the arbitrators' "character" in English would be their "buena reputación" in Spanish, which is not what is meant here.*]
   con cualquier carácter in any capacity
cárcel jail, prison
carcelería sufrida (Per) time served [*time already spent in prison that is subtracted from the sentence*]
carecer to lack
   carecer de derecho to lack legal grounds
   carecer de fuerza legal to be unenforceable
   carecer de fundamento to be unfounded
   carecer de importancia to be immaterial
   carecer de valor to be invalid
careo confrontation hearing [*the accused is brought face to face with the witnesses who will testify against him*]
carga 1. burden 2. cargo
   carga de familia dependents
   carga de la prueba burden of proof
   carga de notificarse duty to go to court and take notice of the court's decision of pending matters
   carga impositiva tax burden
   carga probatoria burden of proof
   carga tributaria tax burden
   cargas de la herencia expenses payable by a decedent's estate
   cargas de un trabajo the duties or responsibilities of a job
   cargas familiares dependents
   cargas sociales employment taxes, social security contributions
cargo 1. job, position, office 2. charge, debit
   cargo administrativo managerial position

cargo fiduciario trusteeship
cargo público public office
cargo y abono debit and credit
cargos diferidos deferred charges [*expenditures not recognized as an expense in the period when made, but carried forward as an asset to be written off in future periods*]
cargos indirectos overhead
carnet electoral (Sal) voter registration card
carpeta 1. file 2. (Per) student's desk 3. (Per) Congressman's desk in Congress
carpetazo (Per) Congressional decision made hastily [*by banging on the desks to show approval or disapproval—note that in other countries "dar carpetazo a un asunto" means to table it.*]
carpetero (Per) Congressman who uses intrigue to censure another Congressman through the use of a "carpetazo" (q.v.)
carta letter
    carta compromiso (Arg) engagement letter [*pursuant to which client hires an accountant. Referred to as "carta de mandato" in Spain.*]
    carta de alivio (Arg) comfort letter
    carta de aval letter of guarantee
    carta de cobranza past due notice, dunning letter
    carta de crédito letter of credit
    carta de crédito auxiliar ancillary letter of credit
    carta de crédito rotativa revolving letter of credit
    carta de crédito stand-by stand-by letter of credit
    carta de ciudadanía naturalization papers
    carta de declaraciones (Mex) representation letter [*letter from management to the auditors confirming the fairness of various elements of the financial statements*]
    Carta de Derechos the Constitution, the Bill of Rights
    carta de gerencia (Arg) representation letter [*letter from management to the auditors confirming the fairness of various elements of the financial statements*]
    carta de intención letter of intent
    Carta de las Naciones Unidas The United Nations Charter
    carta de patrocinio comfort letter
    carta de porte bill of lading
    Carta Magna the Constitution
    carga notarial (Per) letter recorded by a notary
    carta orden de crédito (Gua) letter of credit
    carta poder 1. power of attorney [*that is not recorded by a notary*] 2. proxy [*in the context of shareholders' meetings*]
    Carta Política the Constitution
    carta remesa cover letter, transmittal letter
    carta responsiva custodian receipt
    carta rogatoria letters rogatory

carta simple (Per) letter that is not recorded by a notary [*as opposed to a "carta notarial"*]

carta testamentaria letters testamentary

cartel poster, handbill

    prohibido fijar carteles post no bills [*see also "fijar carteles"*]

cartera portfolio

    cartera accionaria stock portfolio

    cartera con riesgo de cobra doubtful accounts

    cartera crediticia loan portfolio

    cartera de créditos loan portfolio

    cartera de pedidos atrasados backlog of orders

    cartera de valores securities portfolio

    cartera demorada non-performing loans, non-performing portfolio, non-performing loan portfolio

    cartera vencida non-performing loans, non-performing portfolio, non-performing loan portfolio

carterista pickpocket

cartilla (Chi) gambling coupon

    cartilla de ahorros passbook, savings book

    cartilla de desplazado (Spa) document for obtaining medical treatment as a temporary resident

    cartilla militar military identity card

    cartilla sanitaria (Spa) health insurance card

cartulario (Nic) notary public

casa house

    casa de bolsa brokerage firm

    casa de cambio foreign exchange firm

    casa de empeño pawnshop

    casa de moneda mint

    casa matriz parent company

    Casa Rosada (Arg) official residence of the President of Argentina

casación

    casación en el fondo reversal on the merits

    casación en la forma reversal on a procedural issue

    casación per saltum (Lat) leapfrogging [*Leapfrogging means that a trial court decision is appealed directly to the supreme court, by "jumping" over the intermediate court of appeals.*]

casado en primeras nupcias married in first wedlock

casar 1. to marry, to wed 2. to match securities offered and bought at the same price 3. to set aside on appeal, to overturn, to reverse

    casarse por lo civil to get married in a registry office

casco hard hat [*worn by workers for protection*]

casero lessor, landlord

casilla judicial attorney's mailbox in the courthouse

casillero
    casillero criminal (Mex) criminal record [*also called "antecedentes penales"*]
    casillero judicial 1. (Mex) criminal record [*also called "antecedentes penales"*] **2. (Ecu)** room in the courthouse where attorney's mailboxes are located
caso case, event
    caso de incumplimiento event of default
    caso dudoso borderline case
    caso fortuito act of God
castigo penalty, punishment, fine
    castigo corporal corporal punishment
catálogo de cuentas chart of accounts
catastrar to calculate the tax value of property ←—
catastro real estate register   ╱——
categoría de emisores class of issuer
cateo search of a house pursuant to a warrant
    cateo y secuestro de bienes search and seizure
caución bond posted by another for a person in custody
    caución bursátil pledge of securities
    caución de arraigo (Mex) bond for court costs
    caución de no ofender bond posted by a person who has committed an offense to guarantee that he will not commit it again
    caución de rato bond posted by an attorney who has not received a power of attorney from his client. [*The bond guarantees that the client will ratify all the attorney's acts on his behalf.*]
    caución de un administrador bond posted by board member to guarantee the faithful performance of his duties
    caución juratoria (Arg) promissory oath to observe a certain course of conduct [*when there is no bond*]
caucionar su manejo to guarantee the faithful performance of his duties
caudal 1. wealth 2. fortune
    caudal hereditario decedent's estate
    caudal privativo de cada uno de los cónyuges the separate property of each of the spouses [*as opposed to "community property"*]
    caudal público public assets
    caudal relicto decedent's estate
    caudal social partnership/corporate assets [*depending on whether the "sociedad" is a partnership or a corporation*]
causa 1. case, lawsuit 2. cause [*of a contract—similar to the common law notion of "consideration"*]
    causa de disolución cause of dissolution
    causa de pedir (Mex) cause of action

causa eximente exonerating circumstance
causa petendi (Lat) cause of action, ground for a claim
causa pública the public good, the public welfare
causa sobreviniente supervening cause
causahabiente successor in interest, assign, assignee
causal grounds
    causal de divorcio grounds for divorce
    causal de desahucio grounds for eviction
    causal del despido grounds for dismissal
causante 1. decedent 2. taxpayer
    causante de impuestos taxpayer
causar
    causar cosa juzgada to be res judicata
    causar ejecutoria to go into effect, to become enforceable
    causar estado to enter a final judgment, to definitively end a case
    causar impuestos to be subject to taxes
    causar instancia to try a case and hand down a judgment
    causar intereses to earn interest
    causar jurisprudencia to establish a binding precedent
cautelarmente as a precaution, to be on the safe side
cebe (Spa) certificate of deposit from the Bank of Spain [*short for "certificado de depósito del Banco de España*]
cedear (Arg) Argentine depositary receipt [*short for "certificado de depósito argentino"*]
cedente assignor
ceder to assign
cedes (Mex) certificate of deposit [*short for "certificado de depósito bancario a plazo"*]
cédula
    cédula con efectos de patente para ejercer la profesión de X (Mex) identification card that constitutes a license to practice the profession of X
    cédula de citación (Spa) summons
    cédula de ciudadanía (Col, Ecu) identity card for citizens
    cédula de empadronamiento (Mex) VAT registration certificate
    cédula de emplazamiento (Spa) summons
    cédula de extranjería (Col) identity card for resident aliens
    cédula de habitabilidad (Spa) certificate of fitness for occupancy
    cédula de identidad (Bol, Chi, Ven) identity card
    cédula de licencia final (Ecu) certificate of final discharge from the armed forces
    cédula de notificación (Per) official notice of court decision
    cédula de vecindad (Gua) identity card
    cédula hipotecaria mortgage-backed security
    cédula jurídica (Cos) corporate identification number

cédula prendaria (Cos) asset-backed security
cédula sumaria lead schedule [*details the components of an amount appearing on a financial statement*]
cédula testamentaria codicil [*to a will*]
cédula tributaria (Ecu) certificate of tax payment
cédula verde (Arg) automobile registration papers
cedulación (Col, Ven) process of issuing identity cards ⸺
cefepista (Ecu) member of the Concentración de Fuerzas Populares
celda 1. cell [*in a prison*] 2. cubicle [*in an office*]
celebrar
    celebrar un contrato to enter into a contract
    celebrar una asamblea to hold a meeting
    celebrar una reunión to hold a meeting
    celebrar una vista to hold a hearing
cenetista (Spa) member of the Confederación Nacional de Trabajo
censo electoral roll of registered voters
central
    Central de Anotaciones (Spa) Bank of Spain's book-entry office for public debt
    central de depósito de valores central securities depository
    central de riesgo credit-reporting agency, credit bureau
centro de readaptación social (Mex) correctional facility
ceñirse to conform to, not go beyond the bounds of, to be limited to
ceplata (Mex) silver certificate [*short for "certificados de plata"*]
ceprofi (Mex) tax incentive certificate [*short for "certificado de promoción fiscal"*]
certificado certificate
    certificado de abono forestal (Cos) tax refund certificate for forests planted [*Person planting a forest is given a tax refund of 100,000 colones per hectare planted.*]
    certificado de abono tributario (Col, Cos, Pan) tax credit certificate [*Tax incentives are given to promote nontraditional exports. Companies in certain industries that export products manufactured in the country may apply for tax credits in the form of a certificate. These certificates are based on the value added to the product. They can be used to pay taxes and import duties.*]
    certificado de adición certificate of patent improvement
    certificado de buena conducta certificate of good conduct [*issued by the police to certify that a person has no criminal record*]
    certificado de defunción death certificate
    certificado de depósito warehouse receipt [*Bonded warehouses have the power to issue warehouse receipts (certificados de depósito) that banks may accept as collateral. A warehouse receipt demonstrates ownership of*

the goods deposited in the warehouse. Endorsing the warehouse receipt can transfer ownership of the goods. Attached to the warehouse receipt is a collateral receipt (bono de prenda or vale de prenda). Endorsing the collateral receipt can transfer the security interest in the goods. If the debtor does not pay back the loan when due, the holder of the bono de prenda held as collateral can request that the warehouse owner sell the goods at private auction, and the creditor will be paid from the proceeds of the auction.]

certificado de depósito argentino (cedear) (Arg) Argentine depositary receipt [*receipt issued by an Argentine bank to an Argentine who has bought shares abroad. The receipt can be traded on the Buenos Aires Stock Exchange.*]

certificado de depósito bancario a plazo (cedes) (Mex) certificate of deposit

certificado de la Tesorería de la Federación (cetes) (Mex) Federal Treasury Certificates

certificado de goce (Gua) retired share benefits

certificado de inafectabilidad (Mex) certificate of exemption from appropriation

certificado de matrimonio marriage certificate

certificado de movimiento (Chi) certificate of account activity

certificado de nacimiento birth certificate

certificado de origen certificate of origin

certificado de participación (Mex) certificate of investment [*negotiable instrument representing right to a proportional ownership interest in trusts, property and income from property*]

certificado de participación inmobiliaria (CPI) (Mex) certificate of investment in a real estate trust

certificado de participación ordinario (CPO) (Mex) certificate of trust investment

certificado de plata (ceplatas) (Mex) silver certificate

certificado de promoción fiscal (Mex) tax incentive certificate [*document issued by the Secretaría de Hacienda y Crédito Público evidencing the right of its holder to credit the amount thereof against any federal tax owed*]

certificado de trabajo certificate of employment

certificado definitivo formal certificate

certificado global global certificate

certificado provisional interim certificate [*a certificate of shares, bonds, or other securities issued pending preparation of a formal certificate or payment in full on installment issues*]

cesantía 1. (Mex) dismissal, layoff **2. (Col, Per)** severance pay **3. (Chi)** unemployment

cesar (Mex) to fire someone, lay someone off

cesar en sus funciones to cease to hold office

cesión
    cesión de créditos assignment of accounts receivable
    cesión de derechos assignment of rights
    cesión de un contrato assignment of a contract
cesionario assignee
cetes (Mex) federal treasury certificates [*short for "certificados de la tesorería de la Federación*]
chantaje blackmail
chantajear to blackmail
chapa **1. (Arg)** name plate **2. (Mex)** lock **3. (Par)** slate of candidates, a political party's ticket
chartismo charting [*chart analysis of stock prices*]
cheque check
    cheque a favor de X check made out to X
    cheque al contado check made out to cash
    cheque bancario cashier's check [*check drawn by a bank on itself*]
    cheque causal (Gua) earmarked check [*indicates the reason why it was written*]
    cheque certificado certified check [*business or personal check stamped with bank's certification*]
    cheque conformado (Spa) certified check
    cheque cruzado crossed check [*two parallel lines across the face of the check indicate that it must be paid into a bank account and not cashed over the counter—not used in the US*]
    cheque de caja cashier's check [*check drawn by a bank on itself*]
    cheque de gerencia cashier's check [*check drawn by a bank on itself*]
    cheque de otra plaza (Chi) own-of-town check [*drawn on a bank in another city*]
    cheque de plaza (Chi) local check [*drawn on a local bank*]
    cheque de ventanilla counter check
    cheque de viajero traveler's check
    cheque diferido postdated check
    cheque en blanco blank check
    cheque en descubierto bad check
    cheque para abono en cuenta check for deposit only
    cheque posdatado postdated check
    cheque posfechado postdated check
    cheque postdativo postdated check
    cheque sin fondos bad check, rubber check [*check that bounces*]
chequera checkbook
chicanas delaying tactics used to gain advantage in a lawsuit
chicanero lawyer who utilizes delaying tactics

chicharros (Spa) cats and dogs [*speculative stocks that have short histories of sales, earnings, and dividend payments*]
chiquitaje (Arg) trading by small investors
cierre patronal lock-out
cifra
    cifra de desocupados unemployment rate
    cifra de negocios (Spa) revenues, sales
    cifra global lump sum
    cifras arábigas Arabic numerals
    cifras romanas Roman numerals
circulación de capitales circulation of capital
circulante
    circulante activo current assets
    circulante monetario money in circulation
    circulante pasivo current liabilities
circular (Mex) administrative directive [*contains general rules applicable to the internal operations of federal or state governments or to the procedures to follow in order to comply with a given law or decision. The main difference between a "reglamento" and a "circular" is that a reglamento usually clarifies a law, while a circular clarifies one decision, order or one specific provision thereof.*]
circunscripción judicial (Ven) judicial circuit
circunstancia
    circunstancias agravantes aggravating circumstances
    circunstancias atenuantes extenuating circumstances
    circunstancias eximentes exonerating circumstances
citación summons
    citación a comparecer a estar a derecho summons to appear, to enter an appearance
    citación cautelar (Spa) summons to a person who is likely to have committed a crime, ordering him to appear and make a statement before the investigating judge or prosecutor [*If he fails to appear, he will be arrested.*]
    citación con apercibimiento subpoena
    citación en garantía impleader [*procedure by which a third party is brought into a suit between a plaintiff and defendant in which the third party may be liable so as to settle all claims in a single action—also called "llamamiento en garantía"*]
    citación en incidente appeal on a point of law
    citación para sentencia summons of plaintiff and defendant to hear judgment
    citación personal personal service [*also called "in hand" service, i.e., the notice is served directly on the person concerned*]
    citación por carteles summons by substituted service

citación por cédula (Ven) summons by substituted service and publication [*If the process server cannot find the person to be served, a notice will be posted on the person's door or office and also published in two newspapers.*]

citar 1. to summon 2. to give notice

    citar a juicio to summon, to subpoena

    citar a testigos to subpoena witnesses

    citar por edictos to give notice by publication [*in the newspaper of a legal notice called an "edicto"*]

    citar por telefonema (Mex) to give notice by telephone

citatorio summons

ciudadanía citizenship

ciudadano citizen [*Citizens are also referred to as "nationals."*]

clases de acciones classes of shares

cláusula clause, article

    cláusula arbitral arbitration clause

    cláusula Calvo (Mex) Calvo Clause [*Art. 27 of the Mexican Constitution, pursuant to which foreigners are prohibited from seeking assistance from their own government with regard to disputes or assets or contractual rights to property in Mexico*]

    cláusula compromisoria arbitration provision [*provision whereby parties agree to submit future disputes to arbitration*]

    cláusula de no competencia covenant not to compete

    cláusula de exclusión sindical closed shop clause

    cláusula de obligación de medios best efforts clause [*obligation to use one's best efforts to achieve the purpose of the contract*]

    cláusula pari passu pari passu clause

    cláusulas de cajón (Mex) boilerplate clauses

    cláusulas de escala diferencial escalator clauses

    cláusulas de estilo customary clauses

clave 1. key 2. code

    clave catastral real estate tax code

    clave de pizarra (Mex) ticker symbol [*abbreviation that identifies a security for trading purposes*]

    clave única de identificación tributaria (CUIT) (Arg) taxpayer ID

    clave única de registro de población (Mex) unique population registration code

cliente 1.client 2. customer [*Businesses that sell goods have "customers," and those that sell services have "clients."*]

    clientes por aplicar unapplied customer deposits

coacción coercion, duress

coactivo coercive

coadyuvante coadjutor

coadyuvar to formally assist as coadjutor

cobertura 1. hedging 2. coverage [*in the context of insurance*]
  cobertura amplia comprehensive [insurance] coverage
  cobertura cambiaria exchange rate hedge
  cobertura cruzada cross hedge
  cobertura directa direct hedge
  cobertura larga long hedge
  cobertura rodante rolling hedge
  cobertura selectiva selective hedge
cobrar 1. to charge 2. to earn 3. to collect
  cobrar un cheque to cash a check
  cobrar un premio to collect a prize [*in a lottery*]
cobro 1. collection 2. charge
  cobro de comisiones fee income [*in the context of banking*]
  cobros anticipados advance payments from customers [*also
    referred to as "deferred income"*]
codicilo codicil
código code
  código adjetivo procedural code
  Código Civil Civil Code
  **Código Civil para el Distrito Federal en materia común y
    para toda la República en materia federal (Mex)** Civil
    Code for the Federal District in Local Matters and for the
    Entire Republic in Federal Matters
  código comentado annotated code
  código concordado code with cross-references [*called
    "concordancias"*]
  Código Contencioso Administrativo (Col) Code of
    Administrative Procedure
  Código de Comercio Commercial Code
  Código de Enjuiciamiento Criminal (Ven) Code of Criminal
    Procedure
  **Código de Procedimiento Civil (Bol, Chi, Col, Dom, Ecu, Uru,
    Ven)** Code of Civil Procedure
  Código de Procedimiento Penal (Bol, Col, Ecu) Code of
    Criminal Procedure
  Código de Procedimientos Administrativos (Hon) Code of
    Administrative Procedure
  Código de Procedimientos Civiles (Hon, Mex, Sal) Code of
    Civil Procedure
  Código de Procedimientos Penales (Cos, Mex) Code of
    Criminal Procedure
  Código del Trabajo Labor Code
  Código Fiscal de la Federación (Mex) Mexican Internal
    Revenue Code
  Código Penal Penal Code, Criminal Code
  código penal tipo model penal code
  Código Procesal Civil (Cos, Per) Code of Civil Procedure

Código Procesal Civil y Comercial (Arg) Code of Civil and
Commercial Procedure
Código Procesal Civil y Mercantil (Gua) Code of Civil and
Commercial Procedure
Código Procesal Penal Code of Criminal Procedure
Código Tributario Tax Code
coeficiente
   coeficiente de amortización depreciation rate
   coeficiente de caja (Spa) minimum reserves [*deposit that
banks must keep in the Bank of Spain*]
   coeficiente de capital capital ratio
   coeficiente de disponibilidades quick ratio, acid test ratio
   coeficiente de garantía (Spa) capital adequacy ratio [*ratio of
financial institution's assets to its deposits*]
   coeficiente de liquidez liquidity ratio
cohecho bribery [*of a public official*]
cohonestar to falsify
coinversión joint venture
colación de bienes bringing assets into hotchpot [*return of assets
distributed by the decedent to heirs prior to his death*]
colegio de abogados bar association
colindancias boundaries
colindante adjoining
colindar to adjoin, to be adjacent to
colocación 1. placement 2. underwriting 3. loan [*on a bank's
financial statements*]
   colocación privada private placement
   colocaciones loans
   colocaciones de dudosa cobranza possible loan losses
   colocaciones interbancarias interbank loans
colocador (de una emisión) underwriter
colocar una emisión to underwrite an issue
colorado (Par) member of the Asociación Nacional Republicana
(ANR)
comanditado general partner
comanditario limited partner
comando de la policía (Col) police station
comerciante merchant
   comerciante detallista retailer
   comerciante mayorista wholesaler
   comerciante minorista retailer
comercio
   comercio de cabotaje coasting trade [*domestic maritime trade
between points within a country on the same coast as
opposed to trade between points in two countries*]
   comercio de objetos robados trading in stolen goods
   comercio exterior foreign trade

comercio internacional international trade
comercio interno domestic trade
comicios elections
comisaría (Arg, Per, Spa) police station
   comisaría de familia (Col) office manned by officials of the
   Instituto Colombiano de Bienestar Familiar (ICBF) who
   receive and process complaints (judicial and otherwise)
   exclusively regarding family matters (alimony, spouse abuse,
   child abuse, etc.)
comisario (Dom, Ecu, Gua, Hon, Mex, Ven) statutory auditor,
   statutory examiner [*referred to as "síndico" in Argentina and*
   Uruguay, and as "revisor fiscal" in Colombia and Costa Rica. This
   person is appointed by the shareholders to oversee the acts of
   the board of directors. There is no equivalent in U.S. law.]
comisión 1. fee 2. commercial agency 3. commission 4. committee
   comisión de compromiso commitment fee [*a fee paid by a*
   borrower to a lender in the period between approval and
   disbursement of a loan, so as to reimburse the lender for the
   cost associated with meeting a disbursement request on
   demand]
   comisión de corretaje brokerage fee
   Comisión de las Naciones Unidas para el Derecho Mercantil
   Internacional United Nations Commission on International
   Trade Law (UNCITRAL)
   Comisión de Lucha contra la Piratería (Mex) Anti-Piracy
   Commission
   comisión de mantenimiento (Spa) banking charges
   Comisión Federal de Competencia (Mex) Federal Antitrust
   Commission
   comisión informativa (Spa) advisory board
   comisión mixta joint committee
   comisión permanente standing committee
   Comisión Resolutiva (Chi) Antitrust Court [*established by*
   Executive Order 211]
   comisión rogatoria letter rogatory
   comisiones bancarias bank fees
comisionista sales agent
   comisionista de bolsa (Arg) stock broker
comiso confiscation of prohibited merchandise
comité committee
   comité consultivo advisory committee
   comité de empresa (Spa) works council
   comité ejecutivo executive committee
   comité organizador organizing committee
   comité timón steering committee

como es de público y notorio which is a fact of which the court can take judicial notice
comodante gratuitous lender, gratuitous bailer
comodatario gratuitous borrower, gratuitous bailee
comodato gratuitous loan, gratuitous bailment [*a contract without consideration pursuant to which a fungible object is loaned to another person, who must return it later – also called a "préstamo de uso"*]
compañero de fórmula (Arg, Par) running mate [*in an election*]
compañía
    compañía afianzadora bonding company
    compañía afiliada affiliated company
    compañía anónima (Ecu, Ven) corporation
    compañía controladora holding company
    compañía de economía mixta (Ecu) partly state-owned company
    compañía de responsabilidad limitada (Dom, Ecu, Ven) limited liability company
    compañía en comandita por acciones (Ecu, Ven) partnership limited by shares
    compañía en comandita simple (Ecu, Ven) limited partnership
    compañía en nombre colectivo (Ecu, Ven) general partnership
    compañía fiduciaria trust company
    compañía por acciones stock corporation
comparecencia appearance
comparecer to appear
    comparecer a estar a derecho to enter an appearance
    comparecer ante notario público to appear before a notary public
compareciente the party appearing
comparendo summons
compensación 1. set-off [*of debits and credits*] 2. clearing [*of securities*] 3. compensation
    compensación bancaria check clearing
    compensación de cheques check clearing
    compensación por tiempo de servicios (Per) severance pay [*based on seniority*]
competencia 1. jurisdiction 2. competition
    competencia desleal unfair competition
    competencia en lo penal criminal jurisdiction
    competencia en razón de la materia subject-matter jurisdiction
    competencia en razón de la persona personal jurisdiction [*also called "in personam jurisdiction"*]
    competencia funcional appellate jurisdiction [*i.e., which appellate court can hear which appeals*]

competencia por cuantía jurisdiction based on the amount in controversy
competencia preventiva exclusionary jurisdiction
competencia procesal internacional international procedural jurisdiction
competencia territorial territorial jurisdiction
competitividad competitiveness
cómplice accomplice
cómplice encubridor accessory after the fact
cómplice instigador accessory before the fact
compra a plazos installment purchase
comprador purchaser, buyer
    comprador de buena fe good faith purchaser
    comprador final ultimate purchaser
comprobación de inventario verification of inventory
comprobante receipt, voucher, supporting documentation [*verifying that a transaction took place*]
    comprobante de compra proof of purchase
comprometer
    comprometer en árbitros to submit to arbitration
    comprometerse a to covenant to, to agree to
    Las controversias pueden comprometerse en uno o más árbitros. Disputes may be submitted to arbitration by one or more arbitrators.
compromiso 1. covenant, commitment, obligation 2. agreement to submit to arbitration
    compromiso de árbitros submission to arbitration
compulsa authenticated copy, compared document
compulsar to validate
compurgar (Mex) to finish serving a prison sentece
Comuníquese Let it be known. Let it be made public.
con cualquier carácter in any capacity
con derecho a voto with a right to vote
con derecho a voz with a right to take part in discussions, without a right to vote
con descuento at a discount
con garantía secured
con la venia de la sala may it please the court
con todas las de la ley legally proper, complying with all the requirements set forth by law
concedente grantor
conceder to grant, to award
    conceder la guarda to award custody
concejal member of the city council
concejo city council, town council, municipal council
    Concejo Deliberante (Arg) the deliberating body of a municipio
concentración de empresas merger, business combination

concentración horizontal horizontal combination [*a business combination of companies with similar functions in production or sale of comparable products*]

concentración vertical vertical combination [*combination of companies involved in all steps of production*]

concepto de violación (Mex) legal argument [*made by amparo petitioner that the act violated his constitutional rights*]

concesión 1. concession 2. license

concesionar (Mex) to license

concesionario (Mex) licensee

concluir to make one's closing argument

conclusión 1. termination 2. closing argument 3. finding

> **conclusión de la relación laboral** termination of employment
> **conclusiones de hecho y derecho** findings of fact and conclusions of law
> **conclusiones del tribunal** findings of the court

concordancias cross-references [*in an annotated code or statute*]

concordar to agree, to be in keeping with

> **concuerda fielmente con su original, al que me remito** it is a true copy of the original, to which I refer

concordato preventivo (Arg) agreement with creditors to avoid bankruptcy

conculcar to infringe, to violate

concurrencia

> **concurrencia de delitos** situation in which more than one provision of the criminal code applies to a given set of facts [*synonym of "concurso de delitos"*]
> **concurrencia de normas (Mex)** situation in which two or more laws apply to a certain situation and govern it in differing manners

concurrentes the persons appearing, the persons in attendance

concurrir

> **concurrir a una sesión** to attend a meeting
> **concurrir ante un juez** to appear before a judge

concursar 1. to compete 2. to declare bankruptcy

concurso 1. (Arg) proceeding prior to adjudication of bankruptcy 2. competitive bidding

> **concurso civil (Arg)** bankruptcy proceedings with respect to an individual rather than a merchant [*Therefore, these proceedings are governed by the Civil Code rather than the Commercial Code. This is also referred to as "quiebra civil."*]
> **concurso comercial (Arg)** bankruptcy proceedings with respect to a merchant [*and thus governed by the Commercial Code*]
> **concurso de acreedores** meeting of creditors [*of a non-merchant*]
> **concurso de competencia** competitive bidding

concurso ideal de delitos situation where one action results in several criminal offenses [*e.g., a person shoots at another man, and kills him, but wounds a third party*]

concurso necesario involuntary bankruptcy

concurso preventivo (Arg) reorganization in bankruptcy [*This is a judicial proceeding conducted under the supervision of a court-appointed official (síndico) in which the debtor retains possession of his assets and stops making payments. This proceeding can only be requested by the debtor, never by the creditors.*]

concurso real de delitos situation where a person commits two or more related crimes [*usually results in a penalty less severe than the sum of penalties for the individual crimes*]

concurso resolutorio (Arg) meeting of creditors after the court declares the debtor bankrupt

concusión extortion [*by a judge or public official*]

condena sentence

  condena condicional suspended sentence

  condena contradictoria judgment after trial

condenar to sentence someone

  condenar a muerte to sentence to death, to condemn to death

  condenar en costas to order to pay costs, to assess costs against

  condenar por un delito to convict of a crime

condición 1. condition 2. capacity

  condición resolutoria condition subsequent

  condición suspensiva condition precedent

condominio joint ownership

condonación remission [*forgiveness of a debt*]

conducta conduct, behavior

conductor (Per) tenant, lessee

conexidad consolidation [*of two lawsuits*]

confabulación conspiracy

confesión

  confesión en juicio defendant's answers to oral interrogatories [*The judge asks questions of the defendant that have been previously submitted in the form of "posiciones" by the plaintiff.*]

  confesión espontánea voluntary confession

  confesión expresa express admission

  confesión ficta admission by default, implied admission [*Defendant is silent when asked a question.*]

  confesión llana confession of facts that are favorable to the other side

confirmación confirmation, acknowledgment

conflicto dispute, conflict

conflicto colectivo de derecho collective labor dispute of a legal nature [*seeking the interpretation of a collective bargaining agreement in force*]

conflicto colectivo económico o de intereses collective labor dispute of an economic nature [*seeking to modify the rules in an existing agreement or replace it with another agreement*]

conflicto de intereses conflict of interests

conflicto laboral labor dispute

conflictos de leyes conflicts of laws

conflictos sociales labor disputes

conformación members, makeup of a committee

conformar to be made up of

conforme

    conforme a derecho according to law, in accordance with the law, legal

    conforme a lo antes establecido in accordance with the foregoing

conformidad bancaria reconciliation statement [*also called "conformidad de saldo"*]

confrontación (Mex) police lineup

confrontar to compare documents, to make authenticated copies

    la presente copia fue confrontada con su original this copy was compared with its original

confusión

    confusión de derechos merger of rights [*one person is both debtor and creditor in the same transaction*]

    confusión de deudas merger of debts

    confusión de patrimonios commingling of assets [*combining them such that it cannot be determined which assets belong to whom*]

congresista congressman

congruencia requirement that the judgment meet the petitions of the parties

conjuez alternate judge, associate judge

conjunto

    en su conjunto in the aggregate, in all, all told

conminación judge's warning an accused that he must tell the truth or correct a prior statement

conminar to warn an accused from the bench to tell the truth or correct a prior statement

conmoriencia simultaneous death of two or more persons

conmutación de penas commutation of a sentence [*converting it to a less severe penalty*]

conmutar un castigo to commute a penalty

conocer de un juicio to hear and determine a case, to take cognizance of a case

una asamblea para conocer de los asuntos a meeting to review the matters

conocimiento de embarque bill of lading

    conocimiento de embarque a la orden order bill of lading

    conocimiento de embarque a la salida outward bill of lading

    conocimiento de embarque directo through bill of lading

    conocimiento de embarque marítimo ocean bill of lading

    conocimiento de embarque terrestre inland bill of lading

consagrar to establish

    el recurso que consagra este Código the appeal established by this Code

consanguinidad consanguinity

consejero 1. board member, director 2. adviser

    consejero propietario regular director, full director

    consejero suplente alternate director

consejo

    consejo de administración (Gua, Hon, Mex, Spa) board of directors

    Consejo de Estado (Col) Council of State [*the highest administrative court - the administrative court of first instance is the Tribunal de lo Contencioso Administrativo*]

    Consejo de Europa The Council of Europe

    Consejo de Gabinete (Pan) the Cabinet, the President's Cabinet

    Consejo de la Judicatura (Mex, Ven) Judicature Council, Board of Judges

    Consejo de la Magistratura (Arg) Judicature Council, Board of Judges

    consejo de vigilancia (Per) supervisory board

    Consejo europeo European Council [*This is not the same thing as the Council of Europe.*]

    Consejo Superior de la Judicatura (Col) Judicature Council, Board of Judges

consentimiento consent

    consentimiento tácito implied consent

conservar la fuerza to remain in force

considerando que whereas

considerandos conclusions of law [*the part of the judgment that contains the judge's legal analysis of the case*]

consignación 1. [*civil law*] remittance, offer of payment [*by debtor to creditor*] 2. **(Mex)** [*criminal law*] request by the prosecution for a trial, motion to hold defendant to stand trial 3. **(Col)** deposit [*of money at a bank*]

    consignación en pago deposit for the payment of debt

consignar 1. to remand 2. (Col) to deposit [*money*] 3. to set forth 4. to consign, to ship, to dispatch

    consignar ante el juez de la causa to request to hold for trial

consignar para ser juzgado to hold for trial, to bind over for trial

El contrato de seguro deberá consignarse en documento público. The insurance contract must be set forth in a notarial instrument.

consignatario consignee

consorcio 1. consortium 2. syndicate

consorcio bancario bank syndicate [*an association of large or international banks for the purpose of financing major undertakings*]

consorcio de bancos bank syndicate [*an association of large or international banks for the purpose of financing major undertakings*]

constancia certificate

constancia secretarial clerk's certificate

constancias judiciales court records

constante en un pagaré as evidenced by a promissory note

constar to appear, to be of record, to be set forth

conste por el presente notice is hereby given that; this is to certify that; know all men by these presents; this Agreement witnesseth

constitucionalista constitutional scholar

constitución 1. constitution [*Spanish-speaking lawyers often refer to the Constitution as the "Carta Magna," the "ley de leyes," or the "Texto Fundamental"*] 2. incorporation [*of a company*]

constituir 1. to constitute 2. to set up, to establish 3. to appoint

constituir a su cargo un préstamo to take out a loan

constituir abogado to appoint an attorney, to designate an attorney

constituir heredero to appoint an heir, to designate an heir

constituir quórum to constitute a quorum

constituir reservas to create reserves

constituir una sociedad to incorporate a corporation

constituirse ante notario to appear before a notary

constituirse coadyuvante del Ministerio Público (Mex) to formally assist the District Attorney as a coadjutor

constituirse en garante to act as guarantor of

constituirse en la obligación de hacer algo to be bound to do something

constituirse en mora to be in default

constituirse en un lugar to go to a place, to present oneself at a place, to report to a place

constituirse parte civil to bring a civil suit

consúltese to be submitted to a higher court for approval or review

consumidor final end consumer

consumismo consumerism

contabilidad accounting

contabilidad a base de efectivo cash basis accounting
[*revenues and expenses are accounted for when cash is
received or disbursed—opposite of "accrual basis
accounting"*]
contabilidad ajustada por inflación inflation accounting
contabilidad de costos cost accounting [*system for recording
and reporting measurements of the cost of manufacturing
goods and performing services in the aggregate and in detail*]
contabilidad social social accounting [*the measurement and
reporting, internal or external, of information concerning the
impact of an entity and its activities on society*]
contabilizar to carry on the books
contador accountant
   contador partidor executor appointed to distribute an estate
contaduría 1. accountancy 2. accountant's office
contencioso contentious, litigious, adversary
   **cuando el procedimiento se convierte en contencioso por
   virtud de oposición** when a proceeding becomes
   adversary by reason of an opposition entered. . .
contestación a la demanda the answer to the complaint
contestar to answer
   contestar la demanda to answer the complaint
   contestar traslado to answer the service of a court order
conteste confirmation of testimony given by another witness
continencia de la causa unity of the case [*one judge until judgment
   is entered*]
contingentes contingencies
contrabandear to smuggle
contrabandista smuggler
   contrabandista de armas gunrunner
contrabando smuggling
   contrabando de armas gunrunning
contracautela bond for costs [*when requesting an interim equitable
   remedy (medidas cautelares)*]
contrademanda counterclaim [*also called a "reconvención"*]
contradictoriamente after hearing both sides, so that both sides
   may be heard
contradictorio in the presence of both parties to the action
contraer to contract
   contraer matrimonio to marry, to get married
   contraer matrimonio católico to get married in a Catholic
     ceremony
   contraer matrimonio civil to get married in a civil ceremony
   contraer nuevo matrimonio to remarry, to get remarried
   contraerse (Per, Ven) to apply to, to refer to
contralor government accounting inspector
Contraloría Office of Government Accounting

Contratar y obligarse — to make a contract, bind himself

contraparte the opposing party, the other party, adversary [*if in litigation*]

    contraparte de un contrato the other party to the contract [*Note that "counterpart of a contract" means "copy of a contract."*]

contrapartida offsetting entry

contraprestación consideration [*bargained-for exchange*]

contrario a la prueba against the weight of the evidence

contratación colectiva collective bargaining

contratar to hire, to engage

    contratar un préstamo to take out a loan

    contratar una póliza de seguros to take out an insurance policy

contrato contract, agreement [*Note that the terms are "contract" and "agreement" are often used interchangeably in English.*]

    contrato accidental ad hoc agreement [*agreement entered into to deal with a temporary situation*]

    contrato aleatorio aleatory contract [*contract whose performance by one party depends on the occurrence of a contingent event, e.g., an insurance policy*]

    contrato anulable voidable contract

    contrato atípico contract not provided for in the law, non-legislated type of contract

    contrato colectivo collective bargaining agreement

    contrato conmutativo contract to sell an asset for a specified price [*as opposed to a "contrato aleatorio," an aleatory contract, in which the amount depends on an uncertain event*]

    contrato consensual consensual contract [*valid without any further act—as opposed to a "contrato real" (q.v.)*]

    contrato considerado inexistente contract that is deemed null and void

    contrato de adhesión adhesion contract [*i.e., standard-form contract imposed by the stronger party*]

    contrato de ajuste shipping articles, ship's articles

    contrato de anticresis "antichresis" agreement [*a contract whereby the debtor allows his creditor to enjoy the fruits and produce or rental of the estate he delivers until the obligation is canceled. Specifically, any contract whereby the debtor encumbers a property in favor of his creditor to enable the creditor to collect rent in lieu of payment of the debt*]

    contrato de arrendamiento lease agreement

    contrato de arrendamiento a plazos (Mex) installment lease agreement

    contrato de caución bursátil securities pledge agreement

    contrato de colocación en base a los mayores esfuerzos best efforts underwriting agreement

contrato de colocación en firme firm commitment underwriting agreement

contrato de comisión (Mex) 1. an agreement concerning a commissioned act [*analogous to an agency agreement at common law*] 2. an agreement concerning the payment of a commission

contrato de compra de esperanza purchase of future goods contract

contrato de compraventa sales agreement

contrato de compraventa a plazos con reserva de dominio (Mex) installment sales agreement

contrato de compraventa de acciones stock purchase agreement

contrato de compraventa de bienes muebles bill of sale

contrato de compraventa de fondo de comercio asset purchase agreement

contrato de cuentas en participación (Cos, Ven) joint venture contract [*No joint venture entity is formed. In this type of agreement, there is usually a managing partner who is fully liable and a partner who contributes capital or services in exchange for a stake in the profits of the venture.*]

contrato de depósito (Mex) bailment contract

contrato de doble (Spa) repurchase agreement, repo [*called "reporto" in Mex and "pase" in Arg*]

contrato de emergencia (Per) emergency employment contract [*entered into to meet needs that arise from acts of God or force majeure*]

contrato de enfiteusis (Arg, Chi) contract for a long-term lease of real estate that requires the lessee to make improvements and pay annual rent and permits the lessee to transfer his rights by sale or gift

contrato de enganche (Bol, Ecu) contract to hire persons to work in another location

contrato de equipo (Mex) contract with a union making it responsible for performance of work

contrato de fideicomiso trust agreement

contrato de fiducia trust agreement

contrato de garantía guarantor agreement

contrato de inquilinato urban leasehold agreement

contrato de locación de obra (Arg) construction contract

contrato de locación por temporada seasonal lease

contrato de locación-conducción (Per) lease agreement

contrato de mandato agency agreement

contrato de mediación (Mex) agreement to provide an intermediary service for a fee [*as opposed to providing service for a commission—the intermediary introduces the product to potential buyers (e.g. through catalogs) with the* *understanding that potentially interested buyers will contact the seller directly without any further services required of the intermediary*]

contrato de obra "llave en mano" turnkey contract

contrato de obra pública public works contract

contrato de obras a precio alzado independent contractor agreement

contrato de permuta barter agreement

contrato de prestación de servicios service contract

contrato de suplencia (Per) employee replacement contract [*entered into to replace an employee who is on leave of absence for training or on maternity leave*]

contrato de temporada seasonal contract

contrato de trabajo employment agreement [*There are two types: contrato individual de trabajo and contrato colectivo de trabajo.*]

contrato de trabajo sujeto a modalidad (Per) conditional employment agreement

contrato de tracto sucesivo contract to be performed over a given period of time [*as opposed to a contrato instantáneo, which is to be performed in one act*]

contrato de transacción settlement agreement [*parties make reciprocal concessions to terminate or prevent a dispute*]

contrato estimatorio consignment sales contract

contrato firme de compra take-or-pay contract

contrato formal contract requiring special formalities to be valid

contrato gratuito gratuitous contract [*agreement whereby one party promises to do something without receiving anything in return—this would be unenforceable in the U.S.*]

contrato informal simple contract [*i.e., one not under seal*]

contrato innomidado contract not provided for in the law, non-legislated type of contract

contrato intermitente (Per) intermittent employment agreement [*drawn up to meet needs that are ongoing but cyclical, such as hiring fishermen only when there are fish*]

contrato leonino one-sided contract

contrato-ley (Mex) union contract that the Government has made official for an entire trade or industry

contrato llave en mano turnkey contract

contrato marco master agreement

contrato múltiple contract combining elements of various types of contracts set forth in the law

contrato nominado contract provided for in the law, legislated type of contract

contrato oneroso contract for valuable consideration

contrato por reconversión empresarial (Per) employment agreement entered into because of a change in the

contrato de fideicomiso traslativo de dominio

employer's business [*e.g., the purchase of a new machine may require the temporary hiring of specialized personnel to operate it*]

contrato preliminar preliminary contract
contrato preparatorio preliminary contract
contrato privado contract that is not recorded by a notary
contrato real contract that requires the delivery of the goods covered thereby to be valid [*as opposed to the normal kind of contract, "contrato consensual"*]
contrato sinalagmático bilateral contract
contrato típico contract provided for in the law, legislated type of contract
contrato tipo model contract, standard-form contract
contrato verbal oral contract, parol contract
contravalor equivalent value
contravención infraction, violation
contravenir to violate
contrayente de matrimonio groom [*if male*], bride [*if female*]
contribución
   contribución al seguro de paro forzoso (Ven) contribution for unemployment insurance
   contribución por política habitacional (Ven) national housing policy contribution
   contribución predial real property tax
   contribución sobre ingresos (Pue) income tax
   contribución territorial (Spa) real property tax [*This tax was replaced in 1992 by the "impuesto sobre bienes inmuebles."*]
   contribución territorial rústica y pecuaria (Spa) rural property tax
   contribución territorial urbana (Spa) urban property tax
contribuyente taxpayer
controversia 1. dispute 2. issue, matter in dispute
   controversia de derecho issue of law, question of law
   controversia de hecho issue of fact, question of fact
contumacia failure to appear in court, nonappearance, default
contumaz in contempt of court, in default
convalidar to confirm, to ratify, to validate
Convención de las Naciones Unidas sobre los Contratos de Compraventa Internacional de Mercaderías United Nations Convention on Contracts for the International Sale of Goods
convencional contractual; by agreement
conveniencia advisability
conveniente advisable, appropriate [*not to be translated as "convenient"*]
convenio 1. agreement 2. convention

Convenio de Berna para la protección de las obras literarias y artísticas Berne Convention for the Protection of Literary and Artistic Works

Convenio de la Haya de 1961 The Hague Convention of 1961 [*abolishing the requirement that foreign public documents be legalized*]

convenio ejecutivo executive agreement [*agreement between heads of state, usually pertaining to administrative matters and therefore less formal than an international treaty*]

convenio judicial stipulation

convenios de coordinación fiscal (Mex) tax coordination agreements [*agreements that the Federal Government enters into with state, municipal and DF governments by which a portion of federal revenues are distributed to such entities, provided that they do not levy taxes or contribution requirements on certain acts, activities or items under federal laws*]

conversión 1. conversion 2. translation [*of foreign currency, i.e., "conversión monetaria"*]

convocar a una asamblea to call a meeting

convocatoria notice of meeting

    convocatoria a licitación call for bids, invitation to bid, request for proposals

cónyuge spouse

    cónyuge supérstite surviving spouse

coordinador de la mayoría parlamentaria (Mex) majority whip

copeyano (Ven) member of the Comité Organizador para Elecciones Independientes (COPEI) [*the Social Christian Party*]

copia copy, counterpart [*also called "tanto" and "ejemplar"*]

    copia fiel true copy

    copia legalizada authenticated copy

    copia simple uncertified copy, plain photocopy

copiar a la letra to copy verbatim

copropiedad joint ownership, joint tenancy

copropietario joint owner, joint tenant

corredor

    corredor de aduanas customs broker

    corredor de bolsa stockbroker

    corredor público (Mex) commercial notary

    corredor titulado registered broker

correligionarios fellow party members

correr

    correr el riesgo to run the risk

    correr el velo societario (Arg) to pierce the corporate veil

    correr en autos to be contained in the record

    correr los asientos to post in the books

correr traslado a las partes con las copias que se anexan to serve the parties with the attached copies

corretaje brokerage

corrimiento del velo societario (Arg) piercing the corporate veil [*i.e., making shareholders liable for the debts of the corporation*]

corro (Mex, Ven) trading floor [*of the stock exchange*]

corte

    Corte Internacional de Justicia International Court of Justice (ICJ) [*in The Hague*]

    Corte Superior (Bol, Ecu, Per, Ven) intermediate court of appeals [*whereas a "superior court" in the US is usually a trial court*]

    Corte Suprema de Justicia (Arg, Col, Ecu, Gua, Hon, Pan, Per, Ven) Supreme Court [*In most other Latin American countries, the Supreme Court is called "Suprema Corte de Justicia." In Spain and Cuba it is called the "Tribunal Supremo."*]

    Cortes (las) (Spa) the Spanish Parliament

cortesía internacional comity [*informal and voluntary recognition by courts of one jurisdiction of the laws and decisions of another jurisdiction*]

cosa

    cosa juzgada res judicata

    cosa litigiosa matter in dispute

    cosa pública public property

    cosas fungibles fungible goods

costas

    costas a la accionada en su calidad de vencida costs are awarded against the losing party

    costas judiciales court costs

    costas por su orden Each party shall bear its own court costs.

    costas procesales court costs

    costas y costos (Arg, Per, Uru) court costs and attorneys' fees [*According to Couture's Vocabulario Jurídico, "costas" are "cantidades fijas e inalterables, como el papel sellado y los tributos judiciales, que se adeudan al Estado con ocasión del juicio," whereas "costos" are "cantidades variables que, como los honorarios profesionales, se adeudan a los que prestan servicios a los litigantes o a la justicia."*]

costeabilidad profitability

costeable profitable, cost effective, economically viable, affordable, feasible

costear to pay for

    costearse to pay for itself

costo cost

    costo de reposición replacement cost

    costo de vida cost of living

costo fiscal de las acciones tax basis of the shares
costo histórico historical cost
costo ponderado promedio average weighted cost
costo porcentual promedio (CPP) average cost of funds [*cost to bank of borrowing money*]
costo, seguro y flete cost, insurance and freight (CIF) [*Incoterm*]
costo y flete cost and freight (CFR) [*Incoterm*]
costos de fabricación manufacturing costs [*consist of materials, labor and factory overhead*]
cotejado verified
cotejar to compare [*a document with its original*]
cotejo de documentos verification of documents by comparison with original
cotización share price, price quotation
    cotización de cierre closing price [*on the stock exchange*]
    cotización del dólar exchange rate for the dollar
coyote (Mex) 1. smuggler of immigrants and refugees for profit 2. shyster, unscrupulous lawyer
coyotear (Mex) to smuggle someone across the border to the United States
coyuntura situation, circumstances
coyuntural temporary, short term, ad-hoc, cyclical
creación de pasivo accrual of liability
creador de mercados market maker
credencial 1.membership card 2. badge
    credencial cívica (Uru) voter registration card
    credencial de elector (Mex) voter registration card
crédito
    crédito a la exportación export credit
    crédito al consumo consumer finance
    crédito al mercado margin dealing
    crédito confirmado confirmed credit [*one granted by a bank to a customer on the basis of a commercial transaction, and confirmed, or stated to exist, by the bank in a letter*]
    crédito de contingencia stand-by credit
    crédito de emergencia stop-gap loan
    crédito de habilitación o avío (Mex) working capital loan
    crédito de vivienda mortgage
    crédito documentario letter of credit
    crédito fiscal tax credit
    crédito garantizado secured loan
    crédito hipotecario mortgage loan
    crédito mercantil (Chi, Mex) goodwill
    crédito puente bridge loan [*short-term advance to a customer pending receipt by him of funds from another source*]

crédito refaccionario (Mex) equipment loan [*See Art. 323 of the Ley General de Títulos y Operaciones de Crédito*]

crédito rotativo revolving credit

créditos comerciales trade finance

créditos vencidos past due loans

criterio 1. discernment, judgment 2. opinion 3. criterion (pl. criteria)

    criterio comercial business judgment

    criterio contable accounting policy

    criterio financiero method of financing

    criterio impositivo system of taxation

    criterio jurídico theory of the case [*an interpretation of the law that fits the facts of the case*]

cruce (Mex) cross trade [*a buy order is matched with a sell order on the stock exchange by one broker; also referred to an "operación cruzada"*]

cuaderno record, case file

    cuaderno aparte collateral issues [*matters to be decided apart from the main trial*]

    cuaderno auxiliar official record of preliminary proceedings

    cuaderno de prueba evidentiary file

    cuaderno principal pleadings file [*at the court*]

    cuaderno separado collateral issues [*matters to be decided apart from the main trial*]

cuadrar dos cuentas to reconcile two accounts, to get two accounts to balance

cuadro de financiación (Spa) statement of cash flow

cuantía amount, quantity

    cuantía de la controversia amount in controversy

    cuantía del litigio amount in controversy

cuarta de libre disposición (Ecu) the part of the estate that the testator is free to dispose of as he wishes

cuarta de mejora (Ecu) special bequest of more than the birthright portion

cuartel barracks

    cuartel de bomberos (Nic) fire station

    cuartel de carabineros (Chi) police station

cuarto

    cuarto intermedio (Arg) recess, adjournment [*of a meeting*]

    cuarto oscuro (Arg) polling booth, voting booth

cuasicapital quasi-equity [*loan that is made directly to one of the owners of a company because the company is so leveraged that it cannot take on another loan*]

cuasicontrato quasi contract

cuasidelito unintentional tort [*Unintentional torts are those based on negligence*]

cuasidinero near money [*assets quickly convertible into money, such as savings deposits and government bonds.*]

cubierta (Pue) insurance coverage [*The standard term is "cobertura."*]

cubrir
  cubrir descubiertos de títulos to substitute short positions
  cubrir gastos to cover expenses
  cubrir una vacante to fill a vacancy
cuenta account
  cuenta al descubierto overdrawn account
  cuenta bancaria bank account
  cuenta bloqueada blocked account [*bank account in a currency subject to exchange controls by monetary authorities*]
  cuenta conjunta joint account
  cuenta corriente 1. checking account 2. current account
  cuenta de ahorros savings account
  cuenta de cheques (Mex) checking account
  cuenta de cheques con intereses interest-bearing checking account
  cuenta de compensación clearing account
  cuenta de enlace liaison account
  cuenta de orden off-balance-sheet item
  cuenta de pérdidas y ganancias profit and loss statement
  cuenta de periodificación 1. [*as an asset*] accrued income and prepaid expenses 2. [*as a liability*] unearned income and accrued expenses
  cuenta de utilidad fiscal neta (CUFIN) (Mex) previously taxed earnings account [*There is no tax on dividends distributed out of the prior earnings account.*]
  cuenta eje primary account
  cuenta en descubierto overdrawn account
  cuenta en participación contractual joint venture
  cuenta impaga delinquent account
  cuenta maestra money market checking account
  cuenta no cancelada old unapplied account
  cuenta productiva interest-bearing account
  cuenta puente clearing account
  cuenta saldada closed account
  cuenta sin movimiento inactive account, dormant account
  cuentas colectivas control accounts
  cuentas de balance balance sheet accounts
  cuentas de corretaje trading accounts
  cuentas en gestión past-due invoices
  cuentas por cobrar accounts receivable
  cuentas por cobrar a reaseguradoras reinsurance assets
  cuentas por cobrar comerciales trade receivables
  cuentas por pagar accounts payable
  cuentas vencidas y no liquidadas past-due accounts
  por mi cuenta at my expense

por su cuenta at his/her/your/their expense

cuentapropista self-employed person, freelancer

cuerda (Pue) unit of land measurement approximately equal to one acre

    cuerda floja (Arg) papers that are not part of the court record but are in the file

    cuerda separada matter that is to be settled apart from the main trial

cuerpo del delito corpus delicti

culpa

    culpa aquiliana tort

    culpa concurrente contributory negligence

    culpa cuasidelictual negligence

    culpa delictual gross negligence

    culpa extracontractual tort

    culpa grave gross negligence

    culpa in contrahendo (Lat) negligence in contracting [*e.g., contracting to perform a certain act without first making sure that the necessary permit can be obtained*]

    culpa lata (Lat) gross negligence

    culpa leve ordinary negligence

    por culpa o dolo due to negligence or intentional misconduct

culpabilidad guilt

culpable guilty

culposamente negligently

Cúmplase So ordered.

cumplimiento

    cumplimiento forzado specific performance

    efectivo cumplimiento specific performance

cumplir

    cumplir una condena to serve a sentence

    cumplir y hacer cumplir to comply and ensure compliance with

cuota 1.share 2. installment 3. membership dues

    cuota alimentaria (Arg) alimony

    cuota de facturación billing rate

    cuota de mercado market share

    cuota inicial down payment

    cuota litis contingency fee

    cuota patronal del seguro social employer's social security contribution

    cuota provisoria (Arg) temporary alimony

    cuota social (Arg, Cos, Ven) share of a sociedad de responsabilidad limitada. [*This is called a "parte social" in Mex and a "participación" in Per.*]

    cuotas compensatorias countervailing duties

    cuotas del seguro social (Mex) social security and employment insurance taxes

cuotas sindicales union dues

cupón corrido accrued interest [*on a bond*]

curador 1. guardian [*see "tutor" for a discussion of the difference between tutor and curador*] 2. (Cos) trustee in bankruptcy

curaduría procesal procedural guardianship [*guardian appointed by the court when a party is absent or lacks procedural capacity, or his whereabouts are unknown*]

curatela guardianship [*see "tutela" for a discussion of the difference between tutela and curatela*]

    curatela dativa court-ordered guardianship

    curatela legítima legal guardianship

curia the bar, the court

cursar 1. (Ven) to appear 2. to be pending 3. to send, to dispatch

    la partida de matrimonio que cursa en autos (Ven) the marriage certificate that appears in the file

    la demanda que cursa actualmente por ante el Tribunal (Ven) the complaint that is pending before the court

    los juicios que cursan actualmente en Venezuela (Ven) the lawsuits that are currently pending in Venezuela

custodia custody, safekeeping

dable feasible, possible, practicable

dación en pago accord and satisfaction [*payment of money or other thing of value, usually less than the amount owed or demanded, in exchange for the extinguishment of the debt*]

dado, firmado y sellado signed, sealed and delivered

daño

    daño emergente indirect or consequential damage

    daño extrapatrimonial pain and suffering, emotional distress

    daño material property damage [*also called "daño patrimonial." Note that "material damage" in English is the opposite of "immaterial" i.e., "insignificant" damage.*]

    daño moral 1. pain and suffering, emotional distress 2. damage to reputation

    daño patrimonial property damage

    daño personal bodily injury

    daños a terceros en sus personas personal injury

    daños compensatorios compensatory damages

    daños corporales bodily injury

    daños pecuniarios monetary damages

    daños y perjuicios damages [*Note that although "daños y perjuicios" is usually translated as "damages," technically "daño" means the loss or deterioration of assets as a result of failure to comply with an obligation, whereas "perjuicio" means the deprivation of lawful gains that would have resulted had there been compliance with an obligation. See Articles 2109 and 2111 of the Civil Code for the Federal District of Mexico.*]

dar carpetazo a un proyecto de ley to table a bill [*but see the meaning in Peru under "carpetazo"*]

dar contestación a la demanda to answer the complaint

dar cuenta to give an account

    Antes de hacer la relación deben los relatores dar cuenta a la Corte de todo vicio u omisión substancial que notaren en los procesos. Before reporting on the case to the judge, the staff attorneys must give an account to the court of any material defect or omission that they note in the record.

    dar cuenta al juez to give a report to the judge

dar curso a to handle, to process, to deal with, to start to process

dar en comodato to lend without charge

dar en locación to rent (out)

dar en garantía to pledge, to grant a security interest in

dar fe to certify, attest

    Doy fe. I certify the foregoing. [*Note that "to certify" is transitive in English, and therefore requires a direct object (the foregoing).*]

dar por desierta la apelación to declare that the term for appeal has expired

dar por resuelto to terminate [*a contract*]

dar por terminado to terminate [*a contract*]

dar razón to give information, explain

dar traslado to serve notice of something on somebody

dar vistas a las partes to make the record available for inspection by the parties

darse de alta en Hacienda (Spa) to get on the tax rolls, to register with the tax authorities

darse por citado to accept a summons

darse por enterado to acknowledge service of notice

darse por notificado to accept a summons

darse por satisfecho to admit having received the price of a sale

dativo court-appointed

de *The titles of sections of laws in Spanish often begin with "de," which can be omitted in English translation, i.e., "De las sociedades anónimas" can be translated "Corporations."*

de acuerdo con lo aquí dispuesto in accordance with the provisions hereof

de común acuerdo by mutual agreement

de cujus (Lat) decedent

de curso forzoso as legal tender

de este domicilio a resident of this city

de igual tenor identical

de la que tomo razón which I have recorded, annotated

de lege ferenda (Lat) legislative policy [*concerning the law as it ideally should be*]

de lege lata (Lat) existing law [*concerning the law as it actually is*]

de ley required by law
de mandato judicial (Uru) by order of the court
de manera pura y simple unconditionally
de mi conocimiento personally known to me
de no haber mediado dicha circunstancia otherwise
de obligatoriedad jurídica legally binding
de oficio sua sponte, on his/her/their own motion
de oficios domésticos (Gua, Ven) a housewife, a homemaker
de parte by one of the parties to the action
de parte o de oficio by request or on its own initiative
de plano summarily [*judgment handed down without procedures*]
de pleno derecho 1. by operation of law 2. as a matter of law
de su incumbencia within its jurisdiction
de su libre voluntad of his/her/their own free will
debate sobre el estado de la Nación (Spa) State of the Union
    address
deber duty
    deber de cuidado duty of care
    deber jurídico legal duty, legal obligation
debida forma proper form
decaimiento de un acto administrativo lapse of an administrative
    act [*occurs when the legal or factual prerequisites for its validity
    are no longer present. "Decaimiento" is the opposite of an
    express revocation of the act by the authorities.*]
decidir to decide
    decidir en derecho to follow the law in making decisions
    decidir en equidad to decide as seems equitable
décimo tercer mes (Pan) additional month of salary to which all
    workers are entitled [*It is paid in three "partidas" (installments).
    The primera partida (first installment) is paid in April; the segunda
    partida (second installment) is paid in August; and the tercera
    partida (third installment) is paid on December 15.*]
decisión sobre el fondo decision on the merits
decisorio sworn statement that one party requests of another in a
    proceeding, agreeing to be bound by whatever that other party
    says under oath [*short for "juramento decisorio"*]
declaración
    declaración arancelaria customs declaration
    declaración complementaria amended tax return
    declaración de aduana customs declaration
    declaración de ausencia judicial determination of absence
    declaración de culpabilidad guilty plea
    declaración de dividendos declaration of dividends
    declaración de herederos acknowledgment of heirs
    declaración de impuestos tax return
    declaración de inocencia plea of innocence

declaración de la administración (Mex) representation letter [*letter from management to the auditors confirming the fairness of various elements of the financial statements*]

declaración de obra nueva (Spa) declaration of new construction [*stamp tax is payable at 0.5% of the value declared*]

declaración de puro derecho (Arg) judgment on the pleadings [*The case involves solely a question of law and not a question of fact.*]

declaración de quiebra bankruptcy declaration

declaración de última voluntad last will and testament

declaración de voluntad statement of intent

declaración definitiva (Mex) final tax return

declaración dolosa fraudulent misrepresentation

declaración en ceros (Mex) no-tax-due return

declaración estimatoria (Spa) ruling that grants leave to appeal

declaración fiscal income tax return

declaración indagatoria a suspect's statement given upon interrogation by the judge during the investigation of the case

declaración jurada affidavit

declaración ministerial official interrogation

declaración negativa tax return showing overpayment

declaración positiva tax return showing that taxes are owed

declaración preparatoria (Mex) a suspect's statement given upon interrogation by the judge during the investigation of the case [*called "declaración indagatoria" in other countries*]

declaración provisional (Mex) estimated tax return

declaraciones recitals

declarado pobre allowed to proceed in forma pauperis

declarante affiant, deponent

declarar to state, to testify

declara ser states that he is

declarar ante un juez to testify before a judge

declarar con falsedad to make false statements

declarar culpable a alguien to find someone guilty

declarar procedente to admit, to grant, to uphold

declarar que ha lugar to admit, to grant, to uphold

declarar que no ha lugar to dismiss, to overrule

declarar sin lugar to dismiss, to overrule

declararse culpable to plead guilty

declararse inocente to plead innocent

declaratoria

declaratoria de jurisdicción defendant's defense requesting a judge to stop interfering with a case over which he has no jurisdiction

declaratoria de pobreza (Arg) order allowing the plaintiff to proceed in forma pauperis

declaratoria indagatoria a suspect's statement given upon interrogation by the judge during the investigation of the case

declinatoria motion that the judge recuse himself

decomiso aduanal customs seizure

decretar 1. to enact 2. to order, to issue a decree

decretar el paro to call a strike

decretar pruebas (Col) to order the production of evidence

decrétese be it enacted

se decreta esta ley this law is enacted

decreto (Mex) law applicable to a specific sector or industry

decreto de embargo order of attachment

decreto exento (Chi) decree exempt from review as to its constitutionality and legality [*such constitutional review is called "toma de razón"*]

decreto judicial court order

decreto legislativo legislative decree [*authorized by Parliament; usually involves complex subject matter that would slow down the workings of Parliament*]

decreto ley executive order [*an order issued by a government's executive on the basis of authority specifically granted to the executive branch*]

decreto reglamentario regulation having the force of law

decreto supremo (Bol, Chi, Per) "Supreme Decree" [*regulations issued by the President to implement the laws, which they must not contradict or modify. Before a Decreto Supremo is signed, it must be submitted to the President's entire cabinet (Consejo de Ministros) for discussion and approval. See also "resolución suprema."*]

dedicarse a algo to engage in something [*often best omitted in English translation, e.g., "una compañía que se dedica a la venta de computadoras" can be translated as "a company that sells computers."*]

dedicarse a negocios to do business, to engage in business

¿A qué se dedica? What does he do [*for a living*]?

deducción

deducción de la demanda (Arg) filing of the complaint

deducción fija (Pue) standard deduction

deducción tributaria tax writeoff

deducible deductible

deducir

deducir acción to file a lawsuit

deducir excepciones to file a defense, to assert defenses

deducir tercerías to appear as intervenor, to appear in third-party claim proceedings

deducir una demanda to file a complaint

defensa
    defensa cautiva (Per) requirement that in places where there
    are at least 3 practicing attorneys all court filings be signed
    by a lawyer
    defensa de falta de acción motion to dismiss for failure to state
    a claim upon which relief can be granted
    defensa legítima self-defense
defensor counsel for the defense
    defensor de ausentes public defender, court-appointed
    defender
    defensor de oficio public defender, court-appointed defender
    defensor de pobres public defender
    defensor del pueblo ombudsman
    defensor judicial public defender
    defensora popular (Mex) paralegal who assists poor women
    who have been battered or abandoned by their husbands or
    have other legal problems
defensoría de oficio legal aid
deferir 1. to yield, to submit 2. to refer a case to another court 3. to
    delegate powers or jurisdiction
    deferir juramentos to administer oaths
déficit
    déficit comercial trade deficit
    déficit en cuenta corriente current account deficit
    déficit externo trade deficit
    déficit presupuestario budget deficit
    déficit público federal budget deficit
definitivamente firme como ha quedado la anterior sentencia
    inasmuch as the foregoing is a final and binding judgment
defraudación tributaria (Per) tax fraud
dejar
    dejar a salvo los derechos to preserve the rights
    dejar constancia de to have the record reflect
    dejar seña 1. (Cub) to leave a forwarding address **2. (Arg)** to
    put up a deposit
delegación (Mex) 1. police station 2. city district in Mexico City
    [*Mexico City is divided into 16 delegaciones políticas, which
    are in turn subdivided into colonias*]
delegado (Mex) head of a delegación [*city district in Mexico City*]
deletéreo deadly, lethal
deliberación deliberation
delincuencia organizada organized crime
delincuente criminal, offender
    delincuente habitual habitual offender
    delincuente juvenil juvenile delinquent
    delincuente primario first offender, first-time offender
    delincuente reincidente repeat offender

delinquir to commit an offense
delito
    delito agotado crime whose effects have been completed
    delito calificado aggravated offense
    delito casual unintentional crime, unpremeditated crime
    delito civil 1. tort [*as opposed to "delito penal" (crime)*]
        2. intentional tort [*as opposed to "cuasidelito" (unintentional tort)*]
    delito complejo combined offense
    delito común ordinary crime
    delito conexo related crime, related offense
    delito continuo a continuing crime
    delito contra el honor crime against a person's honor [*such as defamation, false accusation of crime*]
    delito contra la administración de justicia obstruction of justice [*such as perjury*]
    delito contra la administración pública crime against the government [*such as bribery, being an accessory to crime, tax evasion, abuse of authority, etc.*]
    delito contra la fe pública crime involving public instruments [*falsifying public instruments or counterfeiting money*]
    delito contra la honestidad sex crime [*such as rape, adultery, statutory rape*]
    delito contra la libertad crime against a person's freedom [*such as breaking and entering, deprivation of liberty*]
    delito contra la libertad de reunión crime against the freedom of assembly
    delito contra la propiedad crime against property
    delito contra la salud (Mex) drug-related crime, drug traffic
    delito criminal criminal offense
    delito culposo criminal negligence
    delito de asalto robbery
    delito de sangre violent crime
    delito doloso crime committed with malice aforethought, intentional crime
    delito flagrante crime discovered while in progress
    delito formal offense that is a crime even without actual harm
    delito frustrado frustrated crime
    delito grave felony
    delito incruento crime without bloodshed
    delito leve misdemeanor
    delito material offense that must harm to be a crime
    delito mayor felony
    delito menor misdemeanor
    delito pasional crime of passion
    delito patrimonial crime involving theft or fraud [*e.g., robo, abuso de confianza, fraude, cohecho*]

delito penal crime, felony
delito permanente continuing crime
delito preterintencional crime that causes an injury more serious than the one intended or expected
delito privado crime that can only be prosecuted at the victim's request
delito público crime against the State
delito tipificado statutory offense [*one that is defined in the statutes*]
demanda 1. complaint [*the document filed to commence a civil lawsuit*] 2. demand
   demanda agregada aggregate demand [*the total of intended or ex ante attempts to spend on final goods and services produced in a country*]
   demanda alternativa plea for alternative relief
   demanda analítica plea for alternative relief
   demanda de amparo (Mex) petition for constitutional relief [see *amparo*]
   demanda de mera declaración petition for a declaratory judgment
   demanda en referimiento plea for an injunction, plea for interim relief
   demanda y sus recaudos the complaints and the exhibits thereto
demandado 1. defendant 2. respondent [*in a divorce proceeding*]
demandante 1. plaintiff 2. petitioner [*in a divorce proceeding*]
demandar a alguien to bring an action against someone, to sue someone
demencia insanity
democracia participativa participatory democracy
denegación de justicia denial of justice
denominación
   denominación de origen appellation of origin
   denominación monetaria denomination [*of currency*]
   denominación social name [*of a sociedad anónima, which does not include the name of the owners, as opposed to "razón social," partnership name, which includes the names of the partners*]
denuncia criminal complaint made to the police, reporting a crime to the police
   denuncia de accidente accident report
   denuncia de intestado (hacer) to petition the court to commence intestate succession proceedings and recognize the petitioner as a lawful heir of the intestate
   denuncia intestamentaria (hacer) to petition the court to commence intestate succession proceedings and recognize the petitioner as a lawful heir of the intestate

denuncia de obra muerte (Mex) petition for injunction to prevent new construction

denuncia falsa false accusation, malicious prosecution

denunciante informant, complainant

departamento 1. (Arg, Chi, Mex) apartment **2. (Bol, Col, Sal, Gua, Hon, Par, Uru)** department [*corresponds to state or province in other countries*]

dependencia 1. dependence 2. department, office 3. buildings, rooms 4. premises 5. employees, staff

    en las dependencias de la empresa on company premises

    permanecer en dependencias policiales to remain in police custody

dependiente agent, representative, employee, servant [*employee who routinely transacts a certain type of business on behalf and in the name of the company without a written power of attorney. Employers may be vicariously liable for the acts of their "dependientes."*]

deportación deportation

depositar algo judicialmente to deposit something with the court

depositario depository, trustee, bailee

depositario judicial receiver

depósito 1. deposit 2. warehouse

    depósito a la vista demand deposit

    depósito a plazo time deposit

    depósito central de valores central securities depository

    depósito de aduanas bonded warehouse

    depósito de ahorro savings deposit

    depósito de garantía security deposit

    depósito fiscal bonded warehouse

    depósitos en bancos que devengan intereses interest-bearing deposits in banks

    depósitos en bancos que no devengan intereses non-interest-bearing deposits in banks

    depósitos en tránsito deposits in transit [*deposits that have been made and added to the depositor's check book but have not been listed on the monthly bank statement*]

    depósitos y obligaciones deposits and obligations

depresión monetaria depression

derechista right-wing

derecho 1. right 2. law 3. fee

    derecho a la intimidad right to privacy

    derecho a la vida privada right to privacy

    derecho adjetivo procedural law [*also referred to as "derecho procesal" in Spanish. It is the opposite of derecho sustantivo, substantive law.*]

    derecho administrativo administrative law

    derecho aduanero customs duty

derecho aplicable governing law

derecho ambiental environmental law

derecho bancario banking law

derecho civil civil law

derecho comercial commercial law

derecho comparado comparative law

derecho comunitario EU law

derecho común ordinary law, civil law [*i.e., the contents of the Civil Code*]

derecho constitucional constitutional law

derecho consuetudinario custom, customary law

derecho corporativo corporate law

derecho de acrecer 1. right of accretion [*joint heirs' right to an increase in their portion of the estate because of nonacceptance by others*] 2. (Arg) right of first refusal [*to purchase shares as to which other shareholders did not exercise their preemptive rights to purchase newly issued shares*]

derecho de agremiación right to organize, right to unionize

derecho de asilo right of asylum

derecho de dominio ownership right

derecho de estar en juicio right to sue and be sued

derecho de expedición issuance fee

derecho de familia family law

derecho de fideicomisario beneficial right

derecho de fondo substantive law

derecho de forma procedural law

derecho de gentes public international law [*also referred to as "ius gentium"*]

derecho de importación import duty

derecho de inscripción recording fee

derecho de internación import duty

derecho de llave (Chi, Per) lease premium [*extra amount paid by the assignee to the assignor when a lease is assigned*]

derecho de picaporte (Mex) open-door privilege, free-access privilege [*privilege granted by a senior official to his subordinates that allows them to enter his office without an appointment*]

derecho de postulación right to appoint counsel, right to appoint a representative

derecho de receso (Arg) dissenter's rights [*right of minority shareholders to withdraw from a company with compensation when they dissent to a merger*]

derecho de retiro (Chi) dissenter's rights [*right of minority shareholders to withdraw from a company with compensation when they dissent to a merger*]

derecho de reunión right of assembly

derecho de subscripción subscription right

derecho de tanteo (Per) right of first refusal

derecho de testimonio fee for a certified copy

derecho de trámite aduanal import duty

derecho de visita a los hijos visitation rights [*following divorce*]

derecho del mar law of the sea

derecho del tanto (Mex) right of first refusal

derecho del trabajo labor law

derecho dominical ownership right

derecho en expectativa inchoate right

derecho fiscal tax law

derecho foral (Spa) local law

derecho inalienable inalienable right, vested right

derecho internacional privado conflicts of law [*This is called "private international law" in the UK, but not in the US.*]

derecho internacional público public international law

derecho marítimo maritime law, admiralty law

derecho mercantil commercial law [*Note that the term "mercantile law" is used only in the UK, not in the US.*]

derecho natural natural law

derecho penal criminal law

derecho positivo positive law [*law actually and specifically enacted by the proper authority for the government of an organized society—opposite of natural law*]

derecho potestativo elective right

derecho privado private law [*law that deals with private persons and property, e.g. civil law, commercial law, etc.*]

derecho procesal procedural law

derecho procesal civil law of civil procedure

derecho público public law [*law that deals with individuals' relation to the State; traditionally includes criminal law, administrative law, procedural law, tax law, and public international law*]

derecho societario corporate law (US), company law (UK)

derecho subjetivo personal right, private right

derecho sustantivo substantive law [*as opposed to procedural law, which is called "derecho procesal" or "derecho adjetivo"*]

derecho tributario tax law

derechos 1. rights 2. fees

derechos adquiridos vested rights

derechos aduaneros customs duties

derechos arancelarios customs duties

derechos civiles civil rights

derechos compensatorios countervailing duty [*a retaliatory extra charge that a country places on imported goods to counter the subsidies or bounties granted to the exporters of the goods by their home governments*]

derechos consulares consular fees
derechos de aduana customs duties
derechos de autor copyright
derechos de importación import duties
derechos de leasing leased assets [*on a balance sheet*]
derechos de sello stamp tax
derechos de traspaso lease premiums [*extra amount paid by the assignee to the assignor when a lease is assigned*]
derechos especiales de giro (DEG) special drawing rights (SDRs)
derechos humanos human rights
derechos morales non-pecuniary rights [*rights of the author to his work*]
derechos patrimoniales proprietary rights, pecuniary rights, economic rights [*as opposed to derechos morales, meaning non-pecuniary rights*]
derechos portuarios port dues
derechos preferenciales preemptive rights
derechos reales rights in rem
derechos ribereños riparian rights [*rights of one owning riparian land to have access to and use of the shore and water*]
derechos sobre bienes muebles personal assets
derechohabiente rightful claimant, eligible person, interested party, beneficiary
derivados de industrialización byproducts
derogación de una ley repeal of a law
derogación expresa express repeal
derogación tácita implied repeal [*the contents of later legislation are incompatible with the contents of previous legislation*]
desacato al tribunal contempt of court [*act of offending, provoking or intentionally lessening the dignity or authority of the court*]
desactivación económica economic slowdown
desaduanamiento customs clearance
desaforar 1. to deprive of rights or privileges 2. to disbar
desaforo disbarment
desafuero 1. violation, infringement 2. withdrawal of privileges
desagraviar to compensate, to indemnify, to redress
desahogar asuntos (Mex) 1. to transact business 2. to discuss matters, to take up matters
Pasado a desahogarse el quinto punto del orden del día.
Then, Item 5 on the agenda was taken up.
desahogo de pruebas (Mex) presentation of documentary evidence
desahuciar to evict, to give notice to vacate the premises
desahucio eviction

desalojar to evict
desalojo eviction
desalquilarse to become vacant
desamparar la apelación to abandon an appeal
desapoderamiento effect of a bankruptcy judgment whereby a
    person is deprived of the right to administer or alienate his assets
desarrollar una auditoría to perform an audit
desatender to disregard, to ignore
descargo 1. defense 2. release 3. acquittal
    presentar descargos to present the case for the defense
    Su jefe testificará en su descargo. Her boss will testify in her
        defense.
descapitalización reduction in net worth
descendiente descendant, offspring
desconocer to disavow, to disown, to repudiate [*opposite of
    "reconocer" meaning to acknowledge*]
descontar al valor presente to discount to present value
descubierto insufficient balance to meet obligations, short position
descuento discount
    descuento comercial 1. discounting of bills 2. trade discount
    descuento de créditos en libros receivables financing
desde ahora as of now, henceforth
desechar to dismiss [*a case*], to reject [*a proposal*]
desembolsado fully paid in
desembolso payment
desempleo unemployment
    desempleo friccional frictional unemployment [*person is
        temporarily unemployed between two jobs*]
desestimación de la demanda dismissal of the complaint, finding
    for the defendant
desestimar to deny, dismiss
desfalcador embezzler
desfalcar to embezzle
desfalco embezzlement
desfase lag, delay
desfilar prueba (Pue) to present evidence
desgaste wear and tear
desglosar 1. to remove pages from a judicial record 2. to break
    down (figures), to itemize
desglose 1. removal of documents from the record of a case
    2. breakdown [*procedure after trading when the broker identifies
    the owner of the shares traded*] 3. itemization [*of an invoice*]
desgravación fiscal tax credit, tax relief, tax break [*also called
    "minoración" in Spain*]
desgravar 1. to remove a lien 2. to exempt from tax 3. to be tax
    deductible

(handwritten top margin: deslinde de responsabilidades (Mex.) to investigate / to probe, to examine, search for / or / to clear / to exonerate / to exempt)

designación appointment

designación libre (Mex) unrestricted appointment of judges
[*judges need not be appointed from a special list*]

designación vinculada (Mex) restricted appointment of judges
[*judges can only be appointed from a special list*]

desinteresar a terceros (Arg) to satisfy third-party claims

desintermediación financiera disintermediation

desistimiento de la acción voluntary dismissal, dropping the claim

desistimiento de la acción con reserva dismissal without
prejudice [*i.e., plaintiff can file the action again*]

desistir de una demanda to withdraw a complaint, to drop the claim

deslindar to define the boundaries of a piece of property

desliz cambiario crawling-peg system [*a procedure in which a
currency exchange rate is altered frequently (multiple times a
year), generally to adjust for rapid inflation. Between changes,
the exchange rate for the currency remains fixed.*]

desmaterialización converting certificated shares into book-entry
shares [*i.e., uncertificated shares*]

desocupar to vacate [*a house, an apartment*]

despachante de aduana customs agent

despachar mercancías to release goods from customs

despacho 1. writ of mandamus [*court order to another court of
lesser rank*] 2. order to a judge of lesser rank to perform
procedural act outside the jurisdiction of the court 3. judge's
chambers 4. law firm 5. shipment

despacho aduanero customs clearance

despacho comisorio (Col) writ delegating the authority to
examine evidence to another judge

despacho de aduana customs clearance

despacho de mercancías dispatch of goods

despacho judicial processing of business by the court

despacho privado de un juez judge's chambers

recibió el despacho de abogado (Mex) he was admitted to the
bar

despenalización decriminalization

despido dismissal, layoff

despido improcedente unfair dismissal, dismissal without good
cause

desplazamiento conveyance, transfer

despojo dispossession

destinar to assign, to earmark

destinatario 1. addressee, recipient 2. payee 3. consignee

desvalorización devaluation

desviación de poder abuse of authority, misfeasance,
misapplication of administrative regulations

desvincular el tipo de cambio to unpeg the exchange rate

detallar to itemize

detalle itemization
detallista retailer
detención arrest
deterioro normal normal wear and tear
determinación de paternidad affiliation
deuda debt
    deuda a largo plazo long-term debt
    deuda a reaseguradoras reinsurance payable
    deuda amortizada retired debt
    deuda cobrable collectible debt
    deuda de una cosa cierta obligation to deliver a specific asset
    deuda exigible account receivable
    deuda externa foreign debt
    deuda exterior foreign debt
    deuda incobrable uncollectible debt, bad debt
    deuda líquida liquidated debt
    deuda mancomunada joint debt
    deuda prioritaria senior debt
    deuda pública government debt
    deuda subordinada junior debt, subordinated debt
    deudas a bancos y corresponsales due to banks and
        correspondents
    deudas a plazo payments not yet due
    deudas devengadas accrued liabilities
    deudas fiscales tax liabilities, taxes payable
    deudas incobrables canceladas bad debts written off
    deudas tributarias tax liabilities, taxes payable
deudor debtor
    deudor hipotecario mortgagor
    deudor judicial judgment debtor
    deudores diversos other receivables [*on a balance sheet*]
    deudores solidarios debtors who are jointly and severally liable
devengar intereses to earn interest, to accrue interest, to bear
    interest
devolución de su dinero your money back
devolutivo to a higher court [*as opposed to appealing to the very
    court that issued the order*]
devolver
    devolver el expediente al tribunal inferior to remand the case
        to the lower court
    devolver un préstamo to pay back a loan
día day
    día bancario banking day
    día civil calendar day
    día de asueto day off, holiday
    Día de la Toma Presidencial (Mex) Presidential Inauguration
        Day [*December 1 every six years*]

día de raya (Mex) payday
día feriado holiday
día festivo holiday
día hábil 1. business day 2. court day
día inhábil non-business day
día inhábil bancario non-banking day, bank holiday
día laborable business day
día natural calendar day
a tantos días vista payable on the date stated
diario
    diario de egresos de caja cash disbursements journal [*also called "diario de salidas de caja"*]
    diario de ingresos de caja cash receipts journal [*also called "diario de entradas de caja"*]
    Diario Oficial (Uru) Official Gazette of Uruguay
    Diario Oficial de la Federación (Mex) Official Gazette of Mexico
dictamen advisory opinion
    dictamen con reservas qualified opinion [*paragraph in accountant's report that describes an exception to the basis of accounting used by the reporting entity in the preparation of its financial statements*]
    dictamen con salvedades qualified opinion
    dictamen fiscal (Mex) tax opinion [*Companies above a certain size in Mexico are required to have a public accountant certify that the tax liability in their returns has been correctly determined.*]
    dictamen jurídico legal opinion
    dictamen médico diagnosis
    dictamen pericial expert opinion
    dictamen sin salvedades unqualified opinion
dictaminador aduanero customs examiner
dictaminar estados financieros (Mex) to audit financial statements
dictar
    dictar providencias to deliver, to render, to hand down a ruling
    dictar sentencia to deliver, to render, to hand down a judgment
difamación defamation
    difamación escrita libel
    difamación verbal slander
diferencial spread
diferencia
    diferencias entre la utilidad gravable y la contable differences between taxable and ordinary income
    diferencias negativas de cambio foreign exchange losses
diferimiento adjournment
diferir to adjourn, to postpone
dilación probatoria term for producing evidence

diligencia 1. court order 2. being first [*in the context of recording intellectual property rights*] 3. proceeding

diligencia de embargo attachment proceedings

diligencia de pruebas taking of evidence

diligencia del buen padre de familia the care of a reasonable man

diligencia ordinaria ordinary care

diligencia posesoria delivery of possesion

diligencias legal formalities

diligencias para mejor proveer proceedings to obtain additional evidence [*Final judgment is postponed until further or better evidence is produced.*]

diligencias preliminares discovery in advance of filing suit [*e.g., to determine a potential defendant's address*]

diligencias preparatorias discovery in advance of filing suit [*e.g., to determine a potential defendant's address*]

diligenciamiento

diligenciamiento de citación service of a summons, service of process

diligenciamiento de emplazamiento service of a summons

diligenciamiento de notificación service of notice

diplomado 1. graduate 2. certificate course

diputado congressman

Dirección de Vialidad (Arg) Highway Authority

dirección general administrative offices, headquarters, head office

Dirección General de Averiguaciones Previas (Mex) Administrative Office of Preliminary Investigations

Dirección General de Impuestos Internos (Dom) Dominican Internal Revenue Service

Dirección General de Impuestos Nacionales (Col) Colombian Internal Revenue Service

Dirección General de la Tributación Directa (Cos) Costa Rican Internal Revenue Service

Dirección General Impositiva (Arg) Argentine Internal Revenue Service

Dirección General Jurídica y de Estudios Legislativos (Mex) Office of Legal Affairs and Legislative Studies

Dirección Regional de Fiscalías (Col) Regional Government Attorney's Office

directiva (Col, Cos, Pan, Ven) board of directors [*short for "junta directiva"*]

director 1. director 2. manager [*In countries where the board of directors is called the "directorio" (Arg, Bol, Chi, Par, Per, and Uru) or the "junta directiva" (Col, Cos, Ven), the Spanish word* <u>director</u> *means "director" in the sense of "member of the board of directors." The officers are called "gerentes." In countries where the board of directors is called the "consejo* *de administración" (Gua, Hon, Mex, Spa), the Spanish word director refers to the officers. For example, the "director general" would be the "Chief Executive Officer." The board members are called "consejeros" (Mex) or "administradores" (Spa).]*

director propietario regular director [*as opposed to "alternate director"*]

director suplente alternate director [*as opposed to "regular director"*]

directorio (Arg, Bol, Chi, Par, Per, Uru) board of directors

dirigir atento exhorto to send letters rogatory [*to another judge*]

dirimir to settle [*a dispute*]

disipador spendthrift

disminución

disminución de capital capital decrease

disminución de la renta reduction of the rent

disolución dissolution, termination

disolución de la sociedad conyugal separation of marital property

disolución de las personas jurídicas dissolution of legal entities

dispensa dispensation, exemption, privilege

dispensable excusable

disponer to provide, to stipulate

disponiéndose que provided that

disposición 1. provision 2. drawdown [*of a loan*]

disposición discrecional (Mex) legal provision leaving discretion to the judge

disposición en efectivo cash advance

disposición legal statutory provision, legal provision

disposición vinculada (Mex) legal provision leaving no discretion to the judge

disposiciones transitorias transition provisions

última disposición last will and testament

distracción de fondos misappropriation of funds, embezzlement

distracto (Arg) mutual rescission of a contract

distraer fondos to embezzle funds, to misappropriate funds

distribución de utilidades distribution of earnings

distribuible available for distribution

dividendo dividend

dividendo en acciones stock dividend

dividendo provisional interim dividend

divendendos activos dividends payable

dividendos acumulados accrued dividends

dividendos acumulativos cumulative dividends

dividendos decretados declared dividends

dividendos devengados accrued dividends

dividendos distribuidos dividends paid

dividendos en suspenso deferred dividends

dividendos ganados dividends earned

dividendos pasivos call for subscribed capital

dividendos por pagar dividends payable

divisas foreign currency

división split-up [*parent company is divided into two or more separate companies into which all the parent's assets and liabilities are distributed*]

    división de poderes separation of powers [*executive, judicial and legislative*]

División Fiduciaria Trust Department [*of a bank*]

divorcio 1. divorce 2. (Col) women's jail

    divorcio administrativo (Mex) uncontested divorce [*short for "divorcio voluntario administrativo"—It can be granted by the "juez del registro civil" after one year of marriage when both spouses are of age and no children were born of their marriage.*]

    divorcio contencioso contested divorce

    divorcio judicial (Mex) uncontested divorce [*short for "divorcio voluntario judicial"—If one of the spouses is a minor, or children have been born of their marriage, they must petition the "juez de lo familiar" (family court judge) for divorce.*]

    divorcio necesario contested divorce

    divorcio no contencioso uncontested divorce, no-fault divorce

    divorcio por mutuo consentimiento divorce by mutual consent, no-fault divorce

    divorcio vincular absolute divorce, divorce a vinculo matrimonii [*as opposed to divorce a mensa et thoro, which is legal separation*]

    divorcio voluntario (Mex) uncontested divorce, no-fault divorce [*This is a synonym of "divorcio por mutuo consentimiento." There are two types: "divorcio voluntario administrativo" and "divorcio voluntario judicial."*]

divulgación disclosure

divulgar to disclose

doblar turno to double up on a shift

doble imposición double taxation

doctrina 1. academic writing, academic opinion, the leading authorities, opinion of legal scholars 2. doctrine [*Doctrines are developed by judges in common law countries, and by legal scholars in civil law countries.*]

    doctrina de Calvo Calvo Doctrine [*resident aliens and investors in a country are subject to the laws of that country*]

    doctrina de Drago Drago Doctrine [*the suspension of payments of public debts by a State does not justify armed intervention in that State, much less the occupation of its territory*]

documentación de soporte supporting documentation
documental documentary evidence [*short for "prueba documental"*]
documento 1. document 2. note
   documento de trabajo discussion paper
   documento nacional de identidad (Spa) identity card
   documento privado document that is not recorded by a notary
   documentos a cobrar notes receivable
   documentos contra aceptación documents against
      acceptance (D/A) [*instructions given by a shipper to a bank
      indicating that documents transferring title to goods should
      be delivered only upon acceptance of the attached draft*]
   documentos de conteo count sheets
   documentos glosados documents attached to the record
   documentos justificativos supporting documents, supporting
      documentation
   documentos por cobrar notes receivable [*called "efectos a
      cobrar" in Spain*]
   documentos por pagar notes payable [*called "efectos a pagar"
      in Spain*]
   documentos vencidos unpaid notes
dólar dollar
   dólares preferenciales dollars at preferential rate of exchange
   dólares referenciales dollars at reference rate of exchange
dolo 1. [*in criminal context*] criminal intent, deceit, fraud 2. [*in tort
   context*] gross negligence, intentional misconduct, wanton and
   willful misbehavior
   dolo civil fraud, intentional misconduct
   dolo penal criminal intent [*this is also called "mens rea," Latin
      for "guilty mind"*]
   dolo procesal abuse of process, malicious prosecution
dolosamente 1. intentionally 2. fraudulently, deceitfully
domiciliación payment by standing order
domiciliar la nómina to have one's salary deposited directly to his
   account
domiciliar recibos to pay by standing order
domicilio 1. [*of a person*] registered address, address for notices 2.
   [*of an entity*] registered office, corporate headquarters, principal
   place of business
   de este domicilio a resident of this city
   domicilio comercial corporate domicile, corporation's
      registered address
   domicilio constituido domicile of choice, domicile ad litem
   domicilio convencional domicile of choice, elected domicile
   domicilio conyugal marital domicile
   domicilio de hecho de facto domicile
   domicilio fiscal tax residency
   domicilio habitual usual place of residence

domicilio procesal address for purposes of a lawsuit
domicilio real actual address
    con domicilio real en X y constituyéndolo a todos los efectos procesales en Y with his actual address at X and establishing Y as his address for purposes of this lawsuit
domicilio social registered office, principal place of business
dominio
    dominio eminente eminent domain
    dominio público public domain
    ser del dominio público to be in the public domain
donación gift
    donación entre vivos inter vivos gift
donante donor
donatario donee, recipient
dueño owner
dúplica defendant's rejoinder to plaintiff's reply [*which is called a "réplica"*]
duración 1. term of a contract 2. duration of a company
durar
    durar en su cargo to remain in office, to hold office (for so long)
    durar en sus funciones to remain in office, to hold office (for so long)
ecomarchamo (Cos) vehicle emissions sticker [*to attach to the car's windshield*]
economía
    economía dirigida planned economy
    economía informal informal economy [*cash-only transactions*]
    economía procesal judicial economy
    economías de escala economies of scale
edicto legal notice [*published in the newspaper*]
efectivo en caja y bancos cash on hand and in banks
efecto
    efecto devolutivo without a stay of execution
    efecto resolutivo effect of terminating a contract
    efecto suspensivo with a stay of execution
    efectos comerciales a cobrar (Spa) notes receivable [*called "documentos por cobrar" in other countries*]
    efectos comerciales a pagar (Spa) notes payable [*called "documentos por pagar" in other countries*]
    efectos de comercio commercial paper
    efectos desatendidos (Spa) unpaid notes [*called "documentos vencidos" in other countries*]
    efectos impagados (Spa) unpaid notes [*called "documentos vencidos" in other countries*]
    efectos legales a que haya lugar relevant legal purposes
    efectos públicos government bonds
    para los efectos de for purposes of

egresado (Chi) law school graduate who has not been admitted to the bar [*persons admitted to the bar are "titulados"*]

ejecución

    ejecución de un contrato performance of a contract [*Note that "execution of a contract" in English means "signing of a contract."*]

    ejecución de un laudo arbitral enforcement of an arbitral award

    ejecución de un reo execution of a criminal

    ejecución de una hipoteca foreclosure

    ejecución forzosa specific performance [*of a contract*]

ejecutar

    ejecutar a un reo to execute a criminal

    ejecutar un contrato to perform a contract

    ejecutar una hipoteca to foreclose a mortgage

    ejecutar una sentencia to execute a judgment

ejecutivo hipotecario foreclosure proceeding

ejecutoria final judgment

ejemplar copy, counterpart [*of a contract*]

    dos ejemplares de un mismo tenor a un solo efecto two identical counterparts, each equally binding

ejercer

    ejercer la abogacía to practice law

    ejercer el albaceazgo to act as executor

    ejercer el comercio to be engaged in commerce, to do business

    ejercer el derecho to practice law

    ejercer funciones to hold office

    ejercer la judicatura to serve as a judge, to serve on the bench

    ejercer la profesión legal to practice law

    ejercer su cargo to hold office

    ejercer un derecho to exercise a right

    ejercer una acción to bring an action

    ejercer una actividad en relación de dependencia to be under an employment contract

ejercicio fiscal year

ejercitar

    ejercitar acciones civiles, mercantiles y penales (Mex) to file civil, commercial and criminal actions

    ejercitar el derecho del tanto (Mex) to exercise the right of first refusal

    ejercitar el mandato ante to act before all kinds of

ejidatario (Mex) owner of an ejido

ejido (Mex) ejido [*village lands communally held in the traditional system of land tenure that combines communal ownership with individual use. The ejido consists of cultivated land, pastureland,*

and the townsite (fundo legal). See Art. 27 of Mexican Constitution.]

elegir 1. to elect 2. to select, choose

elemento
    elemento distintivo de la marca distinctive feature of the mark
    elementos coyunturales 1. economic factors 2. temporary factors, short-term factors

elevar
    elevar a escritura pública to put into the form of a notarial instrument
    elevar a segunda instancia to refer a case to a higher court
    elevar a tribunal superior to refer a case to a higher court
    elevar al año to annualize
    elevar en consulta to submit a matter to a higher court for approval or review
    elevar los autos to send the proceedings from a lower court to a higher court
    elevar un recurso to file an appeal

emancipación emancipation [*deeming a minor to be of legal age upon marriage even though he has not yet reached legal age*]

emancipado legally responsible

embargar to attach

embargo attachment [*in an "embargo" the property remains in the debtor's possession, whereas in a "secuestro" the property is taken away from the debtor*]
    embargo precautorio attachment of property to ensure the satisfaction of a judgment [*also called "embargo de precaución" and "embargo preventivo"*]

emisión issue

emisora issuer
    emisora de primera categoría prime issuer

emitir to issue
    emitir un fallo to hand down a judgment, to render a judgment
    emitir un voto to cast a vote

empadronador registrar

empadronamiento voter registration

empate tie vote

empeñar to pawn

empeño pledge

emplazador process server

emplazamiento summons (pl. summonses), service of process

emplazar a huelga to give notice of a strike

empleado employee
    empleado de confianza political appointee
    empleado de plantilla permanent employee
    empleado público government employee
    empleados eventuales temporary workers

empresa company, business, enterprise
   empresa de factoraje financiero financial factoring company
   empresa en marcha going concern
   empresa individual de responsabilidad limitada (Cos) limited liability company with a single member
   empresa matriz parent company
   empresa mixta partly state-owned company
   empresa no lucrativa (Mex) non-profit organization
   empresa pública state-owned company [*Note that "public company" in the US means a company that is publicly traded on the stock exchange.*]
empresario entrepreneur, business owner
empréstito 1. loan 2. debt securities
   empréstito público government loan
en acatamiento a in accordance with, pursuant to
en ambos efectos with stay of execution [*an appeal is made to a higher court (efecto devolutivo) and execution of the order being appealed is stayed (efecto suspensivo)*]
en atención a que in view of the fact that
en base a efectivo on a cash basis
en base al pago on a cash basis
en buen estado in good condition, in good repair
en buen estado de conservación in good order and repair
en buenas condiciones in good condition [*singular in English*]
en cabal juicio of sound mind
en calidad de asesor in an advisory capacity
en caso contrario otherwise
en cifras cerradas al dólar inmediato in figures rounded to the nearest dollar
en conjunto in the aggregate, as a whole
en contumacia in contempt
en cualquier momento at all times, at any time
en cuenta (Chi) without a hearing [*The Court of Appeals can hear an appeal in one of two ways: "en cuenta" and "previa vista de la causa." "En cuenta" is the procedure whereby one of the panels of the Court of Appeals hears an appeal through a private report of one of the court's staff attorneys without any participation by the attorneys for the parties.*]
en debida forma duly, in due form
en desarrollo de in furtherance of
en descubierto overdrawn, in the red
en disolución in liquidation
en efectivo in cash
en el caso de autos in the case at hand, in the instant case
en el curso normal de los negocios in the ordinary course of business
en el fondo on the merits

en el giro normal de los negocios in the ordinary course of business

en especie in kind

en este acto hereby

en este mismo orden de ideas along these same lines; by the same token

en fe de lo cual in witness whereof

en firme binding

en forma enunciativa y no limitativa by way of enumeration and not limitation; including but not limited to

en forma pura y simple unconditionally

en fraude de acreedores with an intent to defraud creditors

en funciones acting [*temporarily holding office, e.g., acting chairman*]

en horas de despacho during business hours [*at a court*]

en igualdad de circunstancias all other things being equal

en la especie in the case at hand

en la inteligencia que with the understanding that

en lo conducente in pertinent part

    que en lo conducente dice the relevant parts of which read as follows

en lo sucesivo hereinafter

en los autos caratulados (Arg) in the case styled

en los autos del juicio señalado al rubro (Mex) in the above-styled case; in the above-captioned case

en mi nombre y en lugar de mí in my name, place and stead

en mora in arrears

en nombre y representación in one's name and on one's behalf; in one's name, place and stead

en orden de turno next on duty

en plena vigencia in full force and effect

en pleno en banc

en pleno siglo XX well into the 20th century

en rebeldía in default, in contempt

en salas in panels

en sede judicial in court, at the courthouse

en su cabal juicio of sound mind, in one's right mind

en su caso if any, if applicable

en su defecto in the absence thereof, otherwise

en su nombre on his behalf

en su oportunidad 1. in due time 2. at the proper time, at the appropriate time

en su procedencia if appropriate, if proper, if well-founded

en tal virtud by virtue thereof

en testimonio de lo cual in witness whereof

en tiempo y forma in due time and proper form

en todo momento at any time, at all times

en trámite pending, in the pipeline

en un solo efecto without a stay of execution [*i.e., the lower court's decision will be implemented while the appeal is being processed*]

en única instancia as a court of first and last resort

en uno y otro caso in either case, in both cases, either way

en uso del poder especial pursuant to the special power of attorney

en vigor in force, in effect

enajenación 1. alienation 2. transfer 3. sale
> **enajenación de acciones** sale of stock
> **enajenación de bienes** sale of goods
> **enajenación a granel** transfer in bulk
> **enajenación de la prenda** foreclosure on the chattels
> **enajenación mental** insanity

enajenador transferor

enajenante transferor

enajenar to alienate, to transfer, to convey, to dispose of

encaje reserve
> **encaje legal (Mex)** reserve requirement [*mandatory cash deposit that credit institutions must maintain in the Banco de México, in relation to their total liabilities*]
> **encajes remunerados** interest-bearing reserves

encarcelamiento imprisonment, incarceration

encartado (Cos, Cub) the accused, the defendant

encausamiento prosecution

encausar to prosecute

encubrimiento being an accessory after the fact [*by hiding a criminal*]

encuesta a pie de urna exit poll

endeudamiento indebtedness
> **endeudamiento con el exterior** foreign indebtedness
> **endeudamiento externo** foreign indebtedness

endosante endorser

endosar to endorse

endosatario endorsee

endoso 1. endorsement 2. rider [*in the context of insurance*]

enervar to void, annul, render invalid

enfiteusis long-term lease of real estate that requires the lessee to make improvements and pay annual rent and permits the lessee to transfer his rights by sale or gift

enganche (Mex) down payment

enjuiciar 1. to sue [*civil case*] 2. to prosecute [*criminal case*]

enmienda amendment

enmendar to amend
> **enmendar un error** to correct an error
> **enmendar una ley** to amend a law

enriquecimiento enrichment
> **enriquecimiento ilegítimo (Mex)** unjust enrichment
> **enriquecimiento ilícito (Per, Spa, Ven)** unjust enrichment
> **enriquecimiento injusto (Mex, Spa)** unjust enrichment

ensañamiento cruelty, barbarity

enseres fixtures

entablar
> **entablar acción** to file suit
> **entablar denuncia** to report a crime to the police, to file a police report
> **entablar juicio hipotecario** to foreclose
> **entablar negociaciones** to open negotiations
> **entablar pleito** to file suit
> **entablar querella** to file charges

entender en una causa to hear a case

entendiéndose que with the understanding that

entera fe y crédito full faith and credit

enterar 1. (Chi, Mex) to pay [*a debt*] **2.** to inform
> **Enterados de su contenido, la ratificaron de conformidad y así la otorgaron firmando todos el día 3 de junio.** Being fully informed of its contents, they stated their agreement therewith and all of them executed it this third day of June.

entero payment

entidad federativa (Mex) state [*one of the states (or the Federal District) of the United Mexican States*]

entrada de capital capital intake
> **entradas al almacén** warehouse receipts
> **entradas y salidas** receipts and disbursements

entrar
> **entrar en funciones** to take office
> **entrar en vigencia** to take effect, to go into force
> **entrar en vigor** to take effect, to go into force

entrega delivery
> **entrega de efectivo** cash advance
> **entrega de la llave** returning the key [*upon termination of a lease*]
> **entrega de una cantidad por el fiduciario** distribution of an amount by the trustee
> **entrega del bien locado** surrender of the leased premises [*upon termination of a lease*]
> **entrega inmediata** special delivery
> **entrega material** physical delivery

entregada
> **entregada derechos pagados** delivered duty paid (DDP) [*Incoterm*]
> **entregada derechos no pagados** delivered duty unpaid (DDU) [*Incoterm*]

entregada en frontera delivered at frontier (DAF) [*Incoterm*]
entregada en muelle delivered ex quay (DEQ) [*Incoterm*]
entregada sobre buque delivered ex ship (DES) [*Incoterm*]
entregar 1. to deliver 2. to distribute [*the assets of a trust*]
entrerrenglonadas interlineations
equidad equity [*Note that "equidad" in Spanish means completely disregarding the law and simply deciding on the basis of what seems fair, whereas "equity" in common law countries is a system of rules parallel to the common law rules.*]
equiparable comparable
    equiparable al contrabando (Mex) possession of goods of foreign origin without proper documentation
equiparar con to equate with
erario public treasury, public funds
erogación outlay, expenditure
error error, mistake
    error de derecho mistake of law [*This is a defense to contract formation, and means a mistake regarding a fact that significantly affects the performance of a contract. Note that in English, the term "error of law" is used in procedural law to describe an erroneous ruling on a legal issue during a trial, which is not what is meant by "error de derecho."*]
    error de hecho mistake of fact [*This is a defense to contract formation, and means a mistake involving the misunderstanding or incorrect application of law to a contract. Note that in English, the term "error of fact" is used in procedural law to describe an erroneous finding of fact by the jury, which is not what is meant by "error de hecho."*]
    error en judicando substantive defects in the court's judgment
    error en procedando procedural error
    error significativo material error
escalafón list of employees by rank or seniority, seniority list, promotions roster
escalamiento breaking and entering, unlawful entry
    escalamiento de precios price escalation
escindente the company that spins off one of its units
escindida the company that is spun off
escisión spin-off [*The parent company contributes only a part of its assets, liabilities and capital to one or more newly formed companies, but the parent company continues to exist.*]
    escisión procesal bifurcation of a cause of action [*as opposed to "acumulación de autos"*]
escribanía (Arg, Uru) office of a notary public
escribano 1. (Arg, Uru) notary public **2. (Per)** court clerk
escrito pleading, petition, writing, document
    escrito de calificación (Spa) bill of particulars

especie valorada — assessed stamp (?)

escrito de conclusiones (Spa) closing brief [*contains the attorney's closing arguments and is also referred to as "alegatos"*]

escrito de contestación responsive pleading

escrito de cuenta (Mex) staff memorandum [*summary of case provided to the judge by a staff attorney*]

escrito de querella charge, criminal complaint

escrito firmado a ruego (Arg) document signed on behalf of an illiterate person

escritura writing, instrument, document

    escritura constitutiva articles of incorporation, charter

    escritura de constitución (Cos, Nic, Per, Spa) articles of incorporation, charter

    escritura de préstamo loan agreement

    escritura de propiedad title deed

    escritura de reformas amendment

    escritura de venta bill of sale

    escritura matriz original instrument

    escritura pública document recorded by a notary, a notarial instrument [*Note that the English term "deed" means a document by which real property is transferred. A power of attorney recorded in an "escritura pública" is not a "deed" in English, so the term "escritura pública" must be translated as "notarial instrument" or "notarially recorded instrument."*]

    escritura social (Chi) articles of incorporation

escriturales (Arg) book-entry shares [*short for "acciones escriturales"*]

escriturar to have a document recorded by a notary

escrutador inspector of elections

escrutinio counting the votes

escuadrón de la muerte death squad

escuchas telefónicas wire tapping, phone tapping

especies fiscales revenue stamps

especulación speculation

espiral inflacionista inflationary spiral

esponsales betrothal agreement, agreement to marry

espontáneamente voluntarily, of one's own accord, at one's own initiative

esposar to handcuff

esqueleto (Ven) blank form

esquema de ganancias compartidas revenue-sharing plan

establecimiento penal prison, correctional facility

estado 1. state 2. status 3. statement

    estado benefactor welfare state

    estado civil marital status

    estado de ánimo frame of mind

estado de asamblea (Chi) state of alert [*one of four "estados de excepción" provided for by the Chilean Constitution*]

estado de cambios en la situación financiera (Mex) statement of changes in financial position

estado de bienestar welfare state

estado de cambios en la inversión de los accionistas (Mex) statement of changes in shareholders' equity

estado de catástrofe (Chi) state of disaster [*one of four "estados de excepción" provided for by the Chilean Constitution*]

estado de cuenta account statement

estado de emergencia state of emergency

estado de evolución del patrimonio neto statement of changes in shareholders' equity

estado de excepción state of emergency

estado de flujos de efectivo (Mex, Pan) statement of cash flow

estado de flujos de fondos (Col) statement of cash flow

estado de guerra state of war

estado de movimientos en el capital contable (Mex) statement of changes in shareholders' equity

estado de origen y aplicación de fondos statement of changes in financial position [*In the UK, this document is called "statement of source and application of funds"*]

estado de pérdidas y ganancias profit and loss statement [*also called an "income statement"*]

estado de posición financiera (Mex) statement of financial position [*synonym of "balance sheet"*]

estado de resultados income statement

estado de sitio state of siege

estado de situación patrimonial (Arg) statement of financial position [*synonym of "balance sheet"*]

Estado Libre Asociado de Puerto Rico Commonwealth of Puerto Rico

estado mayor general staff [*in the military*]

estado patrimonial balance sheet

estados financieros financial statements

estados financieros a fechas intermedias unaudited interim financial statements

estados financieros consolidados consolidated financial statements

estafa 1. fraud, hoax 2. swindling

estafador swindler

estampar un sello to affix a seal

estancamiento stagnation

estanco 1. state-owned monopoly 2. store where goods controlled by the state are sold [*e.g., alcohol, tobacco*]

estanflación stagflation [*situation where a country persistently suffers from both high inflation and high unemployment*]

estar

    estar a derecho (Spa) to appear in court

    estar al resultado de una sentencia to abide by a decision

    estar al sentido literal

        Se estará al sentido literal. The literal meaning shall govern.

    estar en cuarto intermedio (Arg) to be in recess, to be adjourned

    estar en trámite to be pending

estatuir to enact, to stipulate, to provide

estatutario provided by the bylaws [*note that "statutory" in English means "legal" or "previsto por ley"*]

estatutos bylaws

estelionato swindling [*in which the swindler sells, pledges, leases or encumbers property, fraudulently concealing from the victim that the property has already been sold to someone else or is already encumbered by liens or attachments*]

estimación para cuentas incobrables (Mex) allowance for bad debts

estimar

    estimar el riesgo to evaluate the risk

    estimar un recurso to allow an appeal to proceed, to grant the appellant leave to proceed

    estimar una apelación to allow an appeal to proceed, to grant the appellant leave to proceed

    estimar una demanda to entertain a complaint

estímulos fiscales tax incentives

estipulaciones provisions, covenants

estorbar to obstruct

estorbo hindrance, obstruction, impediment

estrado de testigos the witness stand

estudio 1. study 2. law firm 3. movie studio

    estudio de realización feasibility study

    estudio de rentabilidad profitability study

    estudio jurídico (Arg, Uru) law firm, law offices

estupro statutory rape

etiqueta de inventario (Mex) inventory tag

evacuación de pruebas (Ven) production of evidence

evacuar

    evacuar las diligencias to comply with the formalities

    evacuar pruebas (Ven) to produce evidence [*after it has first been "promovido" (offered) and "admitido" (admitted by the judge)*]

    evacuar un testigo (Ven) to produce a witness

    evacuar un traslado to give notice

evacuar una consulta to answer an inquiry

evasión 1. evasion 2. escape

evasión fiscal tax evasion

evicción eviction, dispossession

evolución trend, way in which a situation is likely to evolve, outlook

evolución del negocio business review [*as a heading in an annual report*]

evolución previsible future outlook [*as a heading in an annual report*]

ex nunc (Lat) as of now [*i.e., not retroactive*]

exacción

exacción fiscal levy

exacción ilegal exaction [*an official wrongfully demanding payment of a fee for official services when no payment is due*]

examen anticipado de testigos pre-filing examination of witnesses [*i.e., before the lawsuit is filed*]

excarcelación release from prison

excedente surplus

excedente de capital capital surplus

excedente de efectivo cash surplus

excelentísima cámara (Arg) Honorable Judges of the Court of Appeals

excepción defense

excepción coherente personal defense [*i.e., one that can be asserted only by a person obligated in the legal transaction in dispute*]

excepción de arraigo motion requesting that the plaintiff post bond or bail sufficient to guarantee the payment of costs if he loses the case

excepción de compensación defense that the defendant has given the plaintiff a thing in payment of the claim

excepción de cosa juzgada defense that the matter is res judicata

excepción de defecto legal motion to dismiss for failure to state a claim

excepción de falta de acción motion to dismiss for failure to state a claim [*referred to as "demurrer" in common law pleading (as opposed to the Federal Rules)*]

excepción de falta de personalidad defense that the representative lacks authority to sue on behalf of the plaintiff

excepción de falta de personería defense that the representative lacks authority to sue on behalf of the plaintiff

excepción de incompetencia motion to dismiss for lack of jurisdiction

excepción de litispendencia motion to dismiss on grounds that the claims are already being litigated in another lawsuit

excepción de oscuridad motion for a more definite statement

excepción declinatoria motion to dismiss for lack of jurisdiction or improper venue

excepción dilatoria motion to dismiss [*referred to as "plea in abatement" or "dilatory plea" in common law pleadings (as opposed to the Federal Rules)*]

excepción non adimpleti contractus (Lat) defense that the plaintiff is also in default and therefore cannot demand performance of the contract

excepción perentoria affirmative defense [*referred to as "plea in bar" in common law pleading (as opposed to the Federal Rules)*]

excepción personal personal defense [*i.e., one that can be asserted only by a person obligated in the legal transaction in dispute*]

exceptio veritatis (Lat) truth is a defense to defamation

exclusión del foro disbarment

excluyente de responsabilidad (Mex) defense that a lesser punishment is in order (because of extenuating circumstances)

excusación judge disqualifying himself

excusarse to disqualify oneself, to recuse oneself

exento

exento de derechos duty free

exento de impuestos tax exempt

exequátur exequatur [*authorization to execute a foreign judgment*]

exhibición

exhibición de documentos production of documents

exhibición deshonesta indecent exposure

exhibición personal (Gua, Hon, Nic) habeas corpus

exhibiciones de capital (Mex) capital contributions

exhibiciones no realizadas (Mex) payments not yet made

exhibir (Mex) to make a payment

exhibir documentos to produce documents

exhorto letters rogatory [*formal request from one court to another of equivalent status – Traditionally the word was used when the letters rogatory were sent to another judge in the same country, while "carta rogatoria" was used for judges in another country. However, the two terms are used interchangeably in the Spanish version of the Inter-American Convention on Letters Rogatory.*]

exigibilidad enforceability

exigibilidades current liabilities

exigibilidades a la vista demand deposits

exigir sin derecho to extort

eximir de responsabilidad to release from liability, to hold harmless

existencia

existencia en caja cash on hand

expresar – to state

existencias (Spa) inventory [*called "inventarios" in Mex and "bienes de cambio" in Arg*]
expedición de flete freight forwarding
expediente 1. file 2. record of the proceedings 3. action, proceedings
    expediente de crisis (Spa) statement of financial difficulties [*as required by law prior to laying off staff*]
    expediente de dominio proceedings to establish ownership
    expediente de regulación de empleo (Spa) downsizing plan, layoff plan
    expediente en apelación the record on appeal
expedienteo red tape
experiencia crediticia credit history
explotar una patente to work a patent
exposición de motivos (de una ley) preliminary recitals
expósito foundling, abandoned newborn
expresa o tácitamente expressly or implicitly
expresar to state, to set forth
    El artículo 6 expresa lo siguiente: Article 6 reads as follows:
expresión statement
extemporáneo untimely
externalización outsourcing [*referred to as "tercerización" in Arg*]
extinción 1. termination [*of a contract*] 2. discharge [*of debts or liabilities*]
extorsión extortion
extorsionar to extort
extrabursátil over the counter
extrajudicial out-of-court
extralimitación de funciones ultra vires acts
extravío misplacement
extremo 1. point, issue 2. cause of action
    extremo de la demanda cause of action, claim
    según ese extremo del reglamento according to that provision of the regulation
factoraje factoring [*short-term financing by selling accounts receivable at a discount*]
factura invoice, bill
    factura cambiaria (Col, Gua) commercial invoice
    factura comercial commercial invoice
    factura consular consular invoice [*an instrument that a shipper of goods must present for certification to a consul of the country to which the goods are to be shipped*]
    factura de contribución (Pue) tax bill
    factura pro forma pro forma invoice

facultad power, authority

    facultad de atracción ancillary jurisdiction [*power of court to take jurisdiction over matters that are normally outside its jurisdiction, in order to settle all claims in one court*]

    facultad de derecho law school

    con facultades de sustituir este poder, revocar sustituciones y hacer otras de nuevo with full power of substitution, revocation and delegation

fallar to hand down a ruling, to decide a case, to render a judgment

    fallo, haciendo lugar a lo pedido It is hereby ordered, adjudged and decreed that the petition be, and the same hereby is, sustained/dismissed [*depending on whether the court grants the plaintiff's petition or the defendant's petition*]

fallido insolvent

fallo 1. decision, ruling 2. arbitral award

    fallo plenario decision of an appellate court sitting en banc

falsificación forgery, counterfeiting

falsificar to forge, to counterfeit

falta 1. lack 2. misdemeanor 3. negligence 4. absence

    falta absoluta (Ven) judge's permanent absence [*e.g., because of death*]

    falta accidental (Ven) judge's absence on a one-time basis [*because he does not have jurisdiction*]

    falta de aceptación (Mex) failure to honor a check

    falta de buenos criterios lack of good judgment

    falta de legitimación lack of standing

    falta de personalidad lack of standing

    falta de personería lack of standing

    falta de poder lack of authority

    falta de probidad lack of integrity

    falta de representación lack of authority

    falta grave gross negligence

    falta objetiva strict liability

    falta por enfermedad sick leave

    falta temporal (Ven) judge's temporary absence [*because he is on leave or on vacation*]

faltar al trabajo to be absent from work

fama pública a person's reputation in the community

familia directa immediate family

fe faith

    fe de bautismo baptismal certificate

    fe de conocimiento verification of a person's identity

    fe de vida certificate that a person is still alive

    fe notarial the presumption of accuracy to which a notary's certification is entitled

    fe pública legal authority to attest documents

fecha date

    fecha de constitución date of incorporation [*of a company*]

    fecha de disposición del crédito drawdown date [*date on which a loan is made available*]

    fecha de entrada en vigor effective date

    fecha de vencimiento date of maturity

    fecha de vigencia effective date

    fecha límite deadline

fedatario notary public

fehaciente reliable, trustworthy

    Es necesario que quede de él la debida constancia auténtica y fehaciente. It is necessary that there be an authentic and reliable record thereof.

    mediante notificación fehaciente al banco through reliable notice to the bank

fehacientemente reliably, by any reliable means

    Nos consta fehacientemente su identidad. We are absolutely certain of her identity.

fenecer to expire

feria judicial court holidays [*period during which the courts are not in session*]

feriado judicial court holiday [*day on which the courts are not in session*]

feudatario (Per) tenant property

fiador guarantor

fianza guaranty [*contract between the creditor and the guarantor whereby the guarantor agrees to pay the debtor's debts upon an event of default*]

    fianza de caución surety bond

    fianza de cumplimiento performance bond

    fianza de fiel cumplimiento performance bond

    fianza de licitación bid bond

    fianza de rato bond posted by an attorney who has not received a power of attorney from his client. [*The bond guarantees that the client will ratify all the attorney's acts on his behalf.*]

    fianza de validez bid bond

ficción jurídica legal fiction [*something assumed in law to be true regardless of its truth or accuracy*]

ficha

    ficha de depósito (Mex) deposit slip

    ficha médica medical records

    ficha policial criminal record, arrest record

    ficha rugoscópica palatine record [*description of a person's palate used as a means of identification in forensic science*]

    ficha técnica technical specifications

fideicomisario beneficiary [*of a trust*]

    fideicomisario en primer lugar primary beneficiary

fideicomisario en segundo lugar secondary beneficiary
fideicomisario en tercer lugar tertiary beneficiary
fideicomiso trust
fideicomitente settlor, trustor [*the person setting up the trust*]
fiduciario trustee
figura concept, feature
Ésta es una figura novedosa en nuestro derecho interno.
This is a new concept in our internal law.
figurar to appear, to be listed, to be shown in
Su nombre no figura en la relación. His name is not on the
list.
fijar
fijar audiencia to call a hearing
fijar carteles 1. (Ven) to post a public notice of marriage on the
bulletin board at the Civil Registry [*i.e., the Jefatura Civil*] **2.**
to post bills
fijar el domicilio to establish a place a business
filiación filiation
filiación legítima legitimate descent, being born in wedlock
filiación natural birth out of wedlock, being an illegitimate child
filosofía del derecho jurisprudence
finado 1. [*as a noun*] the decedent, the deceased 2. [*as an adj.*]
deceased
finca 1. (Pue) farm **2.** plantation **3. (Mex)** real estate, real property
finca arrendada leased property
finca destinada a habitación residential property
finca destinada al ejercicio de una industria industrial
property
finca rústica rural property [*synonym of "predio rústico"*]
finca urbana city property [*synonym of "predio urbano"*]
fincar 1. to buy real estate 2. to award [*the standard term is
"adjudicar"*]
**El postor a favor de quien se finque la venta deberá pagar el
precio dentro de 10 días.** The bidder who is awarded the
sale must pay the price within 10 days.
finiquitado closed and terminated
finiquitar 1. to settle and close an account 2. to give an employee
his final paycheck
finiquito 1. release 2. quitclaim 3. final paycheck 4. closing of an
account
firma 1. firm, company 2. signature 3. firm name, corporate name
firma a ruego (Arg) signature on behalf of an illiterate person
firma de puño y letra handwritten signature [*as opposed to a
"facsimile signature"*]
firma facsímil facsimile signature [*not a faxed signature, but a
signature reproduced by rubber stamp*]
firma falsificada forged signature

firma mancomunada joint signature
firma solidaria single signature
firma y sello hand and seal
llevar el uso de la firma social to be authorized to sign on behalf of the company
firmar to sign, to execute
firmado, sellado y otorgado signed, sealed and delivered
firmar de puña y letra to sign in person
Firmó el que supo, pudo y quiso hacerlo. Those willing and able to sign did so.
firmeza finality, definitive character
fiscal 1. district attorney, prosecutor 2. statutory auditor [*short for "revisor fiscal" - Col, Cos*]
fiscal de cámara (Arg) government attorney at an appellate court
fiscal general del estado (Spa) attorney general
Fiscal Nacional Económico (Chi) Head of the Antitrust Commission [*i.e., the Comisión Resolutiva. His representatives in the various regions are called "fiscales regionales."*]
Fiscalía Especial para la Atención de Delitos Electorales (Mex) Special Prosecutor's Office for Electoral Crimes
fiscalización supervision, oversight, inspection
fisco tax authorities, internal revenue service, the Treasury
fluctuación cambiaria exchange gain or loss
flujo de caja cash flow
foja page
a fojas 8 on page 8
foliar to number [*pages*]
folio page
folios útiles pages of text
folleto
folleto bursátil (Spa) prospectus [*called "prospecto" in other countries*]
folleto de admisión (Spa) registration prospectus
folleto de emisión (Spa) issue prospectus
fomento promotion, advancement
fondo 1. fund 2. the merits of the case
fondo amortizante sinking fund
fondo común de inversión (FCI) (Arg) mutual fund
fondo de amortización sinking fund
fondo de caja chica petty cash fund
fondo de comercio (Spa) 1. goodwill 2. going concern [*The sale of a "going concern" is referred to as an "asset purchase" (as opposed to a "stock purchase") in legal English.*]
fondo de comercio negativo (Spa) negative goodwill

fondo de contingencias contingency fund
fondo de estabilización de cambios exchange stabilization
fund
**Fondo de Garantía de Depósitos y Protección Bancaria
(Ven)** Venezuelan Federal Deposit Insurance Corporation
Fondo de Garantía Salarial (Spa) Wage Protection Fund
[*protects workers' wages in the event of bankruptcy or
closure*]
fondo de inversión (Mex) mutual fund
fondo de maniobra working capital
fondo de rescate redemption fund
fondo de retiro retirement fund, pension
fondo fiduciario trust fund
fondo jubilatorio pension fund
Fondo Monetario Internacional (FMI) International Monetary
Fund (IMF)
fondo mutual de inversiones (Ven) mutual fund
fondo mutuo de inversión (Col) mutual fund
Fondo Nacional de las Artes (Arg) National Association for the
Promotion of the Arts
fondo revolvente (Mex) revolving fund [*a fund, provided for a
particular purpose, that is periodically replenished either from
operations or by transfers from other funds*]
fondo rotatorio revolving fund [*a fund, provided for a particular
purpose, that is periodically replenished either from
operations or by transfers from other funds*]
fondo y forma substance and procedure
fondos ajenos borrowed funds
fondos de activos líquidos (Ven) money market funds
fondos propios (Spa) shareholders' equity [*referred to as
"patrimonio neto" in Latin America and "capital contable" in
Mexico*]
fono (Chi) telephone
forajido fugitive, outlaw
foral (Spa) regional
formalización de objeto litigioso (Spa) statement of the grounds
for litigation
formalizar por escrito to reduce to writing
fórmula (Arg, Par) ticket, slate of candidates [*in an election*]
foro the bar
fracción paragraph
    fracción arancelaria (Mex) customs classification
    fracción de campo real property
franco
    franco a bordo free on board (FOB) [*Incoterm*]
    franco a bordo punto de destino delivered ex ship (DES)
      [*Incoterm*]

franco al costado del buque free alongside ship (FAS) [*Incoterm*]

franco en fábrica ex works (EXW) [*Incoterm*]

franco transportista free carrier (FCA) [*Incoterm*]

franco vagón free on rail (FOR) [*Incoterm*]

franquicia 1. franchise 2. deductible [*also called "franquicia de seguro"*]

franquicia arancelaria exemption from customs duties

franquicia impositiva tax exemption

franquicia tributaria tax exemption

franquiciado franchisee

franquiciador franchisor

frapista (Chi) member of the Frente de Acción Popular

fraude fiscal tax evasion

fuente

fuente de ingresos source of income

fuente de riqueza source of wealth

fuero 1. forum 2. local laws, laws in a certain region or city 3. exemption, privilege

fuero civil civil jurisdiction

fuero comercial commercial jurisdiction

fuero común 1. ordinary jurisdiction 2. local court

fuero concurrente concurrent jurisdiction

fuero de atracción 1. (Arg) jurisdiction over all suits instituted against the debtor 2. ancillary jurisdiction [*power of a court to hear cases outside its regular jurisdiction*]

fuero del contrato forum selected in a contract

fuero exterior court of law

fuero externo court of law

fuero federal federal jurisdiction

fuero interior conscience [*as opposed to "fuero exterior," which is a law court*]

fuero parlamentario parliamentary privilege

fuero sindical legal rights of organized labor [*particularly the right of labor union leaders not to be fired or transferred on account of their union leadership*]

fueros y costumbres especiales the local laws and special customs

fuerza force

fuerza irresistible irresistible force [*an unforeseeable event that prevents performance of an obligation under a contract*]

fuerza mayor force majeure

fuerza probatoria probative value [*i.e., weight as evidence*]

fuerza pública law enforcement agencies, the police

fuga

fuga de capitales capital flight

fuga de cerebros brain drain

fuga de procesados escape of prisoners
Fulana de Tal Jane Doe
Fulano de Tal John Doe
fumus boni juris (Lat) credibility of the right invoked [*the right must be credible for the judge to order interim injunctive relief (medidas cautelares). This is similar to the requirement that there be "probable success upon a trial on the merits" for a preliminary injunction to be granted in the US.*]
fumus periculum in mora (Lat) appearance of danger from delay [*This is similar to the US requirement that there be probability of irreparable harm if interim injunctive relief is not granted.*]
función 1. office 2. function
    función administrativa managerial function
    función pública civil service
funcionar to function
    El consejo funcionará válidamente con la mayoría de los consejeros. A quorum of the board shall consist of a majority of the directors.
funcionario civil servant
    funcionario de una sociedad officer of a corporation
    funcionario judicial officer of the court
    funcionario público public official, civil servant
fundador incorporator
fundamentos de derecho legal grounds
fundar to base, to support
    fundado well founded, supported
    fundar una sentencia to base a judgment on the law [*Judges have the duty to "fundar" and "motivar" their decisions. "Motivar" refers to stating the reasons for the decision.*]
    fundo mi derecho en the right to which I am entitled arises from
fundo 1. rural property 2. estate
    fundo dominante dominant estate [*parcel of land that benefits from an easement on a servient estate*]
    fundo legal (Mex) townsite [*part of an ejido*]
    fundo sirviente servient estate [*estate on which an easement is placed for the benefit of another estate*]
fusionada merging company [*in a merger, i.e., the one that is merged out of existence*]
fusionante surviving company [*in a merger*]
fusionar to merge
fusión 1. merger 2. consolidation
    fusión por absorción (Arg) merger [*one or more companies merge into another and cease to exist*]
    fusión por creación (Chi) consolidation [*two or more companies unite to create a new company, and the original companies cease to exist*]
    fusión por incorporación (Chi) merger

fusión por integración (Mex) consolidation
fusión pura (Arg) consolidation
futuros financieros futures [*agreements to buy or sell a specific amount of financial investments at a particular price on a stipulated future date*]
gaceta gazette
    Gaceta Forense (Ven) Supreme Court Reporter
    Gaceta Judicial (Col, Ecu) Supreme Court Reporter
    gaceta oficial official gazette
gafete (Mex) badge [*The standard term is "credencial."*]
ganancia
    ganancia de capital capital gain
    ganancia líquida net profit
    ganancia neta en la venta de acciones net gain from sale of securities
    ganancia neta en operaciones de cambio net gain from foreign exchange transactions
    ganancia por traslación (Per) gain from foreign currency translation
    ganancias 1. profit 2. gain
    ganancias eventuales occasional earnings
    ganancias y pérdidas profit and loss
garante guarantor
garantía 1. warranty, guarantee 2. security deposit [*in a lease*]
    garantía de cumplimiento performance bond
    garantía de mantenimiento de oferta bid bond
    garantía implícita implied warranty
    garantía personal personal guaranty [*e.g., aval or fianza*]
    garantía prendaria pledge
    garantía real collateral
    garantías constitucionales constitutional rights
    garantías individuales constitutional rights
garantizar to warrant, to guarantee
    garantizar el interés fiscal (Mex) to guarantee the payment of any tax that may be found payable
    garantizar un préstamo to secure a loan
gasto
    gasto de capital capital expenditure
    gasto público government spending
    gastos a distribuir en varios ejercicios (Spa) deferred expenses
    gastos administrativos administrative expenses
    gastos anticipados prepaid expenses
    gastos bancarios bank charges
    gastos causídicos court costs
    gastos de acarreo freight costs
    gastos de desplazamiento travel expenses

gastos de elaboración manufacturing expenses [*consist of materials, labor and factory overhead*]

gastos de explotación (Spa) operating expenses

gastos de fabricación manufacturing expenses [*consist of materials, labor and factory overhead*]

gastos de investigación y desarrollo research and development expenses

gastos de operación (Mex, Per) operating expenses

gastos de primer establecimiento (Spa) start-up expenses

gastos de representación entertainment expenses, hospitality expenses

gastos de ventas cost of sales, cost of goods sold

gastos devengados accrued expenses [*expenses that have been incurred but are not recognized in the accounts*]

gastos financieros interest expense [*as an item on a financial statement*]

gastos fiscales tax expenditures [*tax revenue forgone by the government because it has granted tax preferences*]

gastos generales overhead

gastos indirectos overhead

gastos judiciales court costs

gastos no deducibles non-deductible expenses

gastos notariales notarial fees

gastos operativos (Arg) operating expenses

gastos periódicos recurring expenses

gastos por intereses interest expense

gastos procesales court costs

generales personal information, personal data, particulars

Manifiestan ser de las generales consignadas. They state that their personal information is as recorded.

generales de ley general questions asked of witnesses, such as name, nationality, domicile

gerente manager

gestionar 1. to negotiate, to try to arrange 2. to conduct business

gestionar fondos to raise money

gestionar un préstamo to arrange for a loan

gestionar una patente to apply for a patent

gestión 1. management 2. transaction 3. negotiation

gestión de carteras portfolio management

gestión de negocios ajenos quasi-agency [*i.e., handling of another's business without written contract*]

gestor negotiator, promoter, professional intermediary

gestor oficioso unofficial representative

gestoría corporate services company [*company that handles all the paperwork and visits to government offices involved in obtaining a document for its clients*]

gira promocional (Arg, Mex) roadshow [*to promote a new issue of securities*]

girado drawee [*of a draft*]

girador drawer [*of a draft*]

girar 1. to draw 2. to send, to remit 3. to do business
    girar bajo la razón social de to do business as [*d/b/a*]
    girar contra una cuenta to draw on an account
    girar en descubierto to overdraw
    girar exhortos to issue letters rogatory
    girar fondos to draw funds
    girar un cheque to write a check

giro 1. line of business 2. draft
    giro a la vista sight draft
    giro bancario bank draft
    giro doloso de cheques check kiting
    giro de ahorros (Chi) savings account withdrawal
    giro en descubierto overdraft
    giro normal de los negocios ordinary course of business
    giro postal money order
    giro telegráfico wire transfer

golpe de estado coup d'état

golpismo coup mentality

golpista one who takes part in a coup

grado degree, grade
    grado de inversión investment grade
    grado de liquidez degree of liquidity
    grado de parentesco degree of kinship

gratificación bonus

gravable taxable

gravamen encumbrance, lien, tax
    gravamen real real-estate lien

gravar 1. to tax 2. to encumber
    El impuesto sobre la renta grava los ingresos ... Income tax is imposed on income ...
    Esta finca está gravada con una hipoteca. There is a mortgage on this property.
    Se grava con el impuesto a la renta la diferencia entre el valor de adquisición y el valor de enajenación. Income tax is imposed on the difference between the purchase price and sales price.

grupo group
    grupo de ingresos income bracket
    grupo impositivo tax bracket
    grupo sanguíneo blood type

guarda custody [*of children*]

guardador guardian [*includes both "curador" and "tutor" (q.v.)*]

Guardia Civil (Spa) police force

guía
    guía aérea airbill [*a non-negotiable document that evidences the contract between the shipper and the carrier for the carriage of the goods*]
    guía de embarque (Cos) bill of lading
    guía de internación import permit
hábeas corpus habeas corpus
hábeas data (Per) right to public information [*Art. 200(3) of the Peruvian Constitution gives individuals access to public information. They may request that inaccurate information in databases be corrected or destroyed if the improper use of it could impair constitutional rights.*]
haber 1. assets 2. credit side [*of a ledger*]
    haber jubilatorio pension
    haber social corporate assets
    haberes income, earnings, salaries
    haberes diferidos unearned income
haber lugar to lie, to be admissible
    no ha lugar petition denied
habilitar
    habilitar el tiempo to allow judicial acts to be performed on a court holiday
    habilitar los libros to affix the required revenue stamps to the books
hacer
    hacer caso omiso de to dispense with
    hacer constar por escrito to reduce to writing
    hacer cumplir to enforce
    hacer efectivo to enforce
    hacer fe
        Los documentos públicos hacen fe entre las partes contratantes. Notarially recorded documents are authentic evidence of the agreement between the parties to the contract.
        Hacen fe en el Distrito Federal los documentos públicos procedentes del extranjero. Notarially recorded documents from abroad are deemed authentic in the Federal District.
    hacer huelga to go on strike
    hacer la carrera de derecho to get a law degree
    hacer negocio to make money
    hacer presente to point out
    hacer responsable to hold responsible
    hacer saber to give notice of, to inform someone of something
    hacer sus mejores esfuerzos to use one's best efforts
    hacer una denuncia to report a crime to the police, to file a police report

hacer una gestión to do a transaction
hacer uso de la palabra to take the floor
hacer uso del derecho del tanto (Mex) to exercise the right of first refusal
hacer valer to assert
hacer valer un derecho to exercise a right
hacerse constar por escrito to be reduced to writing, to be set forth in writing
hasta donde alcance until it runs out
hecho 1. fact 2. act 3. event
   el hecho tuvo lugar the event took place
   hecho delictivo criminal act [*also referred to as "actus reus"*]
   hecho ilícito civil tort
   hecho imponible taxable event
   hecho jurídico event that creates, modifies, transfers, preserves or extinguishes legal rights or obligations
   hecho lícito lawful act
   hecho litigioso fact in dispute
   hecho voluntario voluntary act
   hechos ajenos a su voluntad events beyond his control
   hechos extintivos mitigating circumstances [*facts such as payment of the debt that wipe out the obligation*]
   hechos gravados taxable events
   hechos impeditivos mitigating circumstances [*facts that make the performance of an obligation impossible, even if the obligation still exists*]
   hechos notorios facts of which the court can take judicial notice [*common knowledge*]
   hechos posteriores subsequent events
heredad estate, tenement
heredero heir [*The "heredero" inherits all or a percentage of an estate, whereas the "legatario" inherits specific assets in an estate.*]
   heredero ab intestado statutory heir, intestate successor
   heredero forzoso forced heir [*by law cannot be excluded*]
   heredero instituido por testamento testamentary heir, heir appointed by will
   heredero legitimario forced heir [*by law cannot be excluded*]
   heredero legítimo statutory heir [*i.e., heir at law if the decedent had died intestate*]
   heredero preterido pretermitted heir [*heir who is omitted from the will*]
   heredero puro y simple unconditional heir [*accepts the estate without the "beneficio de inventario" (q.v.)*]
   heredero universal heir to the entire estate
   heredero voluntario heir testamentary [*someone other than a forced heir who is named as heir in the will*]

herencia inheritance, estate
    herencia legítima inheritance by legal heirs
    herencia vacante unclaimed estate
    herencia yacente part of an estate of which heir has not yet
        taken possession
hermano brother
    hermanos de doble vínculo brothers and sisters of the whole
        blood
    hermanos de medio lado brothers and sisters of the half blood
hijo child, son
    hijo adoptivo adopted child
    hijo de bendición legitimate child
    hijo de crianza foster child
    hijo de familia unemancipated minor
    hijo legítimo legitimate child
    hijo natural illegitimate child, child born out of wedlock
    hijo póstumo posthumous child
hipoteca mortgage
    hipoteca de primer grado first mortgage
    hipoteca de segundo grado second mortgage
    hipoteca en primer lugar first mortgage
    hipoteca en primer término first mortgage
    hipoteca mobiliaria (Ven) chattel mortgage
    hipoteca mueble (Bol) chattel mortgage
    hipoteca revertida reverse mortgage [*mortgage in which the
        borrower receives periodic payments from the lender, based
        on the accumulated equity in the underlying property*]
hoja sheet
    hoja de cálculo spreadsheet
    hoja de depósito deposit slip
    hoja de ruta waybill
    hoja de trabajo worksheet [*used to prepare financial
        statements*]
    hoja tamaño carta (Mex) letter-size paper
    hoja tamaño oficio (Mex) legal-size paper
    hojas guía (Arg) lead schedule [*details the components of an
        amount appearing on a financial statement*]
homicidio manslaughter
    homicidio agravado (Per) murder
    homicidio alevoso first-degree murder
    homicidio calificado (Mex) murder
    homicidio casual involuntary manslaughter
    homicidio con ensañamiento murder
    homicidio concausal contributory homicide
    homicidio consentido euthanasia
    homicidio culposo involuntary manslaughter
    homicidio doloso voluntary manslaughter

homicidio en duelo manslaughter resulting from a duel
homicidio en riña manslaughter resulting from a brawl
homicidio eugenésico ethnic cleansing [*killing people to eliminate "undesirable" elements from the gene pool*]
homicidio pasional murder of passion
homicidio piadoso euthanasia
homicidio por caso fortuito excusable homicide, accidental homicide
homicidio por imprudencia (Mex) manslaughter
homicidio por piedad euthanasia
homicidio preterintencional involuntary manslaughter
homicidio simple intencional (Mex) voluntary manslaughter
homicidio suicidio assisted suicide
homicidio voluntario (Ecu) voluntary manslaughter
homologación 1. standardization 2. ratification, official recognition
homologar 1. to standardize 2. to approve, to ratify, to give official recognition to
honorarios de abogado attorneys' fees
hora hour
  hora de Londres London time
  horas extraordinarias overtime
  horas extras overtime
  horas hábiles business hours
  horas hombre manhours
  horas trabajadas time worked
hostigamiento sexual sexual harassment [*also called "acoso sexual"*]
huelga strike
  huelga con ocupación sit-down strike [*workers refuse to work but remain on employer's premises*]
  huelga de brazos caídos sit-down strike [*workers refuse to work but remain on employer's premises*]
  huelga de solidaridad sympathy strike [*strike to show sympathy with another union that is striking*]
  huelga descabellada wildcat strike [*sudden and unannounced work stoppage while a collective bargaining agreement is still in effect*]
  huelga salvaje wildcat strike [*sudden and unannounced work stoppage while a collective bargaining agreement is still in effect*]
hurtar to steal
hurto theft, larceny
  hurto de tienda shoplifting
  hurto mayor grand larceny
  hurto menor petty larceny
iguala retainer fee, contract for services
igualdad de la ley equal protection of the law

bien impuesto de su contenido — well assessed

ilícitos económicos economic offenses
imagen
> **imagen comercial** trade dress
> **imagen de marca** brand image
> **imagen fiel** *equivalent of the term "to present fairly":*
>> **Los estados financieros expresan, en todos los aspectos significativos, la imagen fiel de la situación financiera de la compañía.** The financial statements present fairly, in all material respects, the financial position of the company. [*boilerplate sentence contained in audit reports*]

impagados unpaid items
impedimento legal disqualification
impertinente irrelevant [*with regard to evidence*]
impetrante de garantías (Mex) petitioner in an amparo proceeding
imponer silencio perpetuo al litigante to impose a gag order on the litigant
importe amount
imposición taxation
> **imposición a plazo fijo (Spa)** time deposit, fixed-term deposit [*called "depósito a plazo fijo" in other countries*]
> **imposición de efectivo (Spa)** cash deposit

imprevisible unforeseeable
imprevisto unforeseen
improcedencia inadmissibility, fact that the action was improperly brought
improcedente inadmissible, not properly filed
improrrogable 1. non-extendible [*when speaking of a term*] 2. that cannot be changed [*when speaking of venue*]
imprudencia negligence
> **imprudencia punible** criminal negligence
> **imprudencia simple** ordinary negligence

impuesto tax
> **impuesto a la renta (Ecu, Per, Uru)** income tax
> **impuesto a la renta agropecuaria (Uru)** tax on agricultural and farming income
> **impuesto a las actividades agropecuarias (Uru)** tax on agricultural and farming income
> **impuesto a las ganancias (Arg)** income tax
> **impuesto a las herencias, asignaciones y donaciones (Chi)** inheritance and gift tax
> **impuesto a las remesas (Col)** remittance tax (on payments remitted abroad)
> **impuesto a los ingresos brutos (Arg)** corporate income tax
> **impuesto adicional (Chi)** tax levied on income of persons not residing or domiciled in Chile
> **impuesto al activo (Mex)** business assets tax

impuesto al consumo suntuario y a las ventas al mayor (Ven) value-added tax

impuesto al patrimonio (Uru) net worth tax

impuesto al patrimonio empresarial (Per) corporate net worth tax

impuesto al patrimonio neto (Arg) individual net worth tax

impuesto al valor agregado (IVA) value-added tax (VAT)

impuesto al valor del patrimonio predial (Per) real-estate equity tax

impuesto de alcabala (Ecu, Per) transfer tax [*on transfers of real estate, ships, and airplanes*]

impuesto de primera categoría (Chi) corporate income tax

impuesto de sisa excise tax

impuesto de promoción municipal (Per) municipal improvement tax

impuesto de traspaso (Cos) transfer tax [*on transfers of real property*]

impuesto específico interno (Uru) specific consumption tax (tobacco, liquor, etc.)

impuesto extraordinario sobre el patrimonio de las personas físicas (Spa) wealth tax

impuesto general a las ventas (Per) value-added tax

impuesto general al valor (Nic) value-added tax

impuesto global complementario (Chi) self-employment tax

impuesto industrial (Spa) production tax

impuesto por recuperar tax refund recoverable

impuesto predial municipal property tax, real estate tax

impuesto retenido withholding tax

impuesto selectivo al consumo (Per) excise tax

impuesto sobre actividades económicas (Spa) business tax [*paid by the self-employed once a year*]

impuesto sobre adquisición de inmuebles (Mex) real-estate transfer tax

impuesto sobre donaciones y sucesiones (Ven) inheritance and gift tax

impuesto sobre el lujo luxury tax

impuesto sobre el valor añadido (IVA) (Spa) value-added tax (VAT)

impuesto sobre incremento de patrimonio de un bien inmueble (Spa) capital gains tax

impuesto sobre la renta (Col, Mex, Spa, Ven) income tax

impuesto sobre la renta de las personas físicas (Spa) personal income tax [*either as a resident – obligación personal*—or as a nonresident—*obligación real*]

impuesto sobre la renta de sociedades (Spa) corporate income tax

impuesto sobre las utilidades de las empresas (Bol) corporate income tax

impuesto sobre producción y servicios Federal Excise Tax

impuesto sobre productos del trabajo (Mex) tax on earned income

impuesto sobre sociedades (Spa) corporate income tax

impuesto sobre sucesiones y donaciones (Spa) inheritance and gift tax

impuesto sucesoral (Col) estate tax

impuesto suntuario luxury tax

impuesto territorial (Cos) real property tax

impuesto único de segunda categoría (Chi) withholding tax on employment income

impuestos declarados per tax return

impuestos especiales (Spa) excise taxes

impuestos internos (Arg) excise taxes

impugnable legally vulnerable

impugnar

impugnar el testimonio to impeach the testimony

impugnar un testamento to contest a will

impugnar una resolución to challenge a resolution

impulso

impulso de parte action by parties to advance the lawsuit

impulso oficial principle of judicial supervision

impulso procesal duty to advance the legal proceedings

imputado (Arg, Chi) the accused

imputarle algo a alguien to accuse someone of something, to charge someone with something

al acusado se le imputa el delito de the defendant is charged with

in claris no fit interpretatio (Lat) There is no need to interpret that which is clear.

in dubio pro reo (Lat) In case of doubt, the verdict must be for the accused.

in extenso (Lat) completely

in fine (Lat) at the end

inafectabilidad agrícola (Mex) farmland that cannot be expropriated or encumbered

inamovilidad judicial irremovability [of judges]

inapelable unappealable

inasistencia a una sesión failure to attend a meeting

incapacidad

incapacidad legal lack of legal capacity

incapacidad mental mental incapacity

incapacidad permanente permanent disability

incapacitado disabled, incapacitated

incapacitado para testar lacking testamentary capacity

incapaz incapable, not qualified
incautación 1. administrative receivership 2. seizure, confiscation
incendiario arsonist
incidente 1. motion 2. collateral issue [*matters not directly related to the main issues in the case*]
    incidente de homologación (Mex) proceedings to make a foreign judgment enforceable in Mexico
    incidentes procedure for handling collateral issues
incidentista mover, party filing the motion
inciso paragraph, section
incoar to commence, to initiate
    incoar el juicio intestado to commence intestate proceedings
    incoar expediente contra to initiate proceedings against
incobrable uncollectible
incomparecencia failure to appear, nonappearance
incompatibilidad conflict of interest
incompetencia lack of jurisdiction
incomunicado in solitary confinement
inconcurrencia failure to appear
inconcuso indisputable, undeniable
incontinenti (Lat) promptly, immediately thereafter
    respondió incontinenti he responded without hesitation
incorporación de una nueva sociedad admission of a new company [*to a group or joint venture—Note that "incorporation of a new company" means "constitución de una nueva sociedad."*]
incorporar un socio to admit a partner
    incorporarse al Colegio de Abogados to be admitted to the bar
    incorporarse como socio de una firma to become a partner at a firm, to "make partner"
incremento
    incremento de patrimonio (Spa) capital gain
    incremento salarial wage increase
inculpado the accused
incumplimiento contractual breach of contract
incurrir
    incurrir en adeudos (Mex) to incur indebtedness
    incurrir en gastos to incur expenses
    incurrir en un delito to commit a crime
indagación investigation
indagatoria investigation
indagatorio investigatory
indefectible undeferable, unpostponable
indemnización 1. indemnification 2. severance pay
    indemnización pecuniaria money damages [*also called "resarcimiento pecuniario"*]

indemnización por accidentes de trabajo workers' compensation

indemnización por años de trabajo severance pay based on years of service

indemnización por despido severance pay

indicadores del desempeño performance indicators

índice 1. index 2. ratio

    índice ácido acid-test ratio, quick ratio [*most liquid current assets divided by current liabilities*]

    índice corriente current ratio [*current assets divided by current liabilities*]

    índice de capitalización capitalization index

    índice de holgura breadth index

    índice de inflación rate of inflation

    índice de liquidez liquidity ratio

    índice de precios al consumidor consumer price index

    índice de precios de consumo (Spa, Uru) consumer price index

    índice de rentabilidad profitability ratio

    índice de solvencia current ratio [*current assets divided by current liabilities*]

    índice de solvencia inmediata quick ratio

indiciado (Mex) the accused [*during the preliminary investigation*]

indicios circumstantial evidence

indistintamente

    Los términos se emplean indistintamente. The terms are used interchangeably.

    Pueden firmar indistintamente. Any one of them, acting alone, may sign.

individuo de número full member

indultar to pardon, to grant amnesty

indulto pardon, amnesty [*by the executive branch*]

inexistencia

    inexistencia de hecho de facto invalidity

    inexistencia jurídica legal invalidity

inexistente null and void

infamante defamatory, calumnious

inflación inflation

    inflación furtiva creeping inflation [*a slow but persistent upward movement in the general price level of as much as 2.5% per year*]

    inflación reptante creeping inflation [*see preceding entry*]

inflacionista inflationary

información

    información ad perpetuam perpetuating testimony [*a procedure for preserving for future use witnesses' testimony* *that might otherwise be lost or unavailable before the trial in which it is intended to be used*]

    información de dominio perpetuation of testimony regarding ownership

    información de posesión perpetuation of testimony regarding possession

    información privilegiada inside information, privileged information

informe 1. report **2. (Ven)** closing argument

    informe de gestión (Spa) management's discussion and analysis (MD&A) [*referred to as "memoria" in Arg*]

    informe del Presidente de la República (Mex) President's State of the Union address

    informe in voce oral argument

    informe jurídico legal opinion

    informe justificado (Mex) the respondent authority's answer to an *amparo* petition

    informe pericial expert witness report

    informe presidencial (Mex) President's State of the Union address

infracción administrative offense

infrascrito the undersigned

infringir to infringe, violate

ingeniero comercial (Chi) business administrator

ingresar 1. to join **2.** to be admitted to

    ingresar dinero en un banco (Spa) to deposit money in a bank

    Ingresó cadáver. He was dead on arrival.

ingreso

    ingreso al colegio de abogados admission to the bar association

    ingreso bruto gross income

    ingreso disponible disposable income

    ingreso en efectivo (Spa) cash deposit

    ingreso neto net income

    ingreso por habitante per capita income

    ingresos revenues, income

    ingresos de operación (Mex, Per) operating income

    ingresos financieros interest income [*as an item on a financial statement*]

    ingresos por dividendos dividends earned

    ingresos por intereses interest income

inhabilidad ineligibility

inhabilitación perpetua (Chi) permanent disqualification from holding public office

inhabilitar to disqualify

inhibido subject to an order enjoining him from disposing of his property

inhibición 1. prohibiting a judge from hearing a case over which he does not have jurisdiction 2. temporary restraining order preventing a debtor from encumbering or selling property

inhibirse to disqualify oneself

inhibitoria motion to have one judge declare that another judge lacks jurisdiction

    inhibitoria provisional temporary restraining order (TRO)

iniciar juicio to bring a lawsuit

iniciativa de ley (Gua, Mex) bill, draft law [*the standard term is "proyecto de ley"*]

iniciativa privada private enterprise

injuria insult

    injuria calumniosa libel or slander that involves falsely accusing someone of a crime

    injuria no calumniosa libel or slander that does not involve falsely accusing someone of a crime

injuriar to insult, to slander

injusticia miscarriage of justice

inmigrado (Mex) permanent resident

inmigrante (Mex) alien who intends to become a permanent resident

inmovilizaciones (Spa) fixed assets [*British term*]; property, plant and equipment [*U.S. term*]

    inmovilizaciones financieras (Spa) long-term investments [*financial fixed assets*]

    inmovilizaciones inmateriales (Spa) intangible fixed assets

    inmovilizaciones materiales (Spa) tangible fixed assets

inmovilizado (Spa) fixed assets [*British term*] property, plant and equipment [*U.S. term*]

    inmovilizado inmaterial (Spa) intangible fixed assets

    inmovilizado material (Spa) property, plant and equipment [*called "tangible fixed assets" in the UK*]

inmuebles, mobiliario y equipo (Per) property, plant and equipment

inmuebles, planta y equipo (Mex) property, plant and equipment

inmunidad immunity

    inmunidad diplomática diplomatic immunity

    inmunidad legal statutory immunity

inoficioso inofficious [*describes a will that unreasonably deprives an heir of his just inheritance*]

Inpreabogado (Ven) [*approximately*] Venezuelan Bar Association [*Inpreabogado is short for "Instituto de Previsión Social del Abogado."*]

inquilino lessee, tenant

Insalud (Spa) Spanish National Health Service [*short for "Instituto Nacional de la Salud"*]

inscripción
    inscripción electoral voter registration
    inscripción en bolsa listing on the exchange
insoluto unpaid
insolvencia insolvency
inspección
    inspección de una planilla (Pue) audit of a tax return
    Inspección General de Hacienda (Uru) Corporate Records
        Office
    Inspección General de Justicia (Arg) Corporate Records
        Office
    inspección judicial judicial inspection
    inspección personal del tribunal personal inspection of a thing
        or place by the judge
instalar una asamblea (Mex) to convene a meeting
instancia 1. instance, stage of a judicial process 2. petition
    instancia dilatoria dilatory plea
institución
    institución calificadora de valores securities rating institution
    institución de banca múltiple full-service bank
    institución de crédito lending institution
    institución de fianzas bonding company
    institución de herederos designation of heirs [*either in the will
        (testate succession) or by law (intestate succession)*]
    institución fiduciaria fiduciary institution
    institución financiera financial institution
    institución financiera de primera línea first-tier bank, leading
        bank
instituir heredero to appoint an heir, to designate an heir
    heredero instituido en una cosa cierta heir appointed to take
        a certain thing
instituto
    instituto de menores (Arg) reform school
    Instituto de Previsión Social del Abogado (Ven) Venezuelan
        Bar Association
    Instituto Nacional de Cooperación Educativa (Ven) National
        Institute of Cooperative Education [*This is part of the Ministry
        of Education that promotes training of workers and
        apprentices. Employers of five or more employees who
        engage in commercial or industrial activities must pay a 2%
        payroll tax to this entity.*]
instrucción investigation of a case
    instrucción de las partes making the record available to the
        parties so that can prepare their closing brief [*called an
        "escrito de conclusiones"*]
instructor (Bol) investigating judge [*also called "juez de
    instrucción"*]

instruir un sumario to conduct a preliminary investigation [*i.e, to prepare the groundwork for a criminal prosecution by collecting evidence and specifying charges*]

instrumentar una resolución to implement a resolution

instrumento jurídico legal instrument

insubsistencia 1. invalidity [*of a law*] 2. disqualification [*of a person*]

insumos raw materials, components, ingredients

integración make-up, composition [*of a committee, an account*]

    integración de capital full payment for shares

    integración global (Spa) full consolidation [*of financial statements – called "consolidación global" in other countries*]

    integración nacional (Mex) percentage of domestic raw materials in a product

    integración proporcional (Spa) partial consolidation [*called "consolidación proporcional" in other countries*]

integridad integrity

    integridad del activo de una sociedad the unencumbered assets of a company

    integridad física personal safety, a person's body

        un acto que atentó contra su integridad física an attempt on his life

    integridad moral moral integrity

intendente 1. (Chi, Uru) governor 2. (Ecu) chief of police [*short for "Intendente General de Policía"*] 3. (Spa) quartermaster general

    intendente municipal (Arg, Uru) mayor

intentona golpista attempted coup, coup attempt

intercambio de monedas currency swap

interdicción ban, prohibition

interdicto injunction [*An "interdicto" is always related to ownership or possession. Its main object is protecting ownership or preventing the damage that could occur to persons or things as a result of the negligence or abandonment of an owner or person in possession. It is particularly used in cases involving new or dangerous construction. An "injunction" in the United States is a much broader concept and is used in many other situations.*]

    interdicto de adquirir injunction granting possession [*of inherited assets*]

    interdicto de obra nueva injunction to stop construction

    interdicto de obra peligrosa injunction to stop dangerous construction

    interdicto de obra ruinosa order to demolish a dangerous old building

    interdicto de recobrar injunction restoring possession

    interdicto de retener injunction or restraining order to prohibit interference with possession or ownership

interés interest

    interés activo interest receivable [*lending rate*]

interés compuesto compound interest
interés creado vested interest
interés en obrar standing, legally protectible interest in the litigation
interés jurídico legitimate interest
interés legal statutory interest rate [*also called "legal interest"*]
interés minoritario minority interest
interés pasivo interest payable [*on deposits, savings, etc.*]
interés punitorio penalty interest
interés simple simple interest
intereses a cargo interest payable
intereses cobrados interest earned
intereses de garantía real security interest
intereses de mora default interest, late fee, late charge [*also called "intereses de demora"*]
intereses devengados accrued interest
intereses financieros interest income
intereses ganados interest earned
intereses moratorios default interest, late fee, late charge
intereses por pagar interest payable
intereses sobre colocaciones interest on loans
intereses sobre depósitos interest on deposits
intereses sobre préstamos interest on loans
intereses sobre valores negociables interest on marketable securities
intereses y depósitos en instituciones financieras interest on deposits with financial institutions
intereses y dividendos sobre inversiones interest and dividends on investments
interino interim, acting
interno inmate
interpelación demand for payment
interpelación judicial summons of a witness for questioning
interpelación judicial o extrajudicial judicial or extrajudicial demand
interpelación parlamentaria summons of an official by Congress so that he can give a report on his area of responsibility
interpelar to summon for questioning
interponer
interponer incidente to file a motion
interponer recurso de apelación to file an appeal
interposición filing (of an appeal)
interpretación interpretation, construction [*of a law, a contract, etc.*]
interpretación auténtica interpretation of a law by Parliament
interpretación doctrinal interpretation of a law by legal scholars

interpretación evolutiva interpretation of a law in a manner not contemplated by the legislators, but in keeping with contemporary reality

interpretación extensiva broad interpretation

interpretación restrictiva narrow interpretation

interpretación usual interpretation of a law by a judge

interpretar to interpret, to construe

El contrato debe interpretarse estrictamente. The contract shall be strictly construed.

interregno parlamentario period of time between parliamentary sessions

interrumpir la prescripción to toll the statute of limitations

interrupción de la prescripción tolling of the statute of limitations

intervención en un banco takeover of a bank [*by the regulators*]

intervenir en un banco to take over a bank

interventor 1. receiver 2. inspector

intestado 1. intestate 2. intestate proceedings [*short for "juicio intestado"*]

intimación demand for payment

intimar to demand payment

intuitu pecuniae (Lat) in consideration of money, for good and valuable consideration

intuitu personae (Lat) in express consideration of the person [*as opposed to "intuitu pecuniae"*]

invalidez disability

invalidez permanente permanent disability

invalidez temporal temporary disability

inversión 1. investment 2. (Mex) capital expenditure [*when used in connection with taxes in Mexico, this term often means "an investment in machinery or a building that is depreciated over a period of years," which Americans would call a "capital expenditure"*]

inversión a plazo term investment

inversión de accionistas minoritarios minority interest

inversión de la carga de la prueba shifting of the burden of proof

inversiones disponibles para la venta investment securities available for sale

inversionista investor

inversor investor [*This is the preferred term in Argentina.*]

investigación research

investigaciones a amortizar research and development expenses to be written off

investigaciones en curso research and development in progress

invocar una ley to invoke a statute

irrecurrible unappealable

irreflexión hasty decision, rash decision
irretroactividad de la ley rule against retroactivity
iura novit curia (Lat) The court knows the law. [*Therefore, the parties need not bring the rules to its notice.*]
jactancia slander of title
jefatura de policía police headquarters
    Jefatura Civil (Ven) Office of Vital Statistics, Civil Registry
jefe boss, chief, head
    jefe civil (Ven) registrar, Vital Records Official
    jefe de estado head of state
    jefe de familia (Pue) head of household
    Jefe del Departamento del Distrito Federal (Mex) Mayor of Mexico City
    jefe del ejecutivo the President, the Chief Executive
    jefe político (Ecu) head official of a canton in Ecuador
jerga jurídica legal language, legal jargon, terms of art
    En la jerga jurídica se llama "condición suspensiva". The term of art for this is "condition precedent."
jornada shift, workday
    jornada continuada working day with no break for lunch [*also called "jornada intensiva"*]
    jornada de puertas abiertas open house
    jornada de reflexión (Spa) day before election [*on which campaigning is prohibited*]
    jornada diurna day shift
    jornada intensiva working day with no break for lunch [*also called "jornada continuada"*]
    jornada laboral workday, working day
    jornada mixta swing shift [*partially during the day and partially at night*]
    jornada nocturna night shift
    jornada partida split shift [*working day with a long break for lunch*]
    jornada semanal de 40 horas a 40-hour week
    jornada única (Chi) working day with no break for lunch
jornal daily wage
juanillo (Per) lease premium [*extra amount paid by the assignee to the assignor when a lease is assigned*]
jubilación retirement
    jubilación anticipada early retirement
    jubilación forzosa mandatory retirement
    jubilación voluntaria voluntary retirement
jubilados retired personnel, retirees
judicatura 1. judgeship, the bench 2. the judiciary 3. term of office as judge
juez judge
    juez a quo trial court judge, the court below

juez ad quem appellate court judge, judge on appeal

juez avenidor arbitrator

juez comisionado judge requested to perform a judicial act in his own jurisdiction by a judge in another jurisdiction [*synonym of "juez delegado"*]

juez competente judge of competent jurisdiction

juez de carrera professional judge

juez de comisión judge requested to perform a judicial act in his own jurisdiction by a judge in another jurisdiction

juez de conocimiento judge who heard the case

juez de cruce (Mex) judge of cross-trades [*at the stock exchange*]

juez de derecho trier of law

juez de feria (Uru) judge appointed by the Supreme Court to hear urgent matters while the court is in recess.

juez de fondo trial court judge

juez de grado (Arg) appellate court judge

juez de guardia sitting judge

juez de hecho (Arg) trier of fact

juez de instrucción investigating judge

juez de la causa trial court judge, the court below

juez de letras professional judge [*meaning "judge who is an attorney"*]

juez de lo civil civil court judge

juez de lo concursal bankruptcy court judge

juez de lo criminal criminal court judge

juez de lo familiar family court judge

juez de menor antigüedad most junior judge

juez de paz justice of the peace

juez de turno sitting judge

juez decano senior judge [*judge with the most seniority*]

juez del exequátur judge of the court in which the enforcement of a foreign judgment is sought

juez delegado judge requested to perform a judicial act in his own jurisdiction by a judge in another jurisdiction [*synonym of "juez comisionado"*]

juez exhortado judge to whom letters rogatory are sent

juez instructor investigating judge

juez lego lay judge

juez letrado professional judge [*as opposed to a lay judge*]

juez mixto (Mex) judge of general jurisdiction [*jurisdiction over both civil and criminal matters*]

juez penal criminal court judge

juez promiscuo (Col) judge of general jurisdiction [*jurisdiction over both civil and criminal matters*]

juez propietario (Mex) regular judge

juez que instruye el sumario judge conducting the preliminary investigation

juez sumariante judge conducting the preliminary investigation [*synonym of "juez de instrucción"*]

juez sustanciador judge who examines the evidence

juicio lawsuit, trial, case

    juicio al rubro mencionado the above-captioned case

    juicio arbitral arbitration proceeding

    juicio atractivo proceeding in which an entire estate is at stake

    juicio civil civil trial

    juicio contencioso litigation

    juicio contencioso-administrativo administrative proceeding

    juicio de amparo (Mex) amparo proceeding [*see explanation under "amparo"*]

    juicio de apremio proceedings brought to collect a debt owed

    juicio de cognición (Spa) small-claims proceeding

    juicio de conciliación settlement hearing

    juicio de cuentas repayment proceeding [*in which a public official is ordered to pay back misappropriated or missing funds*]

    juicio de divorcio divorce proceeding

    juicio de exequátur proceeding for enforcement of a foreign judgment

    juicio de faltas misdemeanor proceeding

    juicio de filiación paternity suit, affiliation proceeding

    juicio de garantías (Mex) amparo proceeding [*see explanation under "amparo"*]

    juicio de mensura, deslinde y amojonamiento action to establish boundaries

    juicio de paternidad affiliation proceeding

    juicio de tercería arbitration proceeding

    juicio declarativo (Arg, Spa) declaratory judgment

    juicio declaratorio declaratory judgment

    juicio en segunda instancia appellate proceedings

    juicio ejecutivo a special summary procedure for the enforcement of monetary claims, usually involving attachment ("embargo preventivo")

    juicio ejecutivo hipotecario foreclosure proceeding

    juicio extraordinario summary proceeding

    juicio militar court martial

    juicio no contencioso ex parte proceedings

    juicio oral (Spa) trial [*also referred to as the "plenario," this is the part of criminal procedure that follows the "sumario"—i.e., the investigation*]

    juicio ordinario full trial [*as opposed to a summary proceeding*]

    juicio pericial (Arg) trial by experts [*Where only facts are in dispute, experts known as "peritos árbitros" assist the judge* *in the findings of fact, but it is up to the judge to apply the law and resolve the dispute.*]

juicio petitorio petitory action [*as opposed to a "juicio posesorio"*]

juicio plenario (Spa) trial [*also referred to as the "juicio oral," this is the part of criminal procedure that follows the "sumario"—i.e., the investigation. While the "sumario" is primarily written, the "plenario" is primarily oral.*]

juicio político impeachment proceeding

juicio posesorio possessory action [*as opposed to a "juicio petitorio"*]

juicio rápido (Spa) fast-track criminal proceeding [*also called a "miniproceso"*]

juicio secundario collateral proceedings [*i.e., collateral to the main proceedings*]

juicio señalado al rubro (el) the above-styled case, the above-captioned case

juicio singular proceeding invovling one or more specific rights or assets [*as opposed to a "juicio universal" (q.v.)*]

juicio sucesorio intestado intestate succession proceedings

juicio sucesorio testamentario probate proceeding

juicio sumario summary proceeding

juicio sumarísimo expedited summary proceeding, "fast-track" proceeding

juicio testamentario probate proceeding

juicio universal proceeding involving a person's entire estate [*as in bankruptcy or probate matters*]

juicio verbal oral proceeding

junta 1. meeting 2. board

junta de accionistas shareholders' meeting

junta de acreedores (Arg) meeting of creditors

junta de avenencia (Mex) reconciliation meeting [*in cases of uncontested divorce*]

Junta de Portavoces (Spa) Assembly of Spokesmen [*Each party in Parliament is represented by a spokesman (portavoz), and the spokesmen meet once a year to agree on matters such as agendas for meetings and debates, and the dates and times of parliamentary sessions.*]

Junta del Acuerdo de Cartagena (JUNAC) Cartagena Agreement Board

junta departamental (Uru) departmental legislature [*Uruguay is divided into departments rather than states.*]

junta directiva (Cos, Col, Dom, Gua, Nic, Pan) board of directors

junta electoral (Spa) electoral board [*oversees and administers elections throughout Spain*]

junta especial (Per) meeting of shareholders of a certain series of shares

junta general extraordinaria (Bol, Chi, Ecu, Nic, Per, Spa) extraordinary shareholders' meeting

junta general ordinaria (Bol, Chi, Ecu, Nic, Per, Spa) ordinary shareholders' meeting

junta interventora (Ven) takeover board

junta sindical de bolsa (Mex, Spa) Stock Exchange Council

junta universal (Per, Spa) shareholders' meeting at which all shareholders are present or represented and unanimously agree to hold the meeting [*typical of closely-held corporations—similar to "action by unanimous written consent" in the US*]

Juntas de Conciliación y Arbitraje (Mex) administrative labor courts

jurado 1. jury 2. juror

jurado de conciencia (Col) petit jury

jurado de instrucción (Col) grand jury

Jurado Federal de Ciudadanos (Mex) Federal Jury of Citizens

jurado popular (Mex) people's jury

juramento oath, pledge

juramento de fidelidad pledge of allegiance

juramento decisorio sworn statement that one party requests of another in a proceeding, agreeing to be bound by whatever that other party says under oath [*and therefore is accepted by the judge, rather than being weighed against other evidence*]

juramento falso perjury

juramento indecisorio testimony that is weighed by the judge against the party's other evidence

prestar juramento to take an oath

tomar juramento to swear in, to put under oath

jurar to swear, to pledge

jurar en falso to commit perjury

jurar fidelidad to pledge allegiance

jurisconsulto legal expert

jurisdicción 1. jurisdiction [*"Jurisdicción" is judicial power vested constitutionally, whereas "competencia" is judicial power allocated by the legislature in a statute. Both of these concepts are called "jurisdiction" in English.*] 2. court system (Col)

jurisdicción coactiva (Col) summary jurisdiction

jurisdicción concurrente concurrent jurisdiction

Jurisdicción de lo Contencioso Administrativo (Col) the Administrative Court System [*as opposed to the Ordinary Court System*]

Jurisdicción Ordinaria (Col) the Ordinary Court System [*as opposed to the administrative court system*]

jurisdicción sobre la persona personal jurisdiction, in personam jurisdiction

jurisdicción voluntaria ex parte proceedings

jurisdicción y competencia [*as a heading in a contract*] forum selection

jurisprudencia caselaw, judicial decisions, binding precedent

jurisprudencia constante settled caselaw, established precedent

jurisprudencia sentada settled caselaw, established precedent

jurista legal scholar

justicia 1. justice 2. the courts

Es justicia. (Ven) Let justice be done.

justicia de la Unión (Mex) the federal courts, the federal judiciary

justicia militar the military courts

pedir en justicia to go to court

Justicialismo (Arg) political movement founded by Juan Domingo Perón

justificante voucher, receipt

justo título just title

juzgado court

juzgado accidental (Ven) ad hoc court [*set up to handle a backlog of cases*]

juzgado de circulación (Pue) traffic court

juzgado de familia family court, domestic relations court

juzgado de guardia night court

juzgado de instrucción office of an examining judge or magistrate

juzgado de letras (Hon) court of first instance, trial court

juzgado de lo concursal bankruptcy court

juzgado de lo contencioso-administrativo administrative law court

juzgado de lo civil civil court

juzgado de lo penal criminal court

juzgado de lo social (Spa) labor law court, employment law court

juzgado de mínima cuantía (Bol) small claims court

juzgado de partido (Bol) court of first instance (civil and criminal), trial court

juzgado de paz justice of the peace court

juzgado de sustanciación (Ven) panel of the court that examines the evidence

juzgado de vigilancia (Bol) court that oversees the execution of prison sentences

juzgado letrado de primera instancia (Uru) court of first instance, trial court

juzgado mixto (Mex) court of first instance with both civil and criminal jurisdiction

juzgado promiscuo (Col) court of first instance with both civil and criminal jurisdiction

juzgador judge

labrar un acta to draw up a document

lactancia maternity leave

laguna lacuna

laguna tributaria tax loophole

lagunas del derecho matters as to which the law is silent

lanzamiento eviction, ouster

lapso probatorio time allowed for producing evidence

latifundio very large property, large landed estate

latronicio larceny, theft

laudo award, finding

laudo arbitral arbitral award, arbitration decision

laudo homologado arbitral award that has been approved by a court

legado legacy

legado alternativo legacy in which the legatee must choose between two or more things

legado causal legacy in which the testator states the reason for making it

legado condicional conditional legacy [*only received if certain conditions subsequent do not occur*]

legado modal legacy conditioned on the performance of certain acts or the abstention therefrom

legado puro unconditional legacy

legajo file

legalidad legality

legalización legalization

legalización de créditos (Cos) filing proofs of claim

legatario legatee [*A "legatario" inherits "a título particular," which means that he receives specific assets from the estate, while an "heredero" inherits "a título universal," which means that he receives all or a percentage of the assets of the estate.*]

legislador legislator

legítima

legítima defensa self-defense

legítima efectiva (Ecu) birthright portion of the estate plus any portion added to it [*See Art. 1236 of Civil Code of Ecuador*]

legítima estricta (Pue, Spa) one-third of an estate that the testator by law must leave to his lawful heirs

legítima larga (Per, Pue, Spa) forced two-thirds portion of an estate [*It is composed of the "legítima estricta" and the "tercio de mejora." The legítima estricta (birthright portion) is the third that is divided equally among the lawful heirs, and the* *tercio de mejora is the third that can be left to any or all of the lawful heirs. The remaining one-third of the estate is called the "tercio de libre disposición," of which the testator is free to dispose as he sees fit.*]

legítima rigurosa (Ecu) birthright portion of an estate [*which the testator by law must leave to his lawful heirs--See Art. 1229 of Civil Code of Ecuador*]

legitimación 1. standing 2. right of action

    legitimación activa plaintiff's standing

    legitimación en causa standing to sue, plaintiff's standing

    legitimación pasiva defendant's standing

    legitimación procesal standing

legitimario forced heir

legitimatio ad causam (Lat) standing to sue, plaintiff's standing

leguleyo shyster, incompetent lawyer

lema (Uru) political party

lenocinio procuring, pimping

leonino one-sided

lesión 1. [*in a civil case*] damage 2. [*in a criminal case*] injury

    no existe error ni lesión no error or any excess or inadequacy of consideration exists

    lesión corporal bodily injury

    lesión enorme (Chi, Ecu) heavy damage [*when price received by seller is less than half the value or when price paid is more than what the object was worth*]

    lesión mortal fatal injury

lesionado injured party, victim

lesionar to injure

letra

    letra a la vista sight draft

    letra al cobro collection bill

    letra bancaria bank draft

    letra de cambio bill of exchange, draft

    letra de cambio a la vista sight draft

    letra de cambio a plazo time draft

    letra de cambio causada "concrete" bill of exchange [*the consideration for the obligation and guarantee is mentioned*]

    letra de cambio documentada documentary bill of exchange

    letra de cambio domiciliada domiciled draft [*draft containing a domicile clause which shows where the bill will be honored for payment. In actual practice, drafts are usually domiciled at the bank of the acceptor.*]

    letra de resaca redraft, cross-bill [*a bill of exchange drawn by a holder of a dishonored bill upon either the drawer or the endorser, to recover the amount of the original bill plus the protest fees*]

    letras del tesoro (Spa, Ven) treasury bills

letras por cobrar notes receivable
letrado attorney
levantamiento
> **levantamiento de un cadáver** removal of a dead body by the
>> police following judicial inspection
> **levantamiento de un embargo** dissolution of an attachment
> **levantamiento del velo corporativo (Spa)** piercing the
>> corporate veil [*i.e., making shareholders liable for the debts
>> of a corporation*]

levantar
> **levantar acta** to take the minutes
> **levantar un acta** to prepare, to draw up a document
> **levantar un acta de hechos** to make a record of facts
> **levantar un censo** to take a census
> **levantar un embargo** to dissolve an attachment
> **levantar una encuesta** to conduct a survey
> **levantar una prohibición** to lift a ban
> **levantar una sesión** to adjourn a meeting

ley law
> **ley antimonopolio** antitrust law
> **ley aplicable** governing law
> **ley cambiaria** law of negotiable instruments
> **ley comentada** annotated statute
> **ley complementaria** law that is necessary to give full effect to a
>> provision of the Constitution
> **ley consuetudinaria** customary law
> **Ley de Adquisiciones y Obras Públicas (Mex)** Government
>> Procurement and Public Works Act
> **ley de autorización** enabling act
> **ley de bases** law setting the main guidelines to which
>> subsequent legislation must adhere
> **ley de cuotas compensatorias** countervailing duty statute
> **ley de descanso dominical** blue law
> **Ley de Enjuiciamiento Civil (Spa)** Civil Procedure Act
> **Ley de Enjuiciamiento Criminal (Spa)** Criminal Procedure Act
> **ley de la materia** the law on that topic [*the one being discussed*]
> **ley de la oferta y la demanda** law of supply and demand
> **ley de la situación** lex loci rei sitae [*law of the place where X is
>> situated*]
> **ley de leyes** Constitution
> **ley de los rendimientos decrecientes** law of diminishing
>> returns
> **Ley de Obediencia Debida (Arg)** Due Obedience Act [*ruled that
>> officers below the rank of colonel had acted under orders,
>> and were therefore exempt from criminal responsibility*]
> **ley de orden público** mandatory law [*law that is mandatory
>> because of public policy*]

Ley de Punto Final (Arg) Military Amnesty Act [*prevented judges from trying officers who had not been charged within two months of the law's enactment*]

ley de prescripción statute of limitations

Ley de Procedimiento Administrativo (Spa) Administrative Procedure Act

ley de quórum calificado (Chi) law of lesser status than a "ley orgánica" that nevertheless regulates an important matter

ley del embudo one-sided rule, arbitrary rule, double standards, unequal treatment under the law

¡Ésa es la ley del embudo! There's one rule for you, and another for everybody else! There's one rule for the rich and another for the poor!

Ley del Mercado de Valores (Mex) Stock Market Act

Ley del Organismo Judicial (Gua) Judiciary Act

ley extraordinaria law which, because of the importance of its subject matter, is subject to more stringent requirements for approval by the Legislature (usually a two-thirds majority). [*Note, however, that there is no hierarchical difference between a ley ordinaria and a ley extraordinaria.*]

Ley Federal de Derechos (Mex) Federal Customs Taxes Act [*imposes taxes on trade activities governed by customs regulations*]

Ley Federal de Protección al Consumidor (Mex) Federal Consumer Protection Act

Ley Federal del Trabajo (Mex) Federal Labor Act

Ley General de Títulos y Operaciones de Crédito (Mex) General Law on Negotiable Instruments and Credit Transactions

ley imperativa mandatory law, law that cannot be preempted

ley impositiva tax law

ley marcial martial law

ley natural natural law

ley orgánica 1. internal regulations, law to regulate the internal operations of something 2. implementing act [*law that implements articles of the Constitution*]

Ley Orgánica de la Administración Pública Federal (Mex) Federal Public Administration Act

Ley Orgánica de la Función Judicial (Ecu) Judiciary Act

Ley Orgánica del Poder Judicial (LOPJ) (Per, Ven) Judiciary Act

ley reglamentaria (Mex) law that implements specific articles of the Mexican Constitution [*as opposed to "reglamentos," which implement a particular statute*]

Ley Reglamentaria de los Artículos 103 y 107 de la Constitución Política de los Estados Unidos Mexicanos (Mex) Amparo Act [*This is simply another way of referring to*

Mexico's Ley de Amparo and should be translated as such lest the reader think that there are two different laws.]

ley renunciable law that the parties may contract out of

ley rituaria procedural law [*synonym of "ley adjetiva."* *Sometimes an attorney will use this to refer to a specific procedural law that he has already mentioned in the document.*]

ley supletoria discretionary rule, non-mandatory rule [*rule that either applies in the absence of any express intention to the contrary or fills in where the agreement is silent*]

libelo (Ven) complaint [*i.e., the document filed to commence a civil lawsuit -- synonym of "demanda"*]

liberalización deregulation, loosening restrictions on something

libertad

    libertad bajo caución release on bail

    libertad bajo fianza release on bail

    libertad bajo palabra release on one's own recognizance [*release based simply on the person's oral commitment to appear in court*]

    libertad bajo protesta (Mex) release on one's own recognizance

    libertad civil civil liberty

    libertad condicional parole, probation [*granted after 2/3 of a prison term has been served if convict has observed good behavior*]

    libertad de conciencia freedom of conscience

    libertad de cultos freedom of religion

    libertad de expresión freedom of speech

    libertad de información freedom of information

    libertad de palabra freedom of speech

    libertad de prensa freedom of the press

    libertad de reunión freedom of association

    libertad de sufragio free elections

    libertad por falta de méritos (Mex) dropping charges against a criminal defendant for lack of evidence to make him stand trial

    libertad preparatoria (Mex) parole [*granted after 3/5 of a prison term has been served if the convict has observed good behavior and can get a job*]

    libertad provisional freedom on bail

    libertad vigilada probation

librado drawee

librador drawer

librar to issue

    librar exhortos to issue letters rogatory

    librar oficio to issue an official letter

    librar orden de aprehensión (Mex) to issue an arrest warrant

librar sentencia to pronounce judgment
libre free [*often best translated as "unrestricted" to avoid confusion with "free of charge"*]
   libre comercio free trade
   libre de derechos duty-free
   libre de todo gravamen free and clear of all liens and encumbrances
libreta (Cub) ration card
   libreta cívica (Arg) voter registration card for women [*now replaced by the Documento Nacional de Identidad*]
   libreta de enrolamiento (Arg) voter and draft registration card for men [*now replaced by the Documento Nacional de Identidad*]
   libreta electoral (Per) voter registration card [*This is the primary identity card in Peru.*]
   libreta militar (Ecu, Per) draft card, military record
libro book
   libro auxiliar *see "libro mayor auxiliar"*
   libro de accionistas stock ledger
   libro de actas minute book
   libro de familia (Spa) "Family Book" [*used to record the vital records of all members of a family – no equivalent in the US*]
   libro de varios notary's book of miscellaneous records
   libro diario journal [*the book of original entry, where transactions are recorded as they occur*]
   libro mayor ledger [*the book of final entry*]
   libro mayor auxiliar subsidiary ledger [*as opposed to "general ledger"*]
   libro mayor general general ledger [*as opposed to "subsidiary ledger"*]
   libro talonario stub book [*a book, such as a checkbook containing stubs, which serve as memoranda of checks, receipts, etc. In the UK this is called a "counterfoil book."*]
   libro talonario de acciones stock certificate book
licencia 1. license 2. leave of absence
   gozar de licencia to be entitled to a leave of absence
   licencia con goce de haber (Per) leave of absence with pay
   licencia de funcionamiento (Mex) operating license
   licencia fiscal de actividades comerciales e industriales (Spa) tax on commercial and industrial activities
   licencia fiscal de actividades profesionales y artísticas (Spa) tax on revenue from professional and artistic work
   licencia por maternidad maternity leave
licitación bid, tender, invitation to bid, request for proposals
licitador bidder
lícito legal, lawful, legitimate
licitud lawfulness, legality

lindar to be bounded

    linda por todos sus vientos is bounded on all four sides

línea line

    línea (de parentesco) ascendente ascending line

    línea (de parentesco) colateral collateral line

    línea (de parentesco) descendente descending line

    línea blanca white goods [*e.g. washing machines, refrigerators*]

    línea jurisprudencial a line of cases

    línea revolvente de crédito (Mex) revolving line of credit

liquidación 1. severance pay (to employee fired without cause) 2. settlement 3. liquidation of a company

    liquidación amigable (Ven) voluntary liquidation [*see Art. 898 of the Commercial Code of Venezuela*]

    liquidación de la sociedad conyugal equitable distribution of community property [*upon divorce*]

    liquidación de existencias (Spa) clearance sale

    liquidación de sentencia execution of a judgment

liquidador liquidator

liquidez liquidity

litigante 1. litigator [*when referring to an "abogado litigante"*] 2. litigant [*when referring to the parties*]

litigar to litigate

litigio 1. litigation 2. lawsuit

litisconsorcio joint litigation

    litisconsorcio activo co-plaintiffs

    litisconsorcio mixto co-plaintiffs and co-defendants

    litisconsorcio pasivo co-defendants

litisconsorte joint litigant [*either plaintiffs or defendants*]

litispendencia the time during which a case is pending

llamamiento appointment, designation [*of a person -- as heir, trustee, etc.*]

    llamamiento en garantía impleader [*procedure by which a third party is brought into a suit between a plaintiff and defendant in which the third party may be liable so as to settle all claims in a single action—also called "citación en garantía"*]

llamar 1. to call 2. to appoint, to designate [*a person -- as heir, trustee, etc.*]

    llamar en garantía to implead [*see explanation under "llamamiento en garantía"*]

llave key

    llave de un local (Arg) lease premium [*extra amount paid by the assignee to the assignor when a lease is assigned -- referred to as "derechos de traspaso" in Spain*]

    llave de un negocio (Arg) goodwill

    llave negativa negative goodwill

llegar a un acuerdo to reach an agreement

llevar aparejado to entail

La condena por delito grave lleva aparejada la pérdida de los derechos civiles. Conviction of a felony entails the loss of civil rights.

llevar un registro to maintain a registry

lo actuado the proceedings

lo anterior the foregoing

Lo anterior es copia fiel de un documento que obra en los archivos a mi cargo. The foregoing is a true copy of a record in my custody.

lo dispuesto en el artículo 6 the provisions of Article 6 [*Note that "article" is capitalized in English, but not in Spanish.*]

lo establecido en el artículo 6 the provisions of Article 6

lo estipulado en el artículo 6 the provisions of Article 6

lo normado en el artículo 6 the provisions of Article 6

lo preceptuado en el artículo 6 the provisions of Article 6

lo previsto en el artículo 6 the provisions of Article 6

locador (Arg, Par, Per) landlord, lessor

locatario (Arg, Par) tenant, lessee

logotipo fiscal (Mex) authorized seal representing taxpayer registration with the Ministry of Finance and Public Credit

lonja exchange, marketplace

lote block (of shares)

lucro profit

lucro cesante lost profits

lucro esperado anticipated profits

lucro naciente (Arg) profit earned with borrowed money

lugar place

lugar de los hechos the scene of the crime

lugar, fecha y hora time and place

lustro five-year period [*synonym of "quinquenio"*]

machote (Mex) blank form

magistrado 1. judge [*of an appellate court*] 2. justice [*of a supreme court*] [*Note that "magistrate" in the US refers to a lower court judge with limited jurisdiction, which is the opposite of "magistrado" in Spanish.*]

magistrado ponente judge who writes the opinion of the court

magistrado revisor judge who writes the opinion of the court

magnicidio assassination of a head of state or a public figure

mala administración mismanagement

mala fe bad faith, mala fides

mala praxis (Arg) malpractice

malos tratos mistreatment

malos tratos de obra physical abuse [*grounds for divorce*]

malos tratos de palabra verbal abuse [*grounds for divorce*]

malversación embezzlement, misappropriation

mancomunadamente jointly

mancomunada y solidariamente jointly and severally

mancomunidad solidaria joint and several liability
mandamiento judicial 1. injunction 2. writ [*order of a judge to a subordinate official*] 3. court order
  mandamiento de aprehensión arrest warrant
  mandamiento de comparendo subpoena
  mandamiento de embargo writ of attachment [*either preventivo (pre-judgment attachment) or ejecutivo (pursuant to a writ of execution)*]
  mandamiento provisional preliminary injunction, temporary restraining order
mandante principal
  mandante oculto undisclosed principal
  mandante ostensible disclosed principal
  mandante semi-ostensible partially disclosed principal
mandatario 1. agent 2. proxy 3. legal representative, attorney-in-fact 4. President [*of a country*]
  mandatario estatal (Mex) governor [*head of each state in Mexico is a gobernador*]
  mandatario judicial judicial representative, representative in court
  primer mandatario president
mandato 1. term of office, mandate 2. power of attorney 3. proxy 4. agency
  mandato ad judicia *see "mandato judicial"*
  mandato ad negotia *see "mandato extrajudicial"*
  mandato delegable power of attorney with full powers of substitution
  mandato extrajudicial agency for non-litigious matters [*also called "mandato ad negotia"*]
  mandato judicial 1. judicial power of attorney (for representation in court) [*also called "mandato ad judicia"*] 2. court order [*used in the sense of "mandamiento judicial"*]
mandatum morte dissolvitur (Lat) A power of attorney is terminated by death [*of either the agent or the principal*]
manifestación dolosa fraudulent misrepresentation
manifestar y garantizar to represent and warrant
mano de obra 1. labor, manpower 2. workmanship
  mano de obra indirecta indirect labor costs
mantener registros to keep records
manumisión release of a slave
manutención del cónyuge spousal support
maquiladora in-bond assembly plant, maquiladora [*Mexican plants that receive raw materials and parts from the U.S., process them into finished goods, and ship them back. The materials imported into Mexico are not taxed, and when the resulting finished goods are sent back, only the value added is taxed.*]
maquillaje window-dressing to enhance a share price

marca
    marca blanca generic brand
    marca de comercio trademark [*affixed by a merchant*]
    marca de fábrica trademark [*affixed by a manufacturer*]
    marca de servicio service mark
    marca notoria well known mark [*Well known trademarks are protected whether they are registered or not.*]
    marca registrada registered trademark
    marca sindical union label
marchamo (Cos) vehicle registration sticker
marco 1. framework 2. mark [*currency in Germany and Finland*]
    marco regulatorio regulatory framework
margen margin
    margen bruto de autofinanciación cash flow
    margen comercial profit margin, mark-up
    margen de ganancia profit margin, mark-up
    margen de garantía collateral margin [*difference between the amount of the loan and the value of the collateral*]
    margen financiero net interest income
margesí (Per) list or inventory of property belonging to the State
martillador (Ecu) auctioneer
martillero auctioneer
masa
    masa de la herencia corpus of the estate
    masa de la quiebra bankrupt estate
    masa hereditaria estate [*of a decedent*]
    masa monetaria money supply
    masa salarial total payroll cost
matador (Spa) matador bond [*peseta-denominated bonds issued by foreign institutions*]
materia
    materia común local matters
    materia de mortuales (Gua) estate matters, matters involving a decedent's estate
    materia prima raw material
materiales de oficina office supplies
matrícula judicial (Per) docket number
matrimonio 1. marriage 2. married couple
    matrimonio in artículo mortis marriage under fear of imminent death of one or both parties
matriz 1. original [*of a document*] 2. parent company [*of a company*]
mayor de edad of legal age
mayoría majority
    mayoría absoluta absolute majority
    mayoría de edad majority
    mayoría reforzada supermajority
    mayoría simple simple majority

mayorista wholesaler

medianería party wall [*a wall that separates the adjoining properties of different owners*]

mediano plazo medium term

medicina forense forensic medicine

médico doctor, physician

    médico forense coroner, forensic pathologist, medical examiner

    médico legista (Mex, Col) coroner, forensic pathologist, medical examiner

medidas

    medidas cautelares interim equitable relief

    medidas cautelares innominadas unspecified interim relief [*i.e., not specifying in the contract which interim relief will be granted in case of breach*]

    medidas de apremio coercive measures

    medidas prejudiciales pre-filing discovery [*In Spanish-speaking countries, the law permits a potential plaintiff to request sworn statements and inspection of documents from potential defendants in order to determine whether he has a valid claim and whom to sue. This concept is also referred to as "medios preparatorios del proceso" and as "diligencias preparatorias." Discovery is not permitted in the US until after the complaint is filed.*]

    medidas y colindancias metes and bounds

medio

    medio ambiente environment

    medio circulante money supply

    medios 1. means, resources 2. the media

    medios empresariales business circles

    medios preparatorios del proceso pre-filng discovery [*see explanation under "medidas prejudiciales"*]

mejora (Pue, Spa) additional bequest in a will [*beyond the birthright portion*]

    mejora al local arrendado leasehold improvement

    mejora del embargo extension of the attachment to additional property [*also called "ampliación del embargo"*]

    mejora hereditaria additional bequest in a will [*beyond the birthright portion*]

    mejora útil ameliorating improvement

mejorado (Pue, Spa) beneficiary of a special bequest beyond the birthright portion

memoria 1. annual report 2. **(Spa)** notes to the financial statements [*Prior to 1989, the entire annual report was referred to as the "memoria." Regulations adopted in 1989 refer to the notes as the "memoria."*] 3. **(Arg, Par)** management's discussion and analysis (MD&A) [*An annual report consists of the memoria and the estados financieros.*]

memorial brief [*written argument filed by an attorney*]
menaje de casa household effects, household furnishings
menor
    menor cuantía small claim
    menor de edad minor [*person who is under age*]
menoscabo impairment
    sin menoscabo de su autoridad without diminishing his
        authority in any way
mensualidad monthly payment, monthly installment
mercadeo (Ven) marketing
mercaderías de reventa goods for resale
mercado market
    mercado a la baja bear market
    mercado al alza bull market
    mercado alcista bull market
    mercado bursátil financial market
    mercado cambiario foreign exchange market
    mercado de cambios foreign exchange market
    mercado de capitales capital market
    mercado de crédito credit market, lending market
    mercado de derivados derivatives market
    mercado de dinero money market [*market where short-term*
        debt securities are issued and traded]
    mercado de divisas foreign exchange market
    mercado de futuros futures market
    mercado de valores securities market
    mercado electrónico abierto (Arg) over-the-counter market
    mercado emergente emerging market
    mercado exterior overseas market
    mercado interbancario interbank market [*market in which*
        banks buy and sell money market instruments, such as
        bankers' acceptances, commercial paper, and certificates of
        deposit, usually with maturities of less than one year]
    mercado interior domestic market
    mercado interno domestic market
    mercado mayorista wholesale market
    mercado monetario money market
    mercado nacional domestic market
    mercado negro black market
    mercado primario primary market
    mercado secundario secondary market
mercancías merchandise, goods
    mercancías rescatadas repossessed goods
merced conductiva (Per) rent
merceología (Arg) commodities science
mesa 1. table 2. desk

mesa de dinero money desk [*Deposit-taking institutions must manage their reserves to avoid either reserve shortfalls or excess reserves, because they are penalized for reserve shortfalls, and earn no interest on excess reserves. Typically, the money desk of a financial institution manages the reserve position. Money desk managers can borrow reserve balances from other deposit-taking institutions in the federal funds market if they are short. Unneeded balances can be sold to other deposit-taking institutions in the same market.*]

mesa de entradas (Arg) filing desk

mesa de la junta (Spa) persons presiding over a shareholders' meeting

mesa de partes (Per) filing desk

Mesa del Congreso (Spa) Congressional Board [*consisting of the Presidente, two vicepresidentes, and two secretarios. Its function is to organize parliamentary business, to draw up the agenda, to prepare a draft budget and supervise its implementation, and to evaluate parliamentary papers and documents.*]

Mesa No. 53 del Ministerio Público (Mex) Division 53 of the District Attorney's Office

metálico (Spa) cash

método method

método constante straight-line method of depreciation

método de acumulación a base de intereses interest method of accrual

método de costos promedio average cost method

método de la compra purchase method of accounting [*accounting for a business combination by adding the acquired company's assets at the price paid for them to the acquiring company's assets—opposite of the pooling of interests method*]

método de la fusión de intereses pooling of interests method of accounting [*accounting for a business combination by simply adding together the book value of the assets and equities of the combined companies—This usually leads to a higher reported net income for the combined firms than would be reported if the business combination had been accounted for as a purchase, because the market values of the merged assets are usually greater than their book values.*]

método de línea recta straight-line method of depreciation

método de puesta en equivalencia equity method of accounting

mientras no unless, until

mientras la demanda no haya sido contestada por el demandado until the complaint is answered by the defendant

Ministerio

Ministerio de Economía y Hacienda (Spa) Ministry of Commerce and Finance

Ministerio de Obras Públicas y Urbanismo (Spa) Ministry of Public Works and Town Planning

Ministerio de Relaciones Exteriores, Comercio Internacional y Culto (Arg) Ministry of Foreign Relations, International Trade and Religion

Ministerio de Sanidad y Consumo (Spa) Ministry of Health and Consumer Affairs

ministerio fiscal public prosecutor

ministerio público district attorney, Attorney General's Office, prosecutor, office of the government attorney

Ministerio Pupilar (Arg) official entity that protects the rights of minors who are without legal representation

ministro

ministro de estado (Chi, Ecu, Pan) cabinet minister

ministro de fe pública (Chi) clerk of the court

ministro de fuero (Chi) judge of the Supreme Court or an appellate court who is not a cabinet minister

ministro de la Corte Suprema (Bol, Chi, Ecu) Supreme Court Justice

ministro de la Suprema Corte (Mex, Uru) Supreme Court Justice

ministro en visita (Chi) investigating judge appointed by the Supreme Court in cases of public disturbance that need to be resolved quickly

ministro en visita extraordinaria (Chi) special investigating judge

ministro sin cartera minister without portfolio

ministro subrogante (Chi) alternate judge

ministro sumariante (Chi) prosecutor

ministro supernumerario (Mex) Alternate Justice [*replaces a Supreme Court Justice who is absent*]

primer ministro prime minister

minoración (Spa) tax relief

minorista retailer

minusvalía unrealized loss

minusvalorado undervalued, understated

minuta rough draft, abstract

minutas de abogado (Spa) attorneys' fees

minutario special notarial book of miscellaneous records that parties have opted to record in order to preserve them as admissible evidence

mirista (Bol) member of the Movimiento de la Izquierda Revolucionaria
Miscelánea Fiscal (Mex) annual amendments to the tax law
modelo de utilidad utility patent
modificación modification, amendment [*of bylaws*]
    modificación estatutaria bylaw amendment
Moncloa (Spa) official residence of the Spanish Prime Minister
moneda
    Moneda (la) (Chi) official residence of the President of Chile
    moneda constante constant currency
    moneda corriente legal tender
    moneda de curso legal legal tender
    moneda débil soft currency
    moneda falsa counterfeit money
    moneda fraccionaria fractional currency [*any currency denominated in fractions of the main currency unit, such as centavos to pesos or cents to dollars*]
    moneda fuerte hard currency
    moneda legal legal tender
    moneda nacional local currency
    moneda suelta loose change
monte de piedad pawnshop
montepío 1. pawnshop 2. (Chi, Per) survivor's pension, widow's pension
mora default, arrears
    La mora se producirá de pleno derecho. The debtor shall fall into arrears by operation of law.
mordida (Mex) bribe
morir sin descendencia to die without issue
mortual (Gua) decedent's estate
motivar to state the reasons (los motivos) for something
    Toda resolución del tribunal debe ser motivada. The court must state its reasons for every decision.
movimiento
    movimiento de cuenta account activity
    movimientos de capital changes in capital
múltiple precio-utilidad price-earnings ratio, P/E ratio
muerte death
    muerte civil loss of civil rights
multa fine, penalty
    multa fiscal tax penalty
    multa gubernativa administrative penalty
municipio 1. municipality 2. city hall 3. (Mex) county [*the states are divided into municipios, which are groups of communities*] 4. (Gua) one village or community
muñeco (Mex) trade ticket, order ticket [*at the stock exchange*]
mutualidad mutual benefit association, mutual company

mutualista member of a mutual company
mutuante lender
mutuatario borrower
mutuo loan [*A mutuo is also called a "préstamo de consumo" or a "simple préstamo." It is the opposite of a comodato, which is a "préstamo de uso." All loans made by banks in the US would be "mutuos," and the word can therefore be translated as "loan."*]
nacer 1. to be born 2. to come into being, to arise, to originate from, to accrue
    la fecha en que nazca el derecho the date on which the right accrues
    las obligaciones nacen de la ley obligations are created by law
    un derecho que nace de la falta de pago a right that arises from non-payment
natalidad birth rate
    natalidad dirigida planned parenthood
naturalización naturalization
negativa ficta implied negative response [*presumption that the government has rejected a petition if it does not respond within a predetermined period of time*]
negligencia negligence
    negligencia grave gross negligence
    negligencia manifiesta gross negligence
    negligencia temeraria gross negligence
nivel level, standard
    nivel de cultura standard of education
    nivel de vida standard of living
nivelación convencional de precios collusive price-fixing
no obstante notwithstanding
    no obstante cualquier disposición en contrario notwithstanding any provision to the contrary
    no obstante lo anterior notwithstanding the foregoing
no susceptibles de conversión non-convertible
nombre
    nombre comercial trade name [*"doing business as"*]
    nombre supuesto assumed name, alias
non bis in idem (Lat) the rule against double jeopardy [*i.e., a person cannot be tried for the same crime twice*]
norma rule, standard
    norma dispositiva discretionary rule
    norma imperativa mandatory rule
    normas contables accounting standards
    normas de auditoría auditing standards
    normas de conducta rules of conduct
    normas de seguridad safety standards
    normas técnicas technical standards

normativa
    las disposiciones normativas del presente caso the rules governing this case
    según la normativa vigente under current regulations
nota
    nota de cargo debit memorandum
    nota de crédito credit memorandum
    nota marginal note in the margin
    Las notas que se acompañan forman parte integrante de estos estados financieros The accompanying notes are an integral part of these financial statements.
notaría notary's office
notario público notary public [*Note that the plural form in English is "notaries public." Also note that a notary is called an "escribano" in Arg and Uru.*]
notificación 1. notification, notice 2. service of process [*In Spanish the concepts of both notice and service of notice are covered by the term "notificación."*]
    notificación automática oral notice received by attorneys of actions taken on their pending cases during a periodic sounding of the docket by the trial court
    notificación de la demanda service of the complaint
    notificación en estrados notice of default that is read aloud in the courtroom
    notificación judicial por ujier notice served by a process server
    notificación personal personal service [*also called "in hand" service, i.e., the notice is served directly on the person concerned.*]
    notificación por cédula substituted service [*If the person to be served is not at home, the process server can serve the notice on any other member of the family, or can give it to a neighbor who knows how to read. If the neighbor refuses to accept it, the process server can post it on the door of the litigant's home.*]
    notificación por edicto notice by publication [*Legal notices called "edictos" are published in the newspaper.*]
    notificación por telefonema (Mex) notice by telephone
    notificación por telegrama notice by telegram
notificar to notify
    queda Ud. notificado notice is hereby served upon you
novación novation
novar to novate a contract
nuda propiedad reversionary interest [*the right to dispose of a thing, but not to enjoy it or its fruits, since such right is vested in another person*]
nudo propietario remainderman

nulidad nullity, invalidity, lack of force or effect
nulo y sin valor null and void
numerario cash
número de entrada (Nic) area code [*telephone*]
objeto 1. the subject of a contract 2. purpose
    los bienes objeto del contrato the assets covered by the contract
    objeto social corporate purpose
    la presente ley tiene por objeto the purpose of this law is
oblar impuestos to pay taxes
obligación 1. obligation, duty 2. debenture, debt instrument
    obligación alimentaria obligation to provide support
    obligación alternativa alternative obligation
    obligación conjuntiva joint obligation
    obligación contingente contingent liability
    obligación convencional contractual obligation
    obligación de dar cosa cierta determinate obligation [*i.e., duty to deliver a specific asset*]
    obligación de dar cosa incierta indeterminate obligation [*i.e., duty to deliver an unspecified asset*]
    obligación de hacer affirmative covenant
    obligación de medios best efforts obligation [*obligation to use one's best efforts to achieve the purpose of the contract*]
    obligación de no hacer negative covenant
    obligación dineraria monetary obligation
    obligación garantizada guaranteed obligation
    obligación mancomunada joint obligation
    obligación negativa negative covenant
    obligación propter rem (Lat) obligation binding on the owner of real property
    obligación pura absolute obligation [*as opposed to obligations subject to other conditions*]
    obligación solidaria joint and several obligation
    obligación subsidiaria secondary obligation
    obligación terminante absolute obligation
    obligación tributaria tax liability
    obligaciones al portador bearer bonds
    obligaciones de capital capital liabilities
    obligaciones diversas other liabilities
    obligaciones indizadas indexed debt instruments
    obligaciones nominativas registered debt instruments
    obligaciones quirografarias unsecured debt instruments
    obligaciones subordinadas subordinated debentures
obligacionista bondholder
obligar to be binding on
obligatoriedad binding force
obligatorio compulsory, required

obligatorio para binding on
obra
    obra civil civil engineering work, construction work
    obra social (Arg) health insurance
    obras en proceso construction in progress
    obras públicas public works
obrar
    obra en nuestro poder we are in receipt of
    obrar de buena fe to act in good faith
obrante en autos placed on the record, entered in the record
observancia de la ley compliance with the law
observar
    observar las disposiciones del reglamento to comply with the
        provisions of the regulation
    como puede observarse as may be seen
ocasionar
    los gastos ocasionados al comprador the expenses incurred
        by the buyer
ocupaciones y incautaciones (Col) search and seizure
ocupar la cosa legada to take possession of the legacy
ocurrir ante notario público to appear before a notary public
ocurso (Mex) pleading, petition
ofendido victim of an offense
oferente offeror
oferta 1. offer 2. bid [*in a public tender*] 3. offering
    oferta definitiva firm offer
    oferta monetaria money supply
    oferta para obtener efectivo for-cash offering
    oferta pública de adquisición (OPA) takeover bid
    oferta pública de intercambio (OPI) stock swap
    oferta pública de valores public offering of securities
    oferta pública de venta (Spa) (OPV) public offering
    oferta pública inicial (OPI) initial public offering (IPO)
    la oferta y la demanda supply and demand
ofertante bidder
oficial
    oficial de diligencia (Bol) process server
    oficial de justicia officer of the court
    Oficial del Registro Civil Registrar of Vital Records
    oficial subalterno junior officer
oficial mayor chief of staff
    Oficial Mayor de la PGR (Mex) Chief Administrative Officer of
        the Attorney General's Office
oficialía
    oficialía de partes (Mex) filing desk
    oficilía del registro civil (Mex) Office of Vital Records
    oficialía mayor (Hon, Mex) administrative office

oficialismo representatives of the governing party
oficina office
    oficina central de consignaciones (Mex) office for court filings
    Oficina de Sorteo de Causas y Casilleros Judiciales (Ecu)
        Office of Case Assignments and Attorneys' Mailboxes
    oficina de partes (Chi) filing desk
    oficina recaudadora de rentas (Mex) office of the tax collector
oficio official letter
    que se libre oficio a that an official letter be sent to
    oficios de estilo the customary official notices
ofrecimiento de pruebas offering of evidence [*Evidence is first offered ("ofrecido" in Mex or "promovido" in Ven), then admitted or rejected by the judge (admitido o rechazado), and then produced ("desahogado" in Mex or "evacuado" in Ven).*]
oído el fiscal on the recommendation of the district attorney
opción
    opción de compra call option
    opción de venta put option
operación
    operaciones a plazo forward transactions
    operaciones a premio premium transactions
    operaciones de contado spot transactions, spot trade
    operaciones de contado a hoy same-day spot transactions
    operaciones bursátiles securities trading
    operaciones bursátiles a crédito margin trading [*using borrowed money to buy stock and pledging the stock ("caución bursátil") as security for the borrowed money*]
    operaciones con margen margin transactions [*transactions in which a broker or dealer furnishes credit to facilitate trading in securities or commodities accounts*]
    operaciones cruzadas cross trades [*a buy order is matched with a sell order on the stock exchange by one broker*]
    operaciones de bolsa securities trading
    operaciones de captación deposit transactions
    operaciones de cobertura hedging transactions
    operaciones de doble (Spa) repurchase agreement, repo [*called "reporto" in Mex and "pase" in Arg*]
    operaciones en moneda extranjera foreign currency denominated transactions
    operaciones pasivas de reporto (Mex) securities purchased under agreements to resell
opinión opinion
    opinión asesora advisory opinion
    opinión consultiva advisory opinion
    opinión contraria dissenting opinion
oponer excepciones to assert a defense or move to dismiss

oponerse
 puede oponerse a terceros is binding on third parties, is effective as to third parties, can be enforced against third parties
oponibilidad effectiveness as to third parties
oponible a terceros binding on third parties, effective as to third parties, enforceable against third parties
oportunamente in a timely manner, in due time, at the proper time, in due course
optar
 optar un grado académico (Per) to receive an academic degree
 optar un título (Per) to receive a degree
optimizar to maximize, to optimize
orden order
 orden de aprehensión (Mex) arrest warrant
 orden de cateo (Mex) search warrant
 orden de colaterales collateral line of descent
 orden de comparecencia order to appear
 orden de compra purchase order
 orden de detención arrest warrant
 orden de entrega delivery order
 orden de no innovar (Arg, Chi) order to stay [*When a person files a "recurso de queja" he will often petition for an "orden de no innovar" preventing the lower court from executing its judgment or otherwise proceeding while the appellate court is reviewing the appeal.*]
 orden de prisión preventiva order of pre-trial detention
 orden de registro search warrant
 orden del día agenda, order of business [*Note that a "punto del orden del día" is an "item* _on_ *the agenda," not an "item* _of_ *the agenda"*]
 orden del lado materno maternal line of descent
 orden del lado paterno paternal line of descent
 orden en línea recta direct line of descent
 orden judicial injunction
 orden limitada (Spa) limit order [*on the stock market*]
 orden patronal (Cos) employer's statement of employee's social security contributions
 orden por lo mejor (Spa) market order [*on the stock market*]
 orden público public order, public policy, law and order
 orden sucesorio line of descent
ordenación norm, rule
ordenamiento
 ordenamiento de leyes system of laws, legal systme
 ordenamiento jurídico legal system
ordenanza ordinance

organigrama organizational chart
organismo agency
    organismo administrativo administrative agency
    organismo de control regulatory agency
    organismo ejecutivo executive branch
    organismo internacional international organization [*such as the United Nations*]
    organismo judicial judiciary, judicial branch
    organismo legislativo legislature, legislative branch
    organismo público government agency
    organismos descentralizados (Mex) decentralized regulatory agencies [*independently administered bodies that perform public services, such as the IMSS and INFONAVIT, which are considered separate entities from the Federal Government*]
organizaciones auxiliares de crédito (Mex) auxiliary lending organizations [*examples include almacenes generales de depósito, arrendadoras financieras, sociedades de ahorro y préstamo, uniones de crédito and empresas de factoraje financiero.*]
órgano 1. institution 2. governing body
    Órgano Ejecutivo (Pan) the Executive Branch
    Órgano Judicial (Pan) the Judicial Branch
    Órgano Legislativo (Pan) the Legislative Branch
    órgano jurisdiccional court
    órganos de dirección management
    El órgano supremo de la sociedad es la asamblea de accionistas. The shareholders' meeting is the highest governing body of the company.
oriental (Uru) Uruguayan, from Uruguay
otorgante grantor
otorgado grantee
otorgar 1. to grant 2. to sign, to execute
    otorgar fianza to furnish a bond
    otorgar un crédito to extend credit
    otorgar un documento to execute or sign a document
    otorgar un instrumento to execute or sign an instrument
    otorgar un préstamo to extend a loan
otros gastos other expenses
    otros gastos por intereses other interest expenses
    otros ingresos other income
otrosí supplemental prayer for relief
    otrosí a un contrato supplementary agreement
    otrosí digo I further state
pacto
    Pacto Andino the Andean Pact

pacto comisorio contract clause relating to the rights and duties of the parties upon breach

pacto de cuota litis contingency fee agreement

pacto de no competencia covenant not to compete

pacto de preferencia right of first refusal

pacto de retroventa repurchase agreement

pacto laboral collective bargaining agreement

pacto leonino one-sided agreement

pacto palmario contingency fee agreement with a premium in case of victory

pacto social (Cos, Pan) articles of incorporation

padre putativo putative father

padrón census

padrón de importadores (Mex) list of registered importers

padrón electoral voter registration list, list of registered voters

padrón fiscal (Mex) tax guidelines

pagadero payable

pagadero a la entrega payable upon delivery

pagadero a la vista payable on demand

pagadero a plazos payable in installments

pagadero en un plazo de 30 días payable within 30 days

pagadero por adelantado payable in advance

pagaré promissory note, note

pagaré a la orden negotiable note

pagaré a la vista demand note

pagaré de empresa (Spa) commercial paper

pagarés abstractos (Per) "abstract" promissory notes [*the consideration for the obligation is not mentioned*]

pagarés bancarios con rendimiento liquidable al vencimiento (PRLV) (Mex) promissory notes with yield payable at maturity

pagarés causados (Per) "concrete" promissory notes [*the consideration for the obligation and guarantee is mentioned*]

pago payment

pago a cuenta estimated tax payment

pago a plazos payment in installments

pago anticipado prepayment, advance payment

pago contra embarque cash on shipment (COS)

pago contra entrega cash on delivery (COD)

pago extemporáneo late payment, untimely payment

pago fraccional partial payment

pago indebido unwarranted payment

pago insuficiente underpayment

pago oportuno timely payment

pago parcial partial payment, installment

pago total payment in full

pago virtual del IVA tax credit taken for VAT paid

pagos anticipados prepayments, prepaid expenses
pagos de dividendos dividends paid [*as an item on a financial statement*]
páguese a la orden de pay to the order of
país en vías de desarrollo developing country
pandilla gang
panista (Mex) member of the Partido de Acción Nacional
papel paper
    papel comercial commercial paper
    papel común plain paper, unstamped paper
    papel de actuaciones ordinary paper used as a substitute for sealed paper
    papel moneda paper money
    papel sellado stamped paper
    papel simple plain paper, unstamped paper
    papel timbrado stamped paper
    papel valorado (Per) stamped paper
papeleta 1. (Per) traffic ticket **2. (Spa)** ballot
paquete accionario block of shares
par condicio creditorum (Lat) the equal legal position of all creditors
para abono en cuenta for deposit only
para constancia in witness whereof
para los efectos de esta ley for purposes of this law
para producir efecto to be valid
para que conste for the record, in witness whereof
paradero whereabouts
parado 1. unemployed **2.** out of production **3.** on strike
parágrafo (Col, Pan, Ven) additional clause
paraíso fiscal tax haven
parche (Arg) partial adjustment for inflation
parentesco kinship, relationship
    parentesco civil civil relationship
    parentesco colateral collateral relationship [*a person's blood relatives other than ancestors or issue*]
    parentesco de afinidad relationship by marriage, relationship by affinity
    parentesco de doble vínculo whole-blood relationship [*having the same father and mother*]
    parentesco de medio lado half-blood relationship
    parentesco de simple vínculo half-blood relationship
    parentesco político relationship by marriage, relationship by affinity
    parentesco por consanguinidad relationship by blood, consanguinity
paridad parity
    paridad adquisitiva purchasing power parity

paridad cambiaria exchange rate parity
pariente relative
    pariente colateral collateral relative
    pariente consanguíneo blood relative
    pariente más cercano next of kin
    pariente más próximo next of kin
    pariente político relative by marriage, in-law [*also called "relative by affinity"*]
    pariente por afinidad relative by affinity
    pariente sin afinidad step-relative
paro 1. layoff 2. strike
    paro forzoso unemployment
    paro obrero strike
    paro patronal lockout
parquet (Spa) trading floor [*of the Stock Exchange*]
parroquia parish
parte
    parte actora plaintiff
    parte conducente relevant part, pertinent part
    parte considerativa the whereas clauses of a judgment, the preamble [*also called "los considerandos"*]
    parte contraria the opposing party, the adverse party
    parte contratante contracting party
    parte de policía (el) (Col) police report
    parte de un contrato party to a contract
    parte demandada defendant
    parte demandante plaintiff
    parte dispositiva de una sentencia the operative part of a judgment, the holding
    parte expositiva the preamble
    parte formal person who acts in court on behalf of another
    parte integrante integral part, part and parcel
    parte interesada interested party
    parte más diligente the first party to take action
    parte material person who acts in court in his own name
    parte motivada the whereas clauses
    parte ofendida the injured party
    parte policial (el) (Ecu) traffic ticket
    parte perdidosa the losing party
    parte recurrida respondent, appellee
    ⟶ **parte resolutiva** the operative part of a judgment, the holding
    parte resolutoria the operative part of a judgment, the holding
    parte social (Mex) share of a sociedad de responsabilidad limitada. [*This is called a "cuota social" in Arg and Ven, and a "participación social" in Per.*]
    parte solicitante moving party
partición de la herencia distribution of the estate

participación 1. interest 2. announcement
    participación de los trabajadores en las utilidades (PTU)
      (Mex) employee profit-sharing
    participación en las ganancias profit-sharing
    participación mayoritaria majority interest, controlling interest
    participación minoritaria minority interest
    participación social (Per) share of a "sociedad comercial de
      responsabilidad limitada" [*called "cuota social" in Arg and
      Ven, and "parte social" in Mex*]
    participaciones profit-sharing [*as an item on a financial
      statement*]
participar to inform someone of something
partida 1. item 2. entry 3. installment
    partida compensatoria balancing item
    partida de defunción death certificate
    partida de matrimonio marriage certificate
    partida de nacimiento birth certificate
    partida doble double entry (bookkeeping) [*every transaction is
      reflected in offsetting debits and credits*]
    partida extraordinaria below-the-line entry
    partida informativa memorandum item
    partida ordinaria above-the-line entry
    partida por contra balancing entry
    partida rememorativa memorandum item
    partida simple single entry (bookkeeping)
    partidas a cobrar collection items
    partidas de gastos objects of expenditure
partido
    partido judicial judicial district
    partido político political party
pasante de derecho (Mex) law clerk
pasantía law clerkship, internship
pasar
    pasar a beneficio de to inure to the benefit of
    pasar a cuarto intermedio (Arg) to adjourn, to go into recess
    pasar a disposición judicial to appear in court
    pasar a segundas nupcias to remarry
    pasar ante el notario to attest before a notary
    pasar ante la fe del notario to attest before a notary
pase 1. **(Col)** driver's license 2. **(Arg)** repurchase agreement
    ("repo") [*In Argentina an "operación de pase" is a financial
    transaction in which the buyer of securities agrees to sell them
    back to the seller, and the seller agrees to repurchase them. This
    is known as a "reporto" in Mexico and an "operación de doble" in
    Spain.*]
    pase pasivo (Arg) reverse repo

pasivo
    pasivo a corto plazo short-term debt/liability
    pasivo a largo plazo long-term debt/liability
    pasivo acumulado accrued liabilities
    pasivo circulante current liabilities
    pasivo comercial trade liabilities
    pasivo contingente contingent liabilities
    pasivo corriente current liabilities
    pasivo eventual contingent liabilities
    pasivo exigible current liabilities
    pasivo exigible a la vista demand deposits [*on a bank's balance sheet*]
    pasivo exigible a plazo time deposits [*on a bank's balance sheet*]
    pasivo fijo capital liabilities
    pasivo no exigible capital liabilities
    pasivo patrimonial capital liabilities
    pasivo real current liabilities
    pasivo transitorio unadjusted liabilities, accrued liabilities
patente 1. patent 2. business license 3. (Arg, Chi) license plate
    patente al día in good standing [*i.e., has paid his dues*]
    patente de comercio business license
    patente de industria (Ven) business license
    patente de invención patent [*The phrase "de invención" is used in Spanish to distinguish this "patente" from a "patente de comercio." In English "patent" always refers to inventions. A "patente de comercio" is a business license.*]
    patente municipal (Chi, Ven) business license tax
patria potestad parental authority, legal custody [*i.e, the legal authority to make decisions about the medical, educational, health and welfare needs of a child, as opposed to "physical custody"*]
    ejercer la patria potestad de un menor to exercise parental authority over a child, to have legal custody of a child
patrimonio 1. estate, net assets 2. corpus of a trust, trust assets
    patrimonio de familia homestead [*exempt pursuant to homestead laws from seizure or sale for debt—also called "bien de familia"*]
    patrimonio fideicomitido trust assets, trust corpus, trust res
    patrimonio inmueble federal (Mex) government-owned real property [*such as the land on Mexico's beachfront*]
    patrimonio neto (Arg, Per) shareholders' equity
    patrimonio público (Ven) national wealth
    patrimonio social corporate assets
patrocinar 1. to sponsor 2. (Arg, Chi) to represent at law
patrocinio sponsorship
patronato board of governors of a charitable organization

Patronato de Liberados (Arg) probation board
Patronato del Ahorro Nacional (Mex) National Savings Trust
Patronato Nacional de la Infancia (Cos) National Child
    Welfare Agency
patrón 1. (Mex) employer **2.** standard
    patrón monetario monetary standard
    patrón oro gold standard
patrono employer
paz y salvo (Col, Pan) official certificate that a person does not owe
    taxes to the Government
peculado embezzlement, misuse of public funds
peculio one's own money, private wealth, private resources
pedido order
    hacer un pedido to place an order
    pedido a surtirse cuando haya en existencia back order
    pedido por correo mail order
pedimento 1. request, motion **2. (Mex)** customs entry form
pena 1. penalty **2.** punishment
    pena aflictiva punishment by death or long-term imprisonment
    pena capital capital punishment
    pena contractual contractual penalty
    pena convencional contractual penalty
    pena de muerte death penalty
    pena pecuniaria fine
pensión
    pensión alimentaria 1. alimony **2.** child support
    pensión alimenticia 1. alimony **2.** child support
    pensión de jubilación pension
    pensión vitalicia annuity
percepción de rendimientos receipt of earnings
pérdida loss
    pérdida de un derecho forfeiture of a right
    pérdida en cambios contables book exchange loss
    pérdida en cambios fiscales tax exchange loss
    pérdida fiscal tax loss
    pérdidas fiscales por amortizar tax loss carryforwards
    pérdidas y ganancias profit and loss
perención de la instancia lapsing of a lawsuit because of parties'
    inactivity
perimir (Arg) to lapse
periódicamente from time to time
período de pruebas evidentiary period [*which is tantamount to the
    trial of the case*]
peritaje expert's report, expert testimony
perito expert
    perito caligráfico handwriting expert
    perito valuador expert appraiser

peritos árbitros expert arbitrators who decide the facts in a "juicio pericial" (q.v.)
perjudicial prejudicial
perjuicios damages
permanecer en funciones to remain in office
permuta barter, exchange
perredista (Mex) member of the Partido de la Revolución Democrática
persona person
    persona a cargo dependent
    persona de existencia ideal (Arg) artificial person, legal entity [synonym of "*persona jurídica*"]
    persona de existencia visible (Arg) natural person, individual [synonym of "*persona física*"]
    persona de toda solvencia completely trustworthy person, utterly reliable person
    persona desaparecida missing person
    persona física (Arg, Mex) person, individual [*The standard term is "persona natural."*]
    persona física o moral (Mex) person or entity
    persona jurídica legal entity
    persona moral (Mex) legal entity [*The standard term is "persona jurídica."*]
    persona natural person, individual
    persona natural o jurídica person or entity
    persona por nacer unborn child
    personas de uno y de otro sexo persons of either sex
personaje público public figure
personal personnel
    personal libre non-union workers
personalidad 1. capacity 2. personality
    personalidad jurídica legal personality [*the quality or state of being a legal entity*]
    personalidad procesal legal capacity to sue
personarse to appear [*said only of a party to the case*]
personería legal capacity
personero (Ven) an official [*of the government, of a political party, etc.*]
pertinencia de la prueba relevance of evidence
perturbación
    perturbación del mercado market disruption
    perturbación del orden público disturbing the peace, breach of the peace
pesquisa investigation, inquiry
pesquisar to investigate
petitorio prayer for relief [*in a complaint*]
picapleitos ambulance chaser

picos odd lots [*the number of shares is less than a block*]
pie (Chi) down payment
pignoración security interest in real or personal property [*includes both "anticresis" and "prenda" agreements*]
    pignoración inmobiliaria *see anticresis*
    pignoración mobiliaria pledge
pignorar to pledge
Pinos (los) (Mex) official residence of the President of Mexico
piramidación gross up
piso de remates trading floor
plagiar 1. to plagiarize 2. to kidnap
plagiario 1. plagiarist 2. kidnapper
plagio 1. plagiarism 2. kidnapping
plan plan
    plan de negocio (Mex) business plan
    plan general de contabilidad (Spa) General Chart of Accounts
    plan general de funcionamiento general business plan
planilla 1. form [*synonym of "formulario"*] 2. **(Ven)** receipt for having paid fees 3. **(Mex)** ballot 4. **(Mex)** slate of candidates, ticket 5. **(Cos, Nic)** payroll
    planilla aérea (Ven) special declaration of air cargo entering Venezuela
    planilla de contribución (Pue) tax form, tax return
    planilla de costas bill of costs [*bill setting forth the expenses in connection with a lawsuit that a party seeks to have paid by the opposing party – also called a "pliego de costas"*]
    planilla de distancias (Uru) schedule of distances [*drawn up by the Supreme Court for purposes of computing the deadlines in the case, i.e., the deadlines are extended depending on how far from the court the person in question resides*]
    planilla de ingreso (Spa) deposit slip
    planilla de inscripción registration form
    planilla de precios (Mex) price list
    planilla de retiro (Spa) withdrawal slip
    planilla llave lead schedule [*details the components of an amount appearing on a financial statement*]
plano 1. city map 2. technical drawings
    plano catastrado plat map [*map of a town, section or subdivisions indicating the location and boundaries of individual properties*]
    plano conforme a obra as-built drawing [*in a construction contract*]
    plano de alzada elevation sheet [*construction drawings that illustrate the front and sides of a building*]
    plano de trazado plot plan [*plan showing the location of improvements on a property site*]

planteamiento 1. approach to something, analysis of something, way of looking at something 2. presentation, explanation, depiction, portrayal, statement of the issue
plantear to assert, put forward, set forth
    plantear un asunto to pose an issue, to raise an issue
plantilla payroll, employees [*as a heading in a financial statement*]
plaza location
    plaza bursátil stock exchange site, location of a stock exchange
plazo
    plazo conminatorio deadline for doing something without penalty
    plazo de redención deadline for redemption
    plazo social duration of a company
    plazos escalonados staggered terms
pleito lawsuit, litigation
pleno complete, full
    el pleno de la Corte the Court sitting en banc
pliego
    pliego aparte separate cover
    pliego de condiciones terms of reference, bid documents
    pliego de consignación (Mex) request for pre-trial detention
    pliego de costas bill of costs [*bill setting forth the expenses in connection with a lawsuit that a party seeks to have paid by the opposing party – also called a "planilla de costas"*]
    pliego de especificaciones terms of reference, bid documents
plusvalía capital gain
    plusvalía mercantil (Ecu) goodwill
poder 1. power of attorney 2. possession
    poder adquisitivo purchasing power
    poder apud acta (Lat) power of attorney that is not recorded by a notary but is instead executed before the court clerk
    poder constituyente the framers of the Constitution [*i.e., those who drafted it*]
    poder ejecutivo the Executive Branch
    poder especial para asuntos de comercio exterior special power of attorney for customs matters
    poder general para actos de administración general power of attorney for day-to-day management functions
    poder general para pleitos y cobranzas general power of attorney for litigation and collections
    poder generalísimo (Cos) unlimited power of attorney
    poder generalísimo sin límite de suma (Cos) unlimited power of attorney without monetary restriction
    poder judicial judicial branch, judiciary
    poder legislativo the Legislative Branch, the legislature
    Por este medio confiero poder a X para que, en mi nombre y representación, compre I hereby make, constitute and

appoint X as my lawful attorney-in-fact, to purchase in my name, place and stead ...

poderdante, mi my client [*if attorney is speaking*], my principal [*synonym of "mandante"*]

poderhabiente agent, attorney-in-fact [*synonym of "mandatario"*]

política 1. politics 2. policy

   política corporativa corporate policy

   política exterior foreign policy

   política habitacional (Ven) housing policy contribution [*Contributions must be made at the rate of 2% by the employer and 1% by the employee.*]

   política interior domestic policy

   política monetaria monetary policy

póliza insurance policy

   póliza de acumulación (Ecu) certificate of deposit

   póliza de desalmacenaje (Cos) customs clearance certificate

   póliza de internación (Bol, Chi) customs clearance certificate

ponente judge who writes the court's opinion

poner a la disposición de to submit to

ponerlo en conocimiento de alguien to give notice thereof to someone

ponerse por escrito to be reduced to writing

por concepto de enganche (Mex) as a down payment

por derecho propio on his own behalf

por este simple hecho ipso facto

por este solo hecho ipso facto

por estirpes per stirpes

por las dudas just in case, to be on the safe side

por lo expuesto y fundado for the foregoing reasons and explanations

por ministerio de la ley by operation of law

por partes iguales share and share alike

por sorteos at random, by random selection

por su propia cuenta at his own expense

por su propio derecho on his own behalf

por unanimidad unanimously

porfiriato (Mex) the Porfirio Díaz administration

porfirista (Mex) related to Porforio Díaz or his administration

poseedor de buena fe holder in good faith

posesión possession, enjoyment, taking office

   posesión continua continuous possession

   posesión de mala fe possession in bad faith

   posesión pacífica undisturbed possession

posibles adquirientes eligible buyers

posición

   posición activa en moneda extranjera net foreign currency denominated assets

posición en moneda extranjera foreign currency position
posiciones interrogatories
positiva ficta implied consent [*presumption that the government has granted a petition if it does not respond within a predetermined period of time*]
postor bidder
    el mejor postor the highest bidder
    el segundo postor the next-highest bidder
postulante candidate, bidder
postularse para un puesto público to run for public office
postura bid
    la mejor postura the highest bid
potestad authority, jurisdiction
práctica
    práctica establecida standard practice
    práctica forense practice before the court
    práctica parlamentaria parliamentary procedure
    prácticas comerciales customary business practices
    prácticas desleales de comercio unfair business practices
practicar
    practicar el apeo y deslinde de las tierras to survey and measure the land
    practicar pruebas (Col, Ecu) to examine evidence, to hear evidence
    practicar una auditoría to perform an audit
    practicar una diligencia to carry out a procedural act
    practicar una necropsia to perform an autopsy
    practicar un balance to prepare a balance sheet
preaviso notice of termination of employment [*either by the employer or the employee*]
precaria tenancy at sufferance, tenancy at will
precarista tenant at sufferance, tenant at will
precautorio precautionary
precedente precedent
precio price
    precio al contado spot price
    precio al detal (Pue) retail price
    precio alzado lump sum
    precio aplazado forward price
    precio de adquisición purchase price
    precio de afección sentimental value
    precio de apertura opening price
    precio de catálogo list price
    precio de cierre closing price [*price of the last transaction completed during a day's trading session on an exchange*]
    precio de compra purchase price
    precio de introducción introductory price

precio de mercado market price
precio de plaza market price
precio de realización selling price
precio de venta sales price [*Note that "sale price" (without the "s") means "precio reducido."*]
precio de venta al contado cash price
precio de venta al público retail price
precio global lump sum
precio sombra shadow pricing
precio tope ceiling price
precio unitario unit price
precio vil dumped price, cut-rate price, rockbottom price
predio
    predio dominante dominant estate [*parcel of land that benefits from an easement on a servient estate*]
    predio edificado developed property, improved property [*i.e., things have been built on it*]
    predio enclavado landlocked property
    predio rústico rural land
    predio sirviente servient estate [*estate on which an easement is placed for the benefit of another estate*]
    predio urbano urban property
prefectura de la policía (Ven) police station
prejudicial pre-filing, prior to the lawsuit [*Note that this term does not mean "prejudicial" in English, which is "perjudicial" in Spanish.*]
prelación priority [*of a lender in a secured transaction or of a previously registered patent or trademark*]
    tener igual prelación to rank pari passu
premeditación premeditation
prenda pledge
    prenda agraria chattel mortgage on farm machinery or livestock
    prenda con desplazamiento pledge, pawn [*The creditor takes possession of the collateral until the debt is paid, e.g., a pawnshop, or a bonded warehouse*]
    prenda con registro chattel mortgage, nonpossessory security interest in personal property [*The creditor does not take possession of the collateral and must therefore record his security interest to put third parties on notice of his lien.*]
    prenda fija (Arg) fixed pledge
    prenda flotante (Arg) floating pledge
    prenda mercantil chattel mortgage, nonpossessory security interest in personal property
    prenda registrable (Arg, Par) chattel mortgage, nonpossessory security interest in personal property
    prenda sin desplazamiento de posesión chattel mortgage, nonpossessory security interest in personal property

prenda sin registro pledge, pawn [*The creditor takes possession of the collateral until the debt is paid and therefore does not need to record his security interest.*]

prenda sin tenencia del acreedor (Col) chattel mortgage, nonpossessory security interest in personal property

prepaga (Arg) private health insurance

prepotencia preponderance

prepotente predominant

prescribir en favor de to forfeit to

prescripción statute of limitations

    prescripción adquisitiva adverse possession

    prescripción negativa laches

prescrito barred by the statute of limitations

presenciar un matrimonio (Ven) to preside over a marriage ceremony

presentación

    presentación al pago presentment for payment

    presentación de documentos ante el tribunal filing of documents with the court

presentar

    presentar a la aceptación to present for acceptance

    presentar un informe to render a report, to submit a report

    presentar una declaración to file a tax return

    presentar una demanda ante un tribunal to file a complaint with the Court

    presentar una oferta to submit a bid

    presentar una renuncia a un puesto to tender a resignation from a position

    presentar una solicitud to file an application

    presentarse al trabajo to report for work

    presentarse en concurso to file a petition in bankruptcy

presente hand delivered [*when part of an address*]

    el presente contrato this contract

    en el presente herein

    por el presente hereby

presidente 1. president 2. chairman

    presidente cesante outgoing president, lame-duck president

    presidente del Consejo de Administración Chairman of the Board

    presidente del jurado foreman of the jury

    presidente del tribunal 1. chief justice [*of trial or appellate court*] 2. chief justice [*of the supreme court*]

    presidente ejecutivo (Per) chief executive officer (CEO)

    presidente en funciones acting president, acting chairman

    presidente municipal (Mex) mayor, head official of a municipio [*Mexican states are divided into municipios*]

presidir to preside

presidir una reunión to preside over a meeting
presión fiscal tax burden
prestación
    prestación de fianza posting a bond
    prestaciones (Ven) severance pay
    prestaciones económicas financial assistance
    prestaciones laborales employment benefits
    prestaciones periódicas periodic payments
    prestaciones por desempleo unemployment compensation
    prestaciones sociales welfare
    prestaciones suplementarias fringe benefits
prestamista lender
préstamo loan
    préstamo a sola firma signature loan
    préstamo atado tied loan [*made subject to the condition that the borrower use the loan proceeds in a certain way*]
    préstamo con garantía secured loan
    préstamo con garantía hipotecaria mortgage loan
    préstamo con garantía personal loan with a personal guaranty [*aval or fianza*]
    préstamo con garantía prendaria loan secured by personal property
    préstamo de consumo loan for consumption [*also called a "mutuo"*]
    préstamo de uso loan for use [*also called a "comodato"*]
    préstamo garantizado secured loan [*one that is backed by collateral*]
    préstamo prendario secured loan [*secured by personal property*]
    préstamo quirografario unsecured loan
    préstamo sin intereses interest-free loan
    préstamo sindicado syndicated loan [*a large loan granted or participated in by several banks or lending institutions jointly*]
    préstamo subvencionado soft loan [*a loan providing liberal terms for repayment and sometimes a low interest rate*]
prestar
    prestar consentimiento to give consent
    prestar dinero to lend money
    prestar juramento to take an oath, to be sworn in
    prestar un servicio to perform a service, to render a service
    prestar una fianza to post a bond
prestatario borrower
presunción
    presunción de muerte presumption of death
    presunción fundada justified presumption
    presunción juris et de jure conclusive presumption [*a legal conclusion that cannot be changed by any facts*]

presunción juris tantum rebuttable presumption
presunta responsabilidad (Mex) strong suspicion of guilt
presunto alleged
    presunto asesino the alleged murderer
    presunto extraditado person to be extradited
    presunto responsable (Mex) the suspect
presupuesto budget
pretensión claim, cause of action
preterintencional beyond what was intended
preterición de herederos pretermission of heirs [*i.e., unintentionally not leaving anything to them*]
prevaricación breach of trust, malfeasance of office [*especially by a lawyer or judge*]
prevaricato breach of trust, malfeasance of office [*especially by a lawyer or judge*]
prevención 1. being the first court to hear a case 2. preliminary hearing of a case 3. warning
prevenir 1. to be the first to take jurisdiction over a case 2. to conduct a preliminary hearing 3. to warn
    El Tribunal que haya prevenido en el conocimiento del asunto excluye los demás. The court that took preliminary jurisdiction over the case precludes the jurisdiction of the other courts.
prever to provide for, to contemplate
previa citación individual upon prior notice to each
previa convocatoria in response to notice of a shareholders' meeting
previa habilitación del tiempo necesario having authorized the performance of judicial acts on a day when the court is not in session
previa vista de la causa having heard both sides
previendo la muerte in contemplation of death
previsión social payroll taxes and employee benefits
previsto en el contrato provided for in the contract
priísta (Mex) member of the Partido Revolucionario Institucional (PRI)
prima 1. premium 2. bonus
    prima de emisión additional paid-in capital
    prima de Navidad (Col) Christmas bonus
    prima de seguros insurance premium
    primas netas ganadas net premiums earned
    primas sobre acciones capital stock premiums
    primas y otras pólizas por cobrar premiums and other policyholder receivables
primera instancia first instance
primeras entradas, primeras salidas first in, first out (FIFO)
principio principle

principio de adaptación del proceso principle that the form of procedure must be adapted to the subject matter of the dispute

principio de adquisición procesal rule that evidence produced by one party to a case can be used by the adverse party for his own purposes

principio de concentración rule that all questions in a lawsuit must be settled in one decision

principio de contradicción rule that both parties to a lawsuit must be heard [*basis of the adversarial system*]

principio de controversia rule that the parties must furnish the evidence necessary for a decision

principio de economía procesal rule that the procedure must economize time and cost

principio de eficacia procesal rule that the trial must proceed in an efficient manner

principio de eventualidad rule that evidence must be presented in a timely manner

principio de impulsión procesal rule that the parties must advance the case to its conclusion

principio de inmediación rule that exceptions to a judgment must be made at once

principio de la reserva de ley rule that the executive branch is subject to the rule of law

principio de preclusión rule that evidence must be presented in a timely manner

principio de probidad rule that an action must be in good faith

principio de publicidad rule that the parties may have access to all evidence

principio dispositivo rule that a party is free to file, prosecute and terminate a lawsuit

principio inquisitivo principle that the court may initiate action

principios contables generalmente aceptados generally accepted accounting principles (GAAP)

prisión imprisonment

prisión preventiva pre-trial detention

prisión provisional pre-trial detention

prius pactum per posterius elidetur (Lat) A prior agreement is annulled by a later one.

privilegio de pobreza (Chi) right to proceed in forma pauperis

probable responsabilidad (Mex) strong suspicion of guilt

probable responsable (Mex) the suspect

procedencia admissibility, whether X is in order, whether X is proper

procedente according to the rules, properly filed [*For example, an appeal may be "procedente" (properly filed) but not "fundado" (well founded) and will therefore be dismissed on the merits.*]

proceder 1. to be proper, to be appropriate 2. to proceed to do something

    como mejor proceda en derecho to the extent the law may allow, to the extent permissible by law, to the full extent of the law

    La policía procedió a su detención. The police proceeded to arrest him.

    Procede declarar la nulidad de la acción. It is appropriate to dismiss the case.

    Procede la demanda. The complaint will not be dismissed.

    proceder contra alguien to take legal action against someone

    proceder de mala fe to act in bad faith

    proceder de un contrato to arise out of a contract

    proceder judicialmente to take legal action

    si el caso procede if appropriate, if proper

procedimiento 1. proceedings 2. procedure

    procedimientos contenciosos adversary proceedings

procesado (Mex) the defendant [*after the "auto de radicación" has been issued*]

procesal procedural

procesamiento indictment

proceso 1. case, proceeding, trial 2. (Chi) casefile, record of the case 3. procedure

    proceso del rubro (el) the above-styled case, the above-captioned case

    proceso simulado moot court, mock trial

procurador 1. (Mex) prosecutor 2. "procurador" [*There is no equivalent in the United States. A procurador is a legal assistant who has attended law school and whose function is to act as a liaison between the court and the parties. Procuración is the task of going to court to check on the status of the lawsuit or to file certain documents. However, important documents must bear the signature of the attorney (el abogado patrocinante) for whom the procurador works. Even after they are admitted to the bar, some lawyers continue to work as procuradores because they have no clients of their own or find it more lucrative.*]

    procurador de oficio unofficial "procurador" [*does not have a power of attorney to act on behalf of the client - also called "procurador oficioso"*]

    procurador del número (Chi) "procurador" who has received a license to act as procurador from the court [*as opposed to a "procurador particular"*]

    procurador fiscal public prosecutor

    Procurador General attorney general

    procurador judicial attorney authorized to represent parties in court [*like a barrister in the UK*]

Procuraduría
    Procuraduría Federal del Consumidor (Mex) Federal Consumer Protection Agency
    Procuraduría Federal de Protección al Ambiente (Mex) Federal Environmental Protection Agency
    Procuraduría Fiscal de la Federación (Mex) Office of the Attorney General for Fiscal Matters
    Procuraduría General de la República (Mex) Office of the Attorney General of the Republic, Federal Attorney General's Office
    Procuraduría General del Estado (Ecu) Attorney General's Office

producción en proceso work in progress
producir sus efectos to take effect, to be effective
producto 1. product 2. proceeds
    producto bruto interno (PBI) (Arg) gross domestic product
    producto de la liquidación proceeds of the liquidation
    producto interior bruto (PIB) (Spa) gross domestic product
    producto interno bruto (PIB) (Bol, Cos, Mex, Ven) gross domestic product
    producto nacional bruto (PNB) gross national product
    producto de la venta proceeds of the sale
    productos financieros interest income
    productos por servicios service fees
    productos terminados finished goods [*as an item on a financial statement*]

proemio preamble
proferir una condena to pronounce a sentence
prófugo 1. fugitive from justice 2. draft dodger
profundidad de mercado market depth
progenitor progenitor
prohibición de innovar restraining order
prohibir to prohibit
    queda prohibido it shall be unlawful
promoción pleading, motion
    promoción de pruebas (Ven) offering of evidence [*Evidence is first offered ("ofrecido" in Mex or "promovido" in Ven), then admitted or rejected by the judge (admitido o rechazado), and then produced ("desahogado" in Mex or "evacuado" in Ven).*]
    promociones judiciales legal proceedings
promover
    promover pruebas to offer evidence
    promover reconvención to assert a counterclaim
    promover un juicio to file a suit, to bring an action
    promover una causa to file a suit, to bring an action
    promover una cuestión to raise a question

promulgación de una ley promulgation of a law
prontuario (Arg) criminal record, arrest record
propender to be inclined toward, to tend to
propensión marginal al consumo marginal propensity to consume (MPC) [*the ratio of the additional amount that people will spend for consumption from an additional amount of income*]
propiedad 1. property 2. ownership
    propiedad común common property, joint ownership
    propiedad horizontal condominium ownership
    propiedad industrial patent rights, intellectual property [*Note that "industrial property" in English means "property (such as power plants and factories) used for industrial purposes"*]
    propiedad inmobiliaria real property
    propiedad intelectual intellectual property [*property that is the result of original thought, e.g. copyrights, trademarks, etc.*]
    propiedad particular private property
    propiedades, planta y equipo (Gua, Hon) property, plant and equipment
proponente offeror, bidder
proponer to propose
    proponer a una asamblea to make a motion, to move
    proponer testigo to offer a witness
proposición motion, proposal
propuesta proposal
    propuesta de providencia proposed order
    propuesta y aceptación offer and acceptance [*steps in contract formation*]
prórroga 1. extension [*of a time period*] 2. change [*of venue*]
    prórroga de jurisdicción change of venue
    prórroga voluntaria waiver of improper venue
proscrito outlaw
prospecto prospectus [*called "folleto bursátil" and "folleto de emisión" in Spain*]
protección de sobregiro overdraft protection
protestar 1. to raise an objection 2. to affirm
    Protesto lo necesario. (Mex) Duly affirmed under penalty of perjury.
protesto protest [*the process of legally documenting the maker or drawer's failure to pay an instrument when due*]
protocolización recording in the notarial record book
    Pidió la protocolización del siguiente contrato. He requested to have the following contract recorded in the notarial record book.
protocolizar to record in the notarial record book
    protocolizar las actas to record the documents in the notarial record book, to file the original records with the notary

protocolizar los fondos to enter the funds into the notary public's record

protocolo notarial record book

Proveer de conformidad será justicia. (Arg) If the petition herein is granted, justice will be done.

proveído interlocutory or procedural decision

providencia judicial decision [*there are two types: autos and sentencias*]

    providencia alzable appealable order

    providencia cautelar protective measure

    providencia de mera sustanciación interlocutory order

    providencia judicial court order

    providencia precautoria protective measure [*also called "medidas cautelares"*]

    providencia reservada confidential order [*not to be disclosed to the public because of the nature of the case*]

    providencia revocable reversible error

provisión

    provisión para colocaciones de cobranza dudosa, neta net interest income after provision for possible loan losses

    provisión para cuentas dudosas reserve for bad debt

    provisión para indemnizaciones reserve for severance pay

    provisión para siniestros reserve for property and casualty claims

provisionar to create a provision/allowance

provisiones fiscales estimated advance tax payments

proyecto de ley bill, draft law

prueba

    prueba absoluta irrefutable evidence

    prueba admisible admissible evidence

    prueba aislada uncorroborated evidence

    prueba anticipada evidence produced before a trial [*e.g., the testimony of elderly witnesses, the testimony of terminally ill patients, etc.*]

    prueba circunstancial circumstantial evidence [*also called "prueba de indicios"*]

    prueba concluyente conclusive evidence

    prueba confesional oral testimony of the parties [*in response to "posiciones"*]

    prueba convencional evidence admitted by agreement of the parties

    prueba de cargo evidence for the prosecution

    prueba de indicios circumstantial evidence

    prueba de testigos testimony of witnesses

    prueba documental documentary evidence

    prueba idónea (Mex) conclusive proof

    prueba impertinente irrelevant evidence

prueba indiciaria circumstantial evidence
prueba ineficaz inconclusive evidence
prueba innominada unclassified evidence [*i.e., evidence of a kind not specifically provided for by law*]
prueba instrumental documentary evidence
prueba mediata indirect evidence
prueba nula inadmissible evidence
prueba pericial expert testimony
prueba pertinente relevant evidence
prueba plena conclusive evidence
prueba por constituir evidence developed during trial
prueba por fama pública hearsay evidence
prueba por referencia hearsay evidence
prueba practicada por comisionado evidence examined by a delegate judge
prueba preconstituida evidence existing before trial
prueba semiplena partial evidence, inconclusive evidence [*evidence that must be supplemented in order to prove the fact in question*]
prueba tasada legally weighted evidence [*the effects of this kind of evidence are determined by statute, not by the judge*]
prueba testimonial oral testimony of the witnesses
puesta en equivalencia (Spa) equity method of accounting
puesto de bolsa (Cos) brokerage firm
puja 1. bid 2. amount by which the previous bid must be raised
punto point, item
punto anterior foregoing item
punto de equilibrio break-even point
punto del orden del día item on the agenda
punto muerto break-even point
puntos dispositivos the operative part of a judgment, the holding
puntos resolutivos the operative part of a judgment, the holding
pupilo ward [*person under the guardianship of a "tutor" (q.v.)*]
purgar to clear of a criminal charge
purgar una pena to serve one's sentence, to "do time"
puro unconditional, absolute
quebrado bankrupt
quebrantamiento breach, violation
quebrantamiento de condena violation of a criminal sentence
quebrantamiento de forma violation of procedural rules by a lower court [*ground for casación*]
quebrantamiento de prisión preventiva escape from prison pending trial
quebranto impositivo (Arg) tax loss
quebrar to go bankrupt

quedar
>**El artículo 54 quedará así** Article 54 shall read as follows
>**Las mejoras quedarán en beneficio del locador.**
>Improvements shall become the property of the landlord [*at the end of the lease*].
>**quedar a salvo** to remain intact
>**Toda mejora que se efectúe quedará en favor del inmueble arrendado.** Any improvement that is made shall become a part of the leased premises [*at the end of the lease*].

queja 1. grievance [*in collective bargaining agreement*] 2. appeal to trial court's supervising judge usually with respect to a procedural issue 3. (Chi) special appeal for denial of justice

quejoso (Mex) the petitioner in an amparo proceeding [*also called the "agraviado"*]

querella criminal complaint filed by the victim [*with the intention of becoming a party to the proceedings. See also "denuncia."*]

querellante complainant [*person filing accusation of a crime*]

querellar judicialmente to prosecute

quiebra bankruptcy
>**quiebra casual** unintentional bankruptcy [*also called "quiebra fortuita"*]
>**quiebra culpable (Ven)** bankruptcy due to bad management
>**quiebra culposa (Col, Mex)** bankruptcy due to bad management
>**quiebra fortuita** unintentional bankruptcy, not due to bad management
>**quiebra fraudulenta** fraudulent bankruptcy
>**quiebra simulada** fraudulent bankruptcy

quina (Chi) short list [*of five names*]

quincena two weeks

quinquenio five-year period

quirografario unsecured

quita y espera de las deudas reduction in the amount of the debts or an extension of time for payment thereof

quórum quorum

rábula shyster, incompetent lawyer

radicación 1. filing 2. residence, domicile
>**radicación de una demanda** filing of a complaint
>**radicación temporal** temporary residence

radicar 1. to file 2. to reside, to be domiciled
>**bienes aquí radicados** property located here
>**radicado en el extranjero** resident abroad
>**radicado en sala** assigned to a panel
>**radicar una acción en un tribunal** to bring a case before a court
>**radicar una demanda** to file a complaint
>**radicar una planilla (Pue)** to file a tax return

radicarse to take up residence

Se radica procedimiento de ejecución. Proceedings to
   enforce the award are opened.

rama judicial (Col) judicial branch, judiciary

Ramo de Rústicas (Mex) Rural Property Section

rapiña 1. violent robbery [*of a person*] 2. violent burglary [*of a
   building*]

raponazo (Col) purse snatching

raponero (Col) purse snatcher

rappel (Spa) volume discount

rapto kidnapping, abduction [*for purposes of rape or marriage*]

ratear 1. to distribute pro rata 2. to pilfer, to pinch

ratero pickpocket, petty thief

ratificar de conformidad to state one's agreement thereto

raya (Mex) pay, wages

razón 1. reason 2. ratio

   razón de circulante current ratio

   razón de liquidez liquidity ratio [*measurement of a company's
      liquidity – examples include the current ratio, acid-test ratio,
      etc.*]

   razón de prueba del ácido acid-test ratio, quick ratio [*most
      liquid current assets divided by current liabilities*]

   razón de solvencia current ratio [*current assets divided by
      current liabilities*]

   razón operativa operating ratio

   razón social partnership name [*Technically, a razón social
      includes the names of the owners, e.g., White & Case, while
      a denominación social does not, e.g. The Coca-Cola
      Company. However, this rule is not always followed in
      practice.*]

reafianzamiento backbond [*a bond of indemnification given to a
   surety*]

reajuste económico economic cutback

realengo (Per) free of liens and encumbrances

   **Los vendedores dejan constancia de que las acciones se
      encuentran realengas.** The sellers certify that the shares are
      free of liens and encumbrances.

realizar 1. to perform, to carry out 2. to sell

   realizar la operación inversa to reverse the transaction

   realizar los bienes to convert the assets into cash

   realizar prácticas predatorias to engage in predatory practices

rebaja

   rebaja de impuesto tax deduction

   rebaja de venta sale discount

   rebaja por cantidad quantity discount

rebeldía contempt

recabar 1. to obtain, to succeed in getting 2. to request

recaer

El nombramiento debe recaer en una persona que haya ejercido el cargo de magistrado. The appointment must go to a person who has served as a judge.

El poder ejecutivo recae en el Presidente de la República. The executive power is vested in the President of the Republic.

recargo surcharge

recargo por diferencia de cambio currency adjustment factor (CAF)

recaudación collection

recaudación arancelaria tariff revenue

recaudación de derechos antidumping collection of antidumping duties

recaudación de impuestos tax revenues, tax receipts

recaudación impositiva tax revenues, tax receipts

recaudación tributaria tax revenues

recaudador collector

recaudador de derechos de aduana customs collector

recaudador de rentas tax collector

recaudo 1. collection 2. supporting document

recaudos probatorios supporting documents, exhibits

recepción

recepción definitiva final acceptance [*in a construction contract*]

recepción provisoria provisional acceptance [*in a construction contract*]

receptación receiving stolen goods

receptador 1. fence [*person who receives stolen goods*] 2. accessory after the fact

receptor (Chi) process server

receptor de rentas tax collector

rechazar to reject, to disallow, to refuse, to turn down

recibir

recibir a prueba to admit as evidence

recibir el emplazamiento to accept service of process

recibirse de abogado to get a law degree, to graduate from law school

recibo receipt

recibo de depósito americano American depositary receipt (ADR) [*The term is often left in English.*]

recibo predial real estate tax receipt

recidivista repeat offender, habitual offender

recinto

recinto aduanal bonded warehouse

recinto fiscal bonded warehouse

recinto fiscalizado (Mex) privately-owned bonded warehouse [*See Art. 14 of Mexico's Ley Aduanera*]

reclamación claim

reclamar to sue for recovery of

reclamo claim

reclusión perpetua life imprisonment

reconocer [*in a contract*] to acknowledge

reconocimiento 1. acknowledgment 2. examination, inspection

    reconocimiento aduanero customs inspection

    reconocimiento judicial judicial examination

    reconocimiento pericial expert examination

reconvención counterclaim

reconvenir to file a counterclaim, to assert a counterclaim

recorte

    recorte de personal staff cutback

    recorte de plantilla staff cutback

    recortes sociales cutback in welfare provisions

rectificación de partida ex parte proceedings to correct errors in vital records

rectificatoria (Bol) amended tax return

recuento físico physical inventory

recurrente petitioner, appellant

recurrido appellee, respondent

recurrir a la vía judicial to resort to litigation

recurso 1. recourse 2. remedy 3. appeal

    recurso aclaratoria de sentencia appeal requesting the trial court judge to explain or clarify his judgment

    recurso contra una resolución an appeal from a decision [*not "against" a decision*]

    recurso de aclaración appeal requesting the trial court judge to explain or clarify his judgment

    recurso de alzada appeal to intermediate appellate court

    recurso de apelación appeal (to a higher court)

    recurso de casación appeal to supreme court

    recurso de hábeas corpus writ of habeas corpus

    recurso de homologación (Col) appeal to court against award of arbitrators

    recurso de inaplicabilidad (Chi) writ of inapplicability [*Art. 80 of the Chilean Constitution. Its purpose is to bring before the full Supreme Court the question of a law's constitutionality as that law is sought to be applied in a particular case. If applying the law would violate the Constitution, the Supreme Court will determine that the law is inapplicable in the case (as opposed to declaring it unconstitutional in all cases).*]

    recurso de queja (Chi) petition in error

    recurso de queja por apelación denegada petition in error because of denial of appeal

recurso de reconsideración motion for reconsideration [*also called "recurso de revocatoria"*]

recurso de reclamación (Mex) appeal of a ruling of the Supreme Court or an appellate court in an amparo proceeding

recurso de reforma motion for rehearing in a criminal trial court

recurso de reposición motion for reconsideration of an interlocutory order (in a civil lawsuit in a court of first instance) [*It is also called a "recurso de reconsideración" and a "recurso de revocatoria." In a criminal lawsuit in a court of first instance, this motion is called a "recurso de reforma" It is called a "recurso de súplica" when it is filed in a civil or criminal lawsuit in an appellate court or the supreme court. In Mexico a "recurso de reposición" is a motion for reconsideration of an appellate judge's decision, while a motion for reconsideration of a trial judge's decision is called a "recurso de revocación."*]

recurso de revisión appeal for review, motion for new trial or hearing

recurso de revocación (Mex) motion for reconsideration of an interlocutory order in a civil lawsuit in a court of first instance [*In other countries this is called a "recurso de reposición," which in Mexico is a motion for reconsideration filed in an appellate court.*]

recurso de revocatoria (Arg) motion for reconsideration of an interlocutory order [*in a civil lawsuit in a court of first instance*]

recurso de súplica motion for reconsideration of an interlocutory order in an appellate court or the supreme court

recurso devolutivo an appeal to a higher court [*as opposed to an appeal to the same judge who issued the ruling*]

recurso extraordinario appeal to the supreme court [*not as of right*]

recurso jerárquico (Arg) appeal filed with a higher administrative authority

recurso legal legal remedy

recurso ordinario appeal as of right [*i.e., an appeal to the intermediate court of appeals, as opposed to an appeal to the supreme court, which has discretion not to allow the appeal*]

recursos de un préstamo proceeds of a loan

recusación

recusación con expresión de causa challenge for cause

recusación de un juez recusal of a judge

recusación de un testigo exception to a witness

recusación sin expresión de causa peremptory challenge [*challenge without stating a reason*]

recusar to recuse, to reject, to challenge, to object to
    recusar jueces to challenge judges
    recusar jurisdicción to decline jurisdiction
redactar to draft, to draw up
redada (Spa) police raid [*at one place*], round-up, dragnet [*at several places*]
redargución de falsedad impugning, challenging as false [*a notarially recorded document*]
redargüir de falsedad to impugn, to challenge as false [*a notarially recorded document*]
redimir una hipoteca to pay off a mortgage
rédito income, yield
    rédito imponible taxable income
reducción reduction
    reducción de plantilla lay-off of staff, downsizing
    reducción general across-the-board reduction
redundar en beneficio de to inure to the benefit of
reembolso 1. reimbursement 2. repayment [*of a loan*] 3. refund
    reembolso de derechos de aduana duty drawback, customs drawback [*a refund, in whole or in part, of import duties or taxes on goods that are later reexported or used in the manufacture of other goods for export*]
    reembolso fiscal tax refund
reexpresión restatement
refaccionar to finance
referencia de auditoría audit trail [*a reference to an underlying source document*]
reforma amendment
    reforma tributaria tax reform
    y sus reformas as amended
refrendar to countersign
    refrendar un pasaporte to stamp a passport
refrendo endorsement, countersignature
refugio fiscal tax shelter
regalía pascual (Dom) Christmas bonus
regente (Mex) mayor of Mexico City [*As of July 1997 the Regente has been replaced by a gobernador.*]
regido e interpretado governed and construed
regidor alderman [*member of the ayuntamiento, the governing body of a municipio*]
régimen 1. regime 2. rules governing
    bajo el régimen del Código Civil under the provisions of the Civil Code
    en régimen de reciprocidad on a reciprocal basis
    régimen arancelario tariff treatment
    régimen conyugal de bienes community property system
    régimen de propiedad horizontal horizontal property regime

Registro Nacional de Población - Unique Population (Clave Única) Registry Code = CURP

régimen de reparto (Arg) state-sponsored retirement savings plan

régimen de una asamblea the rules governing a meeting

régimen de visitas visitation schedule [*for non-custodial parent after a divorce*]

régimen patrimonial community property system

regir 1. to rule 2. to govern [*Note that kings* rule *and laws* govern.]

registrador registrar

registro 1. registry 2. search

registro civil office of vital records

Registro de la Escribanía General de Gobierno (Arg) Registry of Notarially Recorded Contracts Entered into by the State

registro de la propiedad real estate registry

registro de propiedad industrial patent and trademarks office

registro mercantil commercial registry

Registro Oficial (Ecu, Par) Official Gazette

registro público public registry

reglamento regulations [*note that the term is plural in English--see also "la ley y su reglamento"*]

reglamento aduanero customs regulations

Reglamento de Conciliación y Arbitraje de la Cámara de Comercio Internacional Rules of Conciliation and Arbitration of the International Chamber of Commerce

Reglamento de la Ley General de Población (Mex) Immigration Regulations

reglamento de régimen interior rules of procedure

regularización de valores (Spa) restatement of assets for inflation

regularizar una situación to straighten out a situation, to put a situation in order

rehabilitación revalidation [*of an expired patent or industrial design*]

rehabilitación del quebrado discharge in bankruptcy

reincorporación al trabajo reinstatement [*in a job*]

reinstalación (Mex) reinstatement [*in a job*]

reintegrar 1. to repay, to pay off 2. to pay 3. to return [*synonym of "devolver"*] 4. to refund

El préstamo ha sido reintegrado. The loan has been paid off.

reintegro (Pue) tax refund

reintegro acelerado accelerated repayment

reintegro de gastos reimbursement of expenses

reintegro del papel valorado (Per) payment of the stamp tax

reivindicación replevin

reivindicación de patente patent claim

relación 1. relationship 2. ratio 3. report on the case by the "relator" (staff attorney) [*as opposed to having the attorneys present the case to the judges in an "informe"*] 4. list

relación de activo fijo a pasivo a largo plazo fixed-asset to long-term debt ratio

relación de canje de acciones share exchange ratio

relación de causalidad causal connection, cause-and-effect relationship

relación de la utilidad neta al activo total ratio of net income to total assets

relación de lo actuado account of the proceedings

relación de responsabilidades de las fincas list of liens on the lands

relación de trabajo employment relationship, employer/employee relationship

relación global comprehensive report

relación laboral employment relationship, employer/employee relationship

relación P/C debt/equity ratio [*stands for "pasivo/capital"*]

relación precio-utilidades price/earnings ratio [*"P/E ratio"*]

relación procesal relationship between the parties to a case

relator staff attorney

relevar de una obligación to release from an obligation

relevo release

rematador auctioneer

remate auction [*also called "almoneda" and "subasta"*]

  remate judicial judicial auction

rematista (Per) auctioneer

remesa

  remesas del exterior remittances from abroad

  remesas en divisas foreign currency remittances

remisión de la deuda release from or forgiveness or cancellation of a debt

remito (Arg) delivery note [*called an "albarán" in Spain*]

remuneración compensation

  remuneración mínima vital (Per) minimum wage

  remuneraciones al personal employee compensation

  remuneraciones pendientes de pago accrued salaries and wages

  remuneraciones y beneficios sociales salaries and employee benefits

  remuneraciones y deudas sociales salaries and employee benefits

rendimiento 1. performance 2. return

  rendimiento de un empleado an employee's performance

  rendimiento sobre activos return on assets (ROA)

  rendimiento sobre capital return on equity (ROE)

renta 1. income, revenue 2. (Mex) rent

  renta anticipada advances from customers [*Note that "prepaid income" is not a correct term because an item should not be* called *"income"* until earned, i.e., when goods are delivered or services are rendered.]

renta corrida accrued income
renta discrecional discretionary income
renta disponible disposable income
renta fija fixed income
renta fiscal taxable income
renta gravable taxable income
renta variable variable income
rentas públicas government revenue
rentabilidad profitability
rentable profitable
renuencia reluctance, unwillingness
renuncia 1. resignation [*from a position*] 2. waiver
renuncia a derechos a waiver of rights
renunciar 1. to resign [*from a position*] 2. to waive 3. to relinquish, to give up
renunciar a la apelación to waive one's right to appeal
renunciar a un derecho to waive a right
renunciar a un puesto to resign from a position, to quit a job
renunciar a una herencia to renounce an inheritance
renunciando al fuero de su domicilio y a cualquier fuero que pudiera corresponderle en razón de su domicilio o por cualquier otro motivo waiving his right to be tried in the courts of his domicile and waiving the jurisdiction of any other forum that he may be entitled to claim because of his domicile or for any other reason
renunciatorio person in whose favor an inheritance is renounced
reo defendant
declarado reo (Chi) committed for trial
reparaciones locativas repairs that are the tenant's responsibility
repartición pública (Arg) government agency
reparto
reparto de dividendos distribution of dividends
reparto de tierras (Mex) distribution of agricultural lands to ejidos
reparto de utilidades distribution of profits
repertorio de jurisprudencia reporter [*published volume of decisions by a court or group of courts*]
repetición action for restitution
repetir to recover a payment made, to "get one's money back"
repetir el monto to recover the amount
repetir el pago to recover the payment
reportado repurchaser [*in a "reporto"*]
reportador repurchasee [*in a "reporto"*]
reportar
reportar gravámenes to be subject to liens

reportar utilidad neta to report net income

reporto (Gua, Mex) repurchase agreement, "repo" [*seller agrees to repurchase securities from the buyer at a specified time*]

representación

    acreditar su representación to prove his authority

    esta representación social federal (Mex) *phrase used to refer to a governmental entity previously mentioned in the document without having to repeat that entity's name*

representada (su) his principal, his client, the person or company he represents

representativo

    las acciones representativas del capital social the shares representing the capital stock

    los títulos representativos de las acciones the certificates representing the shares

reputar to estimate, to judge, to consider

requerimiento request

res nullius (Lat) thing without an owner

resarcible recoverable

resarcimiento de daños recovery of damages

rescatar to repossess

rescindir un contrato to rescind a contract

rescisión rescission [*Note that Peruvian law distinguishes between "rescisión" (rescission), which means terminating a contract on grounds that existed at the time the contract was entered into (such as duress, fraud), and "resolución" (termination), which means terminating a contract on grounds that arose after it was entered into (such as breach).*]

reserva reserve

    reserva de dominio reservation of property rights

    reserva de prueba documental safekeeping of documentary evidence [*usually in the court's safe*]

    reserva estatutaria voluntary reserve [*pursuant to the company's bylaws--Note that "statutory reserve" is "reserva legal."*]

    reserva legal statutory reserve

    reserva libre voluntary reserve

    reserva oculta hidden reserve [*amount by which owners' equity has been understated*]

    reserva para baja de valores (Mex) reserve for depreciation of securities

    reserva para contingencias contingent reserve, reserve for contingencies

    reserva para cuentas incobrables allowance for bad debts

    reserva para eventualidades contingent reserve, reserve for contingencies

reserva para la renovación de los bienes de uso (Arg)
reserve for replacement of vehicles and equipment
reserva reglamentaria (Chi) statutory reserve [*called "reserva legal" in other countries*]
reserva social (Chi) voluntary reserve
resguardar to safeguard
resguardo 1. receipt 2. collateral
   resguardo aduanal customs control
   resguardo de préstamo collateral for a loan
   resguardo negociable marketable collateral
resolución 1. resolution 2. termination [*of a contract*]
   resolución del contrato termination of the contract [*see also "rescisión"*]
   resolución exenta (Chi) decision that is exempt from review as to constitutionality and legality [*the review is called "toma de razón"*]
   resolución judicial court order, judicial decision
   resolución ministerial (Per) regulations issued by a particular division of a ministry
   Resolución Miscelánea (Mex) annual temporary tax regulations
   resolución suprema (Per) regulations issued by the ministries [*They differ from "decretos supremos" in that they need not be brought before the entire Cabinet and do not bear the President's signature, but only his initials.*]
resolver 1. to decide 2. to adopt resolutions
   resolver sobre X to adopt resolutions on X
responder to be liable
   Responden hasta por el monto de su aportación. They are liable up to the amount of their contribution.
responsabilidad 1. responsibility 2. liability
   responsabilidad civil civil liability
   responsabilidad contractual contractual liability
   responsabilidad cuasidelictual liability for unintentional torts
   responsabilidad del hecho de otro vicarious liability
   responsabilidad delictual liability for intentional torts
   responsabilidad extracontractual tort liability
   responsabilidad objetiva strict liability
   responsabilidad profesional professional responsibility
   responsabilidad solidaria joint and several liability
responsabilizar a alguien de algo to lay the blame on someone for something
responsable 1. responsible 2. liable
   responsable en forma solidaria jointly and severally liable
   responsable en primer término primarily liable
   responsable en segundo término secondarily liable
resultado result

resultado acumulado por actualización restatement of retained earnings

resultado cambiario exchange gain or loss

resultado de explotación operating profit or loss

resultado extraordinario extraordinary item [*on a balance sheet – also called "partida extraordinaria"*]

resultado fiscal tax result [*tax profit less tax losses from previous years*]

resultado operativo operating profit or loss

resultado por exposición a la inflación restatement for inflation

resultado por posición monetaria (Mex) restatement for inflation [*referred to as "resultado por exposición a la inflación" in other countries*]

resultado por traslación (Per) translation result

resultados profit or loss

resultados contables book earnings

resultados financieros financial performance

resultandos the facts [*the part of the judgment that summarizes the facts of the case*]

retención de impuestos tax withholding

retención en la fuente withholding at the source

retorno

retorno de las inversiones return on investments

retorno sobre ventas (Col) return on sales

retornos de escala returns to scale [*the relation between a proportional change in inputs to a productive process and the resulting proportional change in output*]

retractación de una oferta withdrawal of an offer

retracto

retracto convencional contractual right to recover a thing sold to someone else [*see Art. 1534 of the Venezuelan Civil Code*]

retracto legal statutory right to recover a thing sold to someone else

retrato portrait

retrato hablado (Mex, Ven) composite picture [*of a suspect*]

retrato robot (Spa) composite picture [*of a suspect*]

reunión

reunión de prensa press conference

reunión del directorio board meeting

revaluación (Mex) adjustment for inflation

revelación disclosure

revisión

revisión adhesiva concurrency by the appellee in the appellant's appeal

revisión de cuentas audit

revisión especial due diligence review
revisor fiscal (Col, Cos) statutory auditor
revista jurídica law review
revocación 1. revocation [*of a law or power of attorney*] 2. reversal [*of a judgment*]
    revocación de administradores removal of board members
revocar 1. to remove [*a person*] 2. to revoke [*a law, a power of attorney*] 3. to reverse, set aside, overturn, vacate [*a judgment*]
rezago 1. **(Mex)** backlog of cases 2. surplus 3. goods seized at customs
riesgo 1. risk 2. exposure
    riesgo bancario credit risk, credit exposure [*the chance of loss through nonperformance of a contract or nonpayment of debt*]
    riesgo cambiario foreign exchange risk
    riesgo de cambio foreign exchange risk
    riesgo del trabajo occupational hazard
    riesgo fiscal tax exposure
    riesgo-país country risk [*the risk of non-repayment of loans by most or all economic agents in a country arising from political, economic, legal or social factors in that country*]
    riesgo profesional occupational hazard
riguroso dominio ownership in fee simple
robo theft, robbery
    robo a mano armada armed robbery
    robo calificado aggravated robbery
rodados (Arg) vehicles [*as an item on a balance sheet*]
rol único tributario (RUT) (Chi) taxpayer I.D. number
rotación turnover
    rotación de activo (Per) ratio of gross sales to total assets
    rotación de cuentas por cobrar trade receivables turnover
    rotación de inventarios inventory turnover
rubricado signed and sealed
rueda trading session [*on the stock exchange*]
    rueda de prensa press conference
    rueda de presos (Spa) police lineup [*called "confrontación" in Mexico*]
rústico rural
saber y entender knowledge and belief
sacar
    sacar en paz y a salvo to hold harmless
    sacar provecho to reap a benefit
sala 1. panel [*of judges*] 2. division [*of a court*]
    Sala Cuarta (Cos) Constitutional Chamber of the Costa Rican Supreme Court
    sala de audiencias del juzgado courtroom
    sala de despacho del tribunal (Ven) courtroom

sala de lo civil civil division
sala de lo penal criminal division
sala de vacaciones pro tem court [*hears cases while the court is in recess*]
sala del juzgado courtroom
salario wages [*received by workers, as opposed to salary (received by professionals)*]
salario justo fair wage
salario mínimo minimum wage
salario mínimo interprofesional (Spa) minimum wage
salario mínimo vital (Ecu) minimum wage
salario mínimo vital y móvil (Arg) index-linked minimum wage
salario mixto wages paid partly in cash and partly in kind
salario neto take-home pay
salario por hora hourly wage
salario social social improvements in lieu of wage increases
salarios caídos backpay
saldar
saldar existencias to sell off inventory
saldar la deuda to pay off the debt
saldo balance
saldo a favor credit balance, positive balance
saldo acreedor credit balance
saldo arrastrado balance brought forward
saldo deudor debit balance
saldo en contra balance owed, negative balance
saldo final closing balance
saldo impago unpaid balance
saldo inicial opening balance
saldo insoluto unpaid balance
saldo pendiente balance outstanding
saldo positivo credit balance
saldo que pasa balance brought forward
saldo traspasado balance carried forward
saldos activos de corresponsales due to correspondents
saldos pasivos de corresponsales due from correspondents
salida
salida a bolsa public offering, going public
salida de bolsa going private
salida de capital capital outflow
salidas de almacén warehouse issues
salidas de caja cash disbursements
salir de bolsa (Spa) to take private
salvamento de voto (Col, Ven) dissenting opinion
salvando las eventualidades barring unforeseen circumstances

salvar
> **salvar las palabras enmendadas y tachadas** to certify the corrections in the document
>
> **salvar voto (Col, Ven)** to dissent from the majority opinion

salvedad de negocio en marcha going concern qualification

salvo aviso unless notified

salvo buen cobro (de un cheque) subject to the due payment (thereof)

salvo buen fin subject to collection

salvo error u omisión errors and omissions excepted

salvo indicación contraria unless otherwise provided

salvo pacto en contrario unless otherwise agreed

sana crítica good judgment [*evaluation of evidence by the judge using his good judgment, as opposed to assigning the weight that is given to evidence by statute. Also called "libre apreciación razonada." See also "apreciación probatoria."*]

sanción sanction, penalty
> **sanción administrativa** administrative sanction
>
> **sanción de las leyes** signing of a statute into law by the head of state

sancionar una ley to sign a statute into law [*as opposed to vetoing it*]

saneamiento 1. write-off, write-down 2. cleaning up the balance sheet 3. putting on sound footing 4. stabilization 5. bailout [*provision of financial aid to a failing company*]
> **saneamiento de la economía** revival of the economy
>
> **saneamiento para el caso de evicción** warranty of title
>
> **saneamiento para el caso de vicios ocultos** warranty against hidden defects
>
> **saneamiento procesal (Per)** correction of procedural defects [*Under Peruvian law, before proceeding to the preliminary hearing, the judge must make sure that he has the express or implied agreement of the litigants that they will not try to hold up lawsuit at a later point by alleging a procedural defect. If the judge finds an excusable defect, he will give the parties time to correct it; if he finds an inexcusable defect, he will dismiss the lawsuit immediately.*]

sanear 1. to correct or cure errors or mistakes 2. to remove encumbrances

sano de juicio of sound mind

seccional (Arg) police precinct

Secretaría Ministry [*The term can also be translated "Secretariat," but that sounds unnatural in English. However, the official translation of NAFTA uses the word "Secretariat."*]
> **Secretaría de Comercio y Fomento Industrial (Mex)** Ministry of Commerce and Industrial Development

Secretaría de Gobernación (Mex) Ministry of the Interior [*Its functions parallel those of the U.S. Immigration and Naturalization Service, including issuance of visas and deportation of aliens.*]

Secretaría de Hacienda y Crédito Público (Mex) Ministry of the Treasury and Public Credit [*Its functions parallel those of the Internal Revenue Service and the Department of the Treasury, among other functions.*]

secretario 1. clerk 2. (Mex) cabinet minister

secretario accidental (Ven) interim clerk [*on duty while the regular clerk is ill or on vacation*]

secretario actuario court clerk

secretario de actas court clerk

secretario de acuerdos court clerk

secretario de estado (Mex) cabinet minister

secretario judicial court clerk

secretario suplente deputy clerk

secretario titular regular clerk

secreto

secreto bancario bank secrecy

secreto de sumario confidentiality of criminal investigations [*such that the accused person's attorney does not have access to them*]

secreto industrial trade secret

secreto profesional attorney-client privilege

secreto profesional médico doctor-patient privilege

secuela

durante la secuela del procedimiento during the course of the procedure

durante la secuela del recurso during the course of the appeal

secuestro 1. seizure 2. kidnapping, abduction 3. sequestration

secuestro convencional sequestration by agreement [*depositing of property in dispute with a neutral third party*]

secuestro de bienes seizure of goods [*in a "secuestro" the property is taken away from the debtor, whereas in an "embargo," the property remains in the debtor's possession*]

secuestro de un avión hijacking

secuestro precautorio preventive seizure [*also called "secuestro provisional"*]

sede 1. seat 2. principal place of business, corporate headquarters

El tribunal tiene su sede en Caracas. The court sits in Caracas.

sedicente so-called

segmento bajo the lower end of the market

seguimiento follow-up

según according to, pursuant to

según consta del acuerdo del directorio as evidenced by a resolution of the Board of Directors

según dispone la Constitución en su artículo 12 as provided by Article 12 of the Constitution

según el caso as the case may be

según todo consta en el documento as is all set forth in the document

seguridad jurídica the rule of law, legal certainty

seguro insurance

seguro a todo riesgo all-risk insurance

seguro colectivo group insurance

seguro contra riesgos casualty insurance

seguro de calderas boiler explosion insurance

seguro de cambio exchange rate hedge

seguro de caución contingency insurance

seguro de cobertura amplia comprehensive insurance, all-risk insurance

seguro de combinado familiar (Arg) homeowners' insurance

seguro de crédito a la exportación export credit insurance

seguro de desempleo unemployment insurance

seguro de incapacidad disability insurance

seguro de invalidez disability insurance

seguro de lucro cesante business interruption insurance

seguro de responsabilidad civil liability insurance

seguro de responsabilidad civil de fabricantes product liability insurance

seguro de responsabilidad profesional errors and omissions insurance [*also called "E&O insurance"*]

seguro de uso y ocupación business interruption insurance [*formerly known as "use and occupancy insurance"*]

seguro de vida colectivo group life insurance

seguro de vida entera whole life insurance

seguro dotal endowment insurance [*also called "seguro de vida dotal"*]

seguros anticipados insurance paid in advance

seguros no devengados unexpired insurance

sellado de actuación (Arg) stamp tax on documents in a lawsuit

sello 1. seal 2.stamp

sello de autorizar authenticating seal

sello fechador date stamp

sello fiscal revenue stamp

sello para autorizar authenticating seal

semana bursátil financial week

Semanario Judicial de la Federación (SJF) (Mex) Supreme Court Reports [*divided into "épocas" - series*]

semanero (Mex) judge who presides for one week

semejante en grado de confusión confusingly similar [*trademark*]

semestral semi-annual

senderista (Per) member of the Sendero Luminoso

sentencia judgment, ruling, decision [*Note that "sentence" in English is "condena" in Spanish. A sentencia in Spanish is usually made up of four parts: (1) the "encabezamiento," stating the date and identifying the court, parties, attorneys, and cause of action; (2) the "resultandos" or "fundamentos de hecho," i.e., a statement of the facts; (3) the "considerandos" or "fundamentos de derecho," which set forth the legal grounds on which the judgment is based; and (4) the "fallo" or "resolutoria," i.e., the holding.*]

> **sentencia absolutoria** 1. [*in a civil case*] judgment for the defendant 2. [*in a criminal case*] acquittal, verdict of not guilty

> **sentencia complementaria (Mex)** judgment on appeal amplifying lower court's judgment

> **sentencia condenatoria** 1. [*in a civil case*] judgment for the plaintiff 2. [*in a criminal case*] guilty verdict

> **sentencia constitutiva** judgment that establishes, modifies or abolishes a right [*such as a paternity suit*]

> **sentencia de antología** landmark opinion, landmark decision

> **sentencia de condena** 1. [*in a civil case*] judgment for the plaintiff 2. [*in a criminal case*] guilty verdict [*also called "sentencia condenatoria"; opposite: sentencia absolutoria*]

> **sentencia de divorcio** divorce decree

> **sentencia de fondo** judgment on the merits

> **sentencia de forma** judgment on a question of procedure

> **sentencia de garantías (Mex)** judgment in an amparo proceeding

> **sentencia de reclusión perpetua** life sentence

> **sentencia de remate** order of judicial sale

> **sentencia declarativa** declaratory judgment [*simply declares the rights of the parties or expresses the opinion of the court on a question of law, without ordering any specific action*]

> **sentencia declaratoria** declaratory judgment [*simply declares the rights of the parties or expresses the opinion of the court on a question of law, without ordering any specific action*]

> **sentencia definitiva** final judgment

> **sentencia ejecutoriada** final and binding judgment (res judicata), final adjudication

> **sentencia en libertad (Mex)** probation

> **sentencia firme** final and binding judgment [*synonym of "sentencia ejecutoriada"*]

> **sentencia incidental** interlocutory judgment

> **sentencia interlocutoria** interlocutory judgment

> **sentencia irrecurrible** unappealable judgment

> **sentencia meramente declaratoria (Mex)** declaratory judgment

> **sentencia ordenatoria (Mex)** opinion on an issue of procedure

sentencia preservativa (Mex) judgment approving temporary injunctive relief

sentenciado en libertad (Mex) convict on parole

seña (Arg) deposit, down payment

separación

    separación de bienes separate ownership of property during marriage [*as opposed to a "sociedad conyugal" (q.v.)*]

    separación de cuerpos legal separation [*of a married couple*]

separo (Mex) holding cell

serenazgo (Per) night watchman services

servicio service

    Servicio de Impuestos Internos (Chi) Chilean Internal Revenue Service

    Servicio Nacional de Impuestos Internos (Bol) Bolivian Internal Revenue Service

    servicios públicos utilities

servidores públicos public servants

servidumbre easement

    servidumbre activa affirmative easement

    servidumbre afirmativa affirmative easement

    servidumbre aparente apparent easement

    servidumbre continua continuous easement

    servidumbre de acueducto easement to run an aqueduct through

    servidumbre de desagüe drainage easement

    servidumbre de paso right of way

    servidumbre de tránsito right of way

    servidumbre negativa negative easement

    servidumbre pasiva negative easement

    servidumbre positiva affirmative easement

    servidumbre real appurtenant easement

    servidumbre voluntaria easement by agreement of the parties

sesión 1. session 2. meeting

    sesión a puerta cerrada closed session

    sesión bursátil trading session [*on the stock exchange*]

    sesión de remates trading session [*on the stock exchange*]

    sesión del Consejo de Administración board meeting [*Note that "session" would be a mistranslation in this context.*]

    sesión plenaria plenary session

sesionar to meet

    El Comité sesionará válidamente con la asistencia de la totalidad de sus miembros. A quorum shall be present at meetings of the Committee if all of its members are in attendance.

sevicia extreme cruelty

sexenio (Mex) Mexican President's six-year term of office

sicario hired assassin, hired gunman, hitman

siefore (Mex) mutual fund specializing in retirement funds [*short for "sociedad de inversión especializada en fondos para el retiro"*]

signos distintivos distinctive marks

sin ánimo de lucro non-profit, not for profit

sin causa without cause, without consideration

sin excepción legal duly qualified [*referring to the witnesses of a will*]

sin lugar not granted, refused, rejected

sin perjuicio de lo anterior without prejudice to the foregoing, the foregoing notwithstanding

sin personalidad jurídica unincorporated

sinalagmático bilateral

sincerarse ante el juez to justify one's conduct to the judge

sindicación unionization

sindicado (Col, Ecu, Ven) the accused, the defendant

sindicato

    sindicato bancario bank syndicate, consortium of banks

    sindicato de colocación underwriting syndicate

    sindicato de empresa company union [*formed by workers at the same company*]

    sindicato de oficios varios mixed union [*formed by workers in various occupations*]

    sindicato gremial craft union [*formed by workers in the same trade*]

    sindicato industrial industrial union [*formed by workers in the same industry*]

    sindicato único mixed union [*includes both blue-collar and white-collar workers*]

síndico 1. trustee in bankruptcy **2. (Arg, Par, Uru)** statutory auditor, statutory examiner [*This person is appointed by the shareholders to oversee the acts of the board of directors. There is no equivalent in U.S. law.*] **3.** legal representative on a municipal council [*also called "síndico municipal"*]

    síndico concursal (Arg) trustee in bankruptcy

    síndico en la quiebra receiver, trustee in bankruptcy

siniestro claim, loss, casualty

    siniestros de la actividad de seguros claims on insurance activities

    siniestros incurridos claims incurred

sistema system

    sistema de acumulación accrual basis accounting [*recognition of revenue when earned and expenses when incurred even if cash has not yet been received or paid. The opposite system is called "cash basis accounting."*]

    sistema de anotaciones book entry positions

    sistema sincronístico instantáneo system whereby a new law takes effect everywhere in a country at the same time [*as* *opposed to "sistema sucesivo," whereby it takes effect in a staggered fashion, depending on distance from the capital city*]

sistema sucesivo system whereby a law takes effect in a staggered fashion throughout the country, depending on distance from the capital city

situación

    situación financiera financial position

    situación jurídica legal status

so pena de under penalty of

soborno bribery [*of a witness, as opposed to "cohecho," which is bribery of a public official*]

sobrecanon (Per) additional tax paid for using or acquiring a public asset

sobrecartar to reissue a court order in writing [*because it was not published or complied with the first time around*]

sobregirar una cuenta to overdraw an account

sobreprecio surcharge

sobreseer 1. to stay 2. to dismiss

sobreseimiento dismissal of proceedings, discontinuance

    sobreseimiento libre dismissal with prejudice

    sobreseimiento provisional dismissal without prejudice

sobresueldo bonus

sobretasa surcharge

social 1. pertaining to a company or partnership 2. labor-related, pertaining to relationships between management and labor

sociedad *This term can mean either "partnership" or "corporation" depending on the context. There is no such generic term in English.*

    sociedad anónima corporation

    sociedad anónima abierta (Chi, Per) "open corporation" [*type of publicly held corporation*]

    sociedad anónima cerrada (Chi) closely held corporation

    sociedad anónima de accionario difundido (Per) diversified ownership corporation [*type of publicly held corporation*]

    sociedad anónima de capital autorizado (SACA) (Ven) closed-end stock corporation [*A company whose subscribed capital is less than the authorized capital and whose shareholders may authorize the administrators to increase the subscribed capital by issuing new shares, up to the limit authorized in the bylaws.*]

    sociedad anónima de capital variable (Mex) open-end stock corporation

    sociedad anónima inscrita de capital abierto (SAICA) (Ven) open-end registered stock corporation [*Less than 50% of the stock belongs to a group of shareholders whose maximum* *investment is equivalent to a determined percentage of the capital.*]

sociedad anónima laboral (Spa) employee-owned company [*similar to an ESOP in the US. 85% of full-time employees must be shareholders and own at least half of the company's stock.*]

sociedad civil professional partnership, non-trading partnership [*There is no such thing as a partnership governed by the Civil Code in the United States, and consequently, there is no such thing as a "civil company" or "civil partnership." This form is used in Spanish-speaking countries primarily by professionals such as lawyers and accountants.*]

sociedad colectiva (Arg, Gua, Per, Spa) general partnership

sociedad comanditaria limited partnership

sociedad comanditaria por acciones partnership limited by shares

sociedad comanditaria simple (Spa) limited partnership

sociedad comercial corporation or business corporation

sociedad controladora holding company

sociedad conyugal community property of husband and wife, joint ownership of property by husband and wife [*as opposed to "separación de bienes" (q.v.)*]

sociedad de capital corporation

sociedad de capital e industria (Arg) a type of limited partnership in which one or more partners invest money and are liable for partnership debts, and one or more partners invest services and are liable only to the extent of undistributed partnership profits

sociedad de compensación y liquidación (Per) securities clearing and settlement company

sociedad de contrapartida (Spa) market maker

sociedad de economía mixta partially state-owned corporation

sociedad de gananciales community property of husband and wife, joint ownership of property by husband and wife

sociedad de hecho de facto corporation

sociedad de información crediticia (Mex) credit bureau, credit-reporting agency

sociedad de inversión (Mex) mutual fund

sociedad de inversión mobiliaria (Spa) security investment company

sociedad de personas partnership

sociedad de responsabilidad limitada (Arg, Mex, Per, Spa) limited liability company [*abbreviated as "S. de R. L." in Mex, "SRL" in Arg, and "SRLtda." in Peru*]

sociedad de tasación (Spa) rating agency [*such as Standards & Poors*]

sociedad dominante (Spa) parent company

sociedad en comandita por acciones (Arg, Mex, Per) partnership limited by shares

sociedad en comandita simple (Arg, Cos, Gua, Mex, Per) limited partnership

sociedad en nombre colectivo (Mex) general partnership

sociedad financiera de objeto limitado (Mex) non-bank bank [*referred to in Spanish as "sofoles"*]

sociedad mandante company granting a power of attorney

sociedad mercantil corporation or business corporation

sociedad mutualista provident society

sociedad nacional de crédito (Mex) government-controlled development bank [*such as Nacional Financiera SNC*]

socio 1. partner [*when referring to the owner of a partnership*] 2. shareholder [*when referring to the owner of a corporation*] 3. partner or shareholder [*when referring to the owner of any sociedad*]

  socio capitalista silent partner [*furnishes capital but no services*]

  socio industrial working partner [*furnishes services but no capital*]

  socio único sole shareholder

  socios o no who may but need not be shareholders

solar lot, plot of land

solicitante petitioner, applicant

solicitar en sede judicial to sue for, to file a lawsuit with respect to

solidariamente severally

solidaridades mutual interests

solidarizarse con to side with

solutio indebiti (Lat) payment of what is not due

solvencia (Ven) certificate of real estate tax payment [*required for any subsequent transaction involving that real estate*]

  solvencia económica financial solvency, credit rating, credit standing

  solvencia moral integrity, good character

solventar la deuda to pay off the debt

someterse a la competencia de los tribunales de la República Mexicana to submit to the jurisdiction of the courts of the Republic of Mexico

sometimiento 1. subjection 2. submission

  sometimiento expreso a la competencia express consent to jurisdiction

  sometimiento tácito a la competencia implied consent to jurisdiction

soplón whistleblower

sorprender la buena fe de alguien (Arg) to mislead someone

sorteo 1. random selection 2. sweepstakes

  sorteo de asuntos distribution of caseloads [*to various judges*]

S.S. Excma. – The Honorable Court

sospechoso (el) the suspect
speuas (Mex) nationwide electronic transfer system [*short for "Sistema de Pagos Electrónicos de Uso Ampliado"*]
su Señoría Your Honor
subarrendador sublessor
subarrendar to sublet
subarrendatario sublessee
subarriendo sublease
subasta auction
    subasta a la baja Dutch auction [*a competitive bidding technique sometimes used in U.S. securities markets, whereby the lowest price necessary to sell the entire amount of securities offered becomes the price at which all securities are sold*]
    subasta pública public auction
subcontratista subcontractor
subcontrato subcontract
subcuentas subsidiary accounts
sublema (Uru) faction [*in a political party*]
subproductos by-products
subrogación subrogation
subsanar 1. to repair 2. to correct (an error) 3. to cure (a breach) 4. to compensate (for damages)
    subsanar el incumplimiento del contrato to cure a breach of the contract
subsecretario assistant secretary, undersecretary
subsidiariamente alternatively, in the alternative
substitución
    substitución cuasipupilar designation of a remainderman to take the place of an heir who is mentally ill [*also called "substitución ejemplar"*]
    substitución de heredero designation of a remainderman
    substitución ejemplar designation of a remainderman to take the place of an heir who is mentally ill [*also called "substitución cuasipupilar"*]
    substitución fideicomisaria creation of a life estate and a remainder [*which is illegal*]
    substitución pupilar designation of a trustee for a protective trust to benefit a minor
    substitución recíproca designation of heirs by reason of reciprocal wills
    substitución vulgar appointment of a remainderman whose estate vests if the prior holder cannot or does not wish to inherit
substituir to replace
subsunción jurídica applying the law to the facts of the case
subvención subsidy

subvención a la exportación export subsidy
subvencionar to subsidize
suceder
    suceder a título particular to take by special right
    suceder a título universal to take by general right
sucesión 1. estate 2. succession
    sucesión forzosa succession required by law
    sucesión intestada intestate succession
    sucesión legítima intestate succession
    sucesión testamentaria testamentary succession
sucursal branch
sueldo salary [*received by professionals, as opposed to wages*]
    sueldo anual complementario (SAC) (Arg) annual bonus
    sueldo base base salary
    sueldo vital (Chi) minimum wage
    sueldos y gratificaciones salaries and bonuses
sufragar los gastos to defray the expenses
sufragio efectivo, no reelección (Mex) "Real Democracy, No
Reelection." [*This slogan was the battle cry of the Mexican
Revolution, which began in 1910. The phrase "no reelección"
refers to Porfirio Díaz, president at the time, who was in his sixth
term. Under the current constitution, Mexican presidents are
allowed to serve only <u>one</u> six-year term called a "sexenio". They
cannot be reelected.*]
sujeto subject
    sujeto activo [*del impuesto*] tax collector
    sujeto del delito penal party to the crime
    sujeto del derecho legal person
    sujeto pasivo [*del impuesto*] taxpayer
sumariado under investigation
sumariar to subject to an investigation
sumario 1. investigation stage of a criminal proceeding [*The "fase
de sumario" is also known as the "fase de instrucción." It is
followed by the "fase de plenario" (the trial) if the investigation
reveals that there are grounds for prosecution.*] 2. summary [*one-
line summary of the nature of the document being filed—referred
to as a "sumilla" in Peru*]
    sumario de supuestos summary of assumptions
sumilla (Per) summary
superávit surplus
    superávit de capital capital surplus [*shareholders' equity in
    excess of the par value of capital stock*]
    superávit de la balanza comercial trade surplus
    superávit en cuenta corriente current account surplus
    superávit ganado earned surplus
    superávit pagado paid-in surplus

superávit por aportación de acciones revaluation of paid-in capital

superávit por revaluación restated surplus

superávit por valuación surplus from appraisal

superávit reservado appropriated surplus

suplencia de la queja deficiente (Mex) court's authority to correct errors or deficiencies in an amparo petition

suplicatorio letters rogatory [*request from a lower judge to one of higher rank—a request to a judge of equal rank is called an "exhorto" and a request to a judge of lower rank is called an "orden" or a "despacho"*]

suposición de valimiento con funcionarios (Ven) false claim of influence over officials [*see Art. 77 of the Ley Orgánica de Salvaguarda del Patrimonio Público*]

supradicho aforesaid, above mentioned

Suprema Corte de Justicia (Dom, Mex, Uru) Supreme Court

supremacía del derecho the rule of law

supuesto supposition

    supuesto lo anterior in view of the foregoing

supuestos macroeconómicos macroeconomic forecasts

surtir efectos to take effect, to become effective, to produce results

suscribir una póliza de seguro to take out an insurance policy

susodicho aforementioned

suspender

    suspender la sesión to adjourn the meeting

    suspender un juicio to stay a trial

suspensión

    suspensión cautelar de una ley suspension of a law until its constitutionality is determined

    suspensión de ejecución stay of enforcement

    suspensión de garantías suspension of civil liberties

    suspensión de oficio (Mex) official suspension of an act in an amparo proceeding [*This is one of two types of "suspensión del acto reclamado" (q.v.). This type is comparable to the injunctive relief sought by way of habeas corpus in the U.S. This suspension may be issued by order of a judge without an adversary hearing upon the preliminary showing by the plaintiff or a friend or relative that the act complained of threatens death, deportation or other acts proscribed by Article 22 of the Mexican Constitution.*]

    suspensión de pagos voluntary bankruptcy petition [*equivalent to Chapter 11 in the US*]

    suspensión del acto reclamado (Mex) suspension of the act complained of in an amparo proceeding [*This is a type of injunctive relief in an amparo proceeding whereby the acts of the respondent authority are enjoined or suspended until a final judgment on the amparo is reached.*]

suspensión provisional preliminary injunction of an act [*until a full evidentiary hearing determines whether the suspensión should be "definitiva" (permanent) or be dissolved.*]

suspensión provisional de la instancia provisional stay of proceedings

suspenso (Mex) the debtor in the context of "suspensión de pagos"

sustanciación hearing a case, trying a case

para la sustanciación y fallo de los negocios urgentes durante las vacaciones for hearing and deciding urgent matters while the court is in recess

sustanciar to try a case

sustituir to replace

con facultades de sustituir este poder revocar sustituciones y hacer otras de nuevo with full power of substitution, revocation and delegation

tabelión notary public

tablilla 1. (Pue) automobile license plate 2. (Cub) bulletin board for announcements

tabulador wage scale

tachadura erasure, obliteration

tachar testigos to challenge witnesses, to impeach witnesses

tachas de los testigos impeachment of witnesses

tácita reconducción extension of the term of a lease by operation of law

talonario (Chi, Spa) checkbook

talón 1. stub 2. (Spa) check

talón bancario (Spa) cashier's check

talón conformado (Spa) certified check

talón de ventanilla (Spa) counter check

talón registrado (Spa) registered check

tanto copy [*of a document*]

tanto de culpa excerpt from the record of a civil proceeding that is used to show guilt and thus bring a criminal proceeding

taquígrafo court reporter

tareas propias de la función duties incidental to the office

tarifa

tarifa aduanal customs tariff

tarifa arancelaria tariff schedule

tarifa para retención mensual monthly withholding rate

tarifas por día per diem rates

tarjar (Chi, Per) to cross out

tarjetas de almacén warehouse quality control cards

tasa 1. rate 2. tax

tasa activa lending rate

tasa de cambio exchange rate

tasa de contribución (Pue) tax rate

tasa de descuento discount rate

tasa de desempleo unemployment rate
tasa de incumplimiento default rate
tasa de interés interbancaria de equilibrio (TIIE) equilibrium interbank interest rate (EIIR)
tasa de interés ordinaria ordinary interest rate
tasa de interés pasiva borrowing rate
tasa de rendimiento (de una obligación) coupon rate
tasa interna de retorno internal rate of return
tasa judicial court filing fee
tasa límite bound rate
tasa nominal nominal rate
tasa pasiva borrowing rate
tasa testigo benchmark rate, reference rate
tasas y gastos fees and costs
tasación appraisal
tasación de costas assessment of court costs
tasación pericial expert appraisal
tasador appraiser
tasar 1. to appraise 2. to limit
tasar la comida to ration food
tasar la libertad to restrict freedom
tasar los precios to regulate prices
taxativamente 1. specifically 2. exhaustively, restrictively
tecnología technology
tecnología de punta advanced technology, state-of-the art technology
tecnología de vanguardia state-of-the-art technology
tecnología objeto de licencia licensed technology
tecnología reservada proprietary technology
temerario 1. reckless 2. frivolous, unjustified, vexatious [*when applied to litigation*]
temeridad 1. recklessness 2. malicious prosecution, abuse of process, frivolous litigation [*synonym of "dolo procesal"*]
tenedor holder
tenedor legítimo holder in due course
tenencia 1. custody [*of children after divorce*] 2. holding 3. (Mex) annual automobile tax [*short for "impuesto sobre tenencia o uso de vehículos"*] 4. possession
tenencia de la tierra real estate holding
tenencia política (Ecu) office of a *teniente político* (q.v.)
tenencias accionarias shareholdings
tener la palabra to have the floor
tener por conveniente to deem proper
tener por presentado acknowledge as having been presented
tener por vencida anticipadamente la deuda to accelerate the debt
tener presente to bear in mind

tener verificativo to be held [*said of a meeting*]
tenerme por parte that I be considered a party to the lawsuit
tenerme por presentado that you enter my appearance
tenerme por revelado de garantizar el interés fiscal (Mex) that
    you hold that I am relieved from furnishing any guarantee as
    security for the payment of any tax that may be found to be
    payable
tenernos por presentados para los efectos legales that you enter
    our appearance for all legal purposes
tenerse por reproducido como si se insertara a la letra (Mex) to
    be incorporated by reference
tengo a la vista I have before me
teniente
    teniente fiscal (Spa) assistant district attorney, deputy
        prosecutor
    teniente político (Ecu) "political deputy," i.e. head official of a
        parish [*Ecuador is divided into provinces presided over by a
        "gobernador." The provinces are subdivided into "cantones,"
        each of which is presided over by a "jefe político." The
        cantones are subdivided into parishes, each of which is
        presided over by a "teniente político."*]
tenor siguiente (es del) it reads as follows
tentativa attempt
    tentativa de delito attempted crime
tequila the "tequila effect" [*refers to the shockwaves that Mexico's
    financial crisis sent through the rest of Latin America. Mexico
    devalued its peso on Dec. 20, 1994, which triggered a 7 percent
    drop in its gross domestic product and sharp drops in stocks and
    the currency.*]
tercera partida (Pan) third installment of the "décimo tercer mes"
    [*annual bonus*]
tercería intervention in a lawsuit
    tercería coadyuvante intervention with a posture that coincides
        with that of the plaintiff or defendant
    tercería de dominio intervention whereby the intervenor seeks
        to be declared owner of the property that is in dispute
    tercería de mejor derecho intervention whereby the intervenor
        claims to have a better right to the property in dispute than
        the litigants
    tercería excluyente intervention whereby the intervenor takes a
        position that is contrary to the position of the litigants
tercerista intervenor, third party
tercerización (Arg) outsourcing [*called "externalización" in Spain*]
tercero third party
    tercero en discordia third party appointed to resolve
        differences or help form a majority when experts or
        arbitrators cannot agree

tercero perjudicado (Mex) the affected third party in an amparo proceeding [*the party who has an interest in preserving and perpetrating the act complained of*]

tercio one-third

tercio de libre disposición (Per, Pue, Spa) the third of the estate that the testator is free to dispose of as he wishes [*also called "cuota de libre disposición"*]

tercio de mejora (Per, Pue, Spa) special bequest of more than the birthright portion

terma (Per) electric water heater

terminación anticipada early termination

terminante absolute

término

término de ejecutoria de una resolución term for execution of a judgment

término de gracia grace period

término de la distancia time required to accomplish something when long distances are involved

término judicial deadline set by the judge

término probatorio evidentiary period

términos de referencia terms of reference (TOR)

terna slate of three candidates

terreno land

terreno edificado developed land

tesis (Mex) excerpt from a Supreme Court decision

tesorería (Spa) cash on hand and in banks [*called "disponibilidades" in other countries*]

testador testator [*person making a will*]

testaferro straw man, front man, agent of an undisclosed principal

testamentaría testamentary proceedings

testamento will, last will and testament

testamento abierto "open" will [*will stated aloud and recorded by notary - there is no equivalent in American law*]

testamento cerrado "mystic" will [*will submitted under seal for recording with notary - there is no equivalent in American law*]

testamento espiritual (Per) poor person's will made orally and without any formalities

testamento inoficioso inofficious will [*will that deprives an heir of his lawful inheritance*]

testamento ológrafo holographic will [*will written in the testator's handwriting - this term is used in the United States*]

testar 1. to make a will 2. to cross out, to delete, to obliterate

Testado no vale. The crossed-out portions should be ignored.

testar un sello to obliterate a seal

testificar to testify

testigo witness

testigo abonado competent witness

testigo auricular hearsay witness [*testifies as to what he has heard*]

testigo conteste witness whose testimony agrees with that of others

testigo de actuación attesting witness [*on the court staff*]

testigo de apremio subpoenaed witness

testigo de asistencia (Mex) attending witness [*sometimes abbreviated "T. de A."*]

testigo de cargo witness for the prosecution

testigo de coartada alibi witness

testigo de descargo witness for the defense

testigo de oídas hearsay witness

testigo de vista eyewitness

testigo desfavorable adverse witness

testigo hábil competent witness

testigo inhábil incompetent witness

testigo instrumental attesting witness, subscribing witness

testigo ocular eyewitness

testigo presencial eyewitness

testigo renuente reluctant witness

testigo singular sole witness

testigo único sole witness

testimonial testimony [*short for "prueba testimonial"*]

testimonio 1. testimony 2. notarial certified copy [*as opposed to a "copia simple"*]

falso testimonio perjury

testimonio fehaciente reliable evidence, genuine evidence, trustworthy evidence

testis unius est testis nullus (Lat) A single witness is no better than having no witnesses at all.

texto text

texto de fuerza legal authoritative text

texto ordenado amended text of a law

texto refundido (Spa) consolidated text of a law [*i.e. incorporating all the amendments into the original text*]

texto único consolidated text of a law

texto único concordado consolidated text with cross-references

tiempo compartido timeshare, timesharing [*ownership or rental of property (often a condominium) on a joint basis with others, allowing each participant to occupy the premises separately on a rotating basis, for a limited period of time*]

timbres de ley tax stamps required by law

tipicidad 1. statutory description of a crime 2. requirement that only crimes set forth in the law be punished 3. requirement that business associations be organized under a legal structure that is provided by law

tipificación de un delito definition of a crime, characterization of an offense

tipo rate

    tipo de cambio exchange rate

    tipo de cambio a futuro forward rate

    tipo de cambio controlado fixed exchange rate

    tipo de cambio de equilibrio equilibrium exchange rate

    tipo de cambio flotante floating exchange rate

    tipo de cambio libre flexible exchange rate

    tipo de cambio real real exchange rate

    tipo de interés interest rate

    tipo de interés interbancario interbank interest rate

    tipo de pignoración bank rate for loans on securities

    tipo interbancario de oferta de Londres London Interbank Offered Rate (LIBOR)

    tipo para la subasta upset price [*the price at which something is exposed to sale by auction, below which it is not to be sold*]

    tipo real effective rate

tironero (Spa) purse snatcher, pickpocket

titular de la cartera minister

título

    título a la orden order instrument

    título al portador bearer instrument

    título de acciones nominativas stock certificate registered in the name of the owner

    título de crédito negotiable instrument

    título de goce (Per) retired share benefits

    título de propiedad title deed

    título definitivo definitive certificate

    título desmaterializado book-entry security [*i.e., uncertificated security*]

    título ejecutivo document proving plaintiff's right of execution [*similar to writ of execution, which is a written demand to bailiff, directing him to execute the judgment of the court*]

    título gratuito (a) without valuable consideration, for free, as a gift

    título nominativo registered certificate [*as opposed to a bearer certificate*]

    título oneroso (a) for valuable consideration

    título opcional warrant

    título precario (a) for temporary use and enjoyment

    título testamentario testamentary right, right under a will

toca (el) (Mex) file, record of the case at the Supreme Court level

toda vez que inasmuch as

toma
>**toma de protesta a los miembros** swearing in of the members
>**toma de razón 1. (Chi)** review by the *Contraloría General de la República* of a *Decreto Supremo*, *Decreto con Fuerza de Ley* or a *Resolución* for constitutionality and legality **2. (Spa)** agreed transaction with a market member outside of normal trading hours

tomador 1. payee [*person to whom a check or promissory note is payable*] 2. beneficiary [*of a letter of credit*]

tomar
>**tomar asistencia** to call the roll
>**tomar dinero a préstamo** to borrow money
>**tomar inventario físico** to take physical inventory
>**tomar la declaración de alguien** to depose someone
>**tomar razón** to make a notation, to record, to make an entry
>**tomar resoluciones** to adopt resolutions

tomo de jurisprudencia reporter [*published volume of decisions by a court or group of courts*]

toque de queda curfew

total total
>**total de ingresos por intereses** total interest income
>**total de mis bienes reales y personales (el)** all my worldly goods
>**total o parcialmente** in whole or in part

traba del embargo levying of the attachment

trabajador worker, employee
>**trabajador accidental** casual worker
>**trabajador autónomo** self-employed person
>**trabajador de confianza** employee in a position of trust
>**trabajador en relación de dependencia** employee under an employment contract
>**trabajador por cuenta ajena** employed person
>**trabajador por cuenta propia** self-employed person

trabajo work
>**trabajo a desgano** slowdown [*a deliberate lessening of work effort without an actual strike, in order to force concessions from the employer*]
>**trabajo a destajo** piece work
>**trabajo a reglamento** work to rule [*a practice whereby workers obey to the letter all laws and rules pertaining to their work, thereby effecting a slowdown*]
>**trabajo con dedicación exclusiva** full-time work
>**trabajo con dedicación simple** part-time work
>**trabajo de utilidad pública (Arg)** community service
>**trabajo en favor de la comunidad (Mex)** community service
>**trabajo eventual** casual labor

trabar embargo to levy an attachment of assets

tradición physical delivery of a thing
    tradición real actual delivery
traductor translator
    traductor jurado (Gua, Spa) sworn translator
    traductor público (Arg) sworn translator
traer aparejada ejecución to be enforceable on its face
tráfico 1. traffic 2. trade, commerce
    tráfico de drogas drug trafficking [*also called "narcotráfico"*]
    tráfico de influencia influence peddling, power dealing
    tráfico entre terceros países cross-trade
    tráfico marítimo shipping
tramitación processing
    ¿Cuánto tarda la tramitación de un pasaporte? How long
        does it take to get a passport?
tramitar to process, to take legal steps
    tramitar ante un tribunal to be pending before a court
    tramitar un crédito to process a loan application
trámite procedures to be followed, formalities, red tape
    estar en trámite to be pending, to be in the pipeline
    de mero trámite routine matters
    realizar un trámite to process a transaction, a filing
    sin más trámite without further formalities
    trámite de estilo routine formalities
    un puro trámite a mere formality
transacción 1. transaction, deal 2. settlement
transar 1. to settle, to compromise, to give in on something 2. to
    trade, to buy and sell 3. (Mex) to cheat, trick, swindle
transcendencia 1. effects, consequences 2. importance,
    significance
transferencia
    transferencia electrónica de fondos electronic fund transfer
    transferencia unilateral unrequited transfer
transformación de una empresa change of corporate form
transfuguismo abandoning one political party for another
transigir to settle
transparencia transparency
    transparencia en el mercado de valores transparency in the
        securities market
    transparencia fiscal pass-through taxation
transporte
    transporte pagado hasta carriage paid to (CPT) [*Incoterm*]
    transporte y seguro pagados hasta carriage and insurance
        paid to (CIP) [*Incoterm*]
trasladar 1. to move from one place to another 2. to transfer
    trasladar una causa to transfer a case
    trasladar una sesión to adjourn a meeting

traslado 1. change of residence 2. transfer of an employee 3. copy of a document 4. making the record available to the parties [*so that they can prepare their closing briefs (called "alegatos" or "escritos de conclusiones"*]

    traslado de impuestos tax shifting [*act by which one party passes to another person the taxes imposed on him*]

    traslado de jurisdicción change of venue

    traslado de la demanda service of process

    traslado fiel y exacto de su original a true and correct copy of the original

traspasar 1. to transfer, to assign 2. to sell

traspaso 1. transfer, conveyance 2. sale

tratado 1. treaty 2. treatise

tratamiento en libertad (Mex) diversion [*suspension of the prosecution of a charge for a period of time during which the defendant participates in a rehabilitation program or makes restitution and after which the charges are dismissed if the rehabilitation or restitution is completed – See Art. 27 of the Mexican Penal Code*]

tribunal court [*In most of Latin America, a "tribunal" is always lower than the supreme court, but in Spain, Cuba, and Puerto Rico, the Supreme Court is called the "Tribunal Supremo."*]

    tribunal colegiado three-judge court

    tribunal competente court of competent jurisdiction

    tribunal correcional (Per) court of criminal appeals

    tribunal de alzada appellate court, court of appeals

    tribunal de apelaciones appellate court

    tribunal de arbitraje arbitral tribunal

    Tribunal de Circuito Circuit Court

    Tribunal de Cuentas (Spa) State Audit Court

    tribunal de faltas (Arg, Uru) police court, traffic court

    tribunal de familia family court, domestic relations court

    Tribunal de la Competencia (Spa) Office of Fair Trading

    tribunal de menores juvenile court

    tribunal de primera instancia court of first instance

    tribunal de última instancia court of last resort

    Tribunal del Jurado (Spa) jury court [*The jury system was introduced in Spain in September 1995. Local courts now use jurors in cases of corruption, murder, embezzlement and arson. A minimum of seven jurors must be in agreement for a guilty verdict.*]

    tribunal fiscal tax court

    tribunal nacional (Arg) federal court [*as opposed to a "tribunal provincial"*]

    tribunal plenario the full court, the court sitting en banc

    tribunal pluripersonal collegiate court

Tribunal Superior de Distrito Judicial (Col) court of appeals [*Trial courts in Colombia are called "juzgados," and the supreme court is called the "Corte Suprema de Justicia."*]
Tribunal Supremo (Pue, Spa) Supreme Court
tribunal unipersonal one-judge court
tribunal unitario (Mex) one-judge court [*The standard term is "tribunal unipersonal."*]
tributación taxation
    Tributación Directa (Cos) Costa Rican Internal Revenue Service [*short for Dirección General de la Tributación Directa*]
tributario 1. tax, tax-related [*as an adjective*] 2. taxpayer [*as a noun*]
tributo judicial filing fee
trimestralmente on a quarterly basis
trimestre quarter
trueque barter, exchange, swap
tuitivo protective, defensive [*of something*]
tutela guardianship [*The difference between "tutela" and "curatela" is based on the degree of incapacity of the person needing a guardian. If the person is a minor or is "interdicto," tutela is used. If the person is an emancipated minor or is "inhabilitado," curatela is used.*]
    tutela dativa court-appointed guardianship
    tutela judicial protection of the law, judicial relief
    tutela jurídica (Mex) protection of the law, judicial relief
    tutela jurisdiccional (Per) protection of the law, judicial relief
    tutela legítima statutory guardianship
    tutela testamentaria testamentary guardianship
tutelar to act as guardian
tutor guardian [*The difference between "tutor" and "curador" is based on the degree of incapacity of the person needing a guardian. If the person is a minor or is "interdicto," a "tutor" is appointed. If the person is an emancipated minor or is "inhabilitado," a "curador" is appointed.*]
    tutor dativo court-appointed guardian
    tutor legítimo legal guardian
udibono (Mex) government bonds denominated in investment units
ultimar los arreglos necesarios to make the necessary arrangements
últimas entradas, primeras salidas (UEPS) last in, first out (LIFO)
ultra petita (Lat) situation where the court grants more than was claimed or settles points not submitted to it [*The phrase literally means "beyond what was demanded."*]
ultraje
    ultraje al pudor (Arg, Per) sexual assault [*taking indecent liberties (such as fondling without consent) with a person of*

the opposite sex—also referred to as "indecent assault" in English and as "atentado al pudor" in Spanish]

ultraje de obra physical insult [*kicking or slapping someone*]

unidad

   unidad de acto continuity of an act

   unidad de fomento (Chi) index-linked unit [*daily indexed unit based on the variation of the preceding month's consumer price index*]

   Unidad de Patrimonio (Col) Robbery Division [*of the Prosecutor's Office - la Fiscalía General de la Nación*]

   Unidad de Vida (Col) Homicide Division [*of the Prosecutor's Office -la Fiscalía General de la Nación*]

unificación de la personería appointment of a single representative [*When various litigants participate in a trial with a common interest, the judge can require them to appoint a single representative.*]

unificar su personería to appoint a single representative

unión *unión libre — common law*

   unión de crédito credit union

   unión transitoria de empresas (Arg) joint venture

uno o varios one or more

urbanismo town planning

urbanización (Ven) city district

urna ballot box

uso

   uso de la palabra (en) having the floor

   uso final end use

   uso y goce pacífico quiet enjoyment [*legal right of an owner in possession to use the property without interference*]

   usos administrativos administrative practices

   usos forenses judicial customs

usuario final end user

usucapión adverse possession

usucapir to acquire by adverse possession

usufructo life estate, use and enjoyment, beneficial ownership

usufructuario beneficial owner

usura usury

usurpación unauthorized appropriation of a right

   usurpación de funciones impersonation of a public official

utilidad

   utilidad financiera net interest income

   utilidad fiscal profit for tax purposes

   utilidad fiscal neta net taxable income

   utilidad monetaria gain on monetary position

   utilidad neta net income

   utilidad neta antes de impuestos net income before tax

   utilidad neta de inversión net investment income

utilidad neta distribuida a accionistas net investment income distributed to shareholders
utilidad por acción (UPA) earnings per share (EPS)
utilidades no distribuidas retained earnings
utilidades por aplicar unappropriated earnings
utilidades retenidas retained earnings
utilización de efectivo cash outlay
vacante vacancy
    cubrir una vacante to fill a vacancy
    se produce una vacante a vacancy occurs
vacatio legis (Lat) period between the publication of a statute in the official gazette and the time it takes effect
vagancia vagrancy
vale 1. promissory note, IOU [*synonym of "pagaré"*] 2. voucher [*synonym of "comprobante"*]
    vale a la vista demand promissory note
    vale de caja cash voucher
    vale de caja chica petty cash voucher
    vale de descuento money-off coupon
    vale de prenda collateral certificate [*see "bono de prenda"*]
    vale obsequio (Arg) gift certificate
valevista bancario (Chi) bank's own promissory note payable on demand
validez por separado (Mex) severability [*of a contract*]
valor 1. value 2. price
    valor a la par par value
    valor a su vencimiento value at maturity
    valor actual present value
    valor agregado value added
    valor catastral official tax appraisal, value for tax purposes
    valor contable book value
    valor de avalúo appraised value
    valor de cambio trade-in value, exchange value
    valor de costo cost value
    valor de desecho (Mex) scrap value
    valor de lista list price
    valor de operación value of transaction
    valor de portada cover price [*of a magazine*]
    valor de reposición replacement value
    valor de rescate surrender value
    valor de rescate en efectivo cash surrender value
    valor del dinero a través del tiempo time value of money
    valor en aduanas customs value, dutiable value, value for customs purposes
    valor en efectivo cash value
    valor en libros book value
    valor global aggregate value

valor justo de mercado fair market value
valor llave (Arg) goodwill [*also called "llave de negocio" in Argentina*]
valor neto de reposición net replacement value
valor nominal 1. par value (shares) 2. face value (bonds)
valor patrimonial proporcional equity value, proportionate share of net worth
valor presente present value [*the amount that must be invested now at a given interest rate to produce a given future value*]
valor probatorio probative value [*the relative weight properly assigned to particular evidence*]
valor real actual value
valor recuperable final (Arg) scrap value
valor reducido a nominal value, a nominal price
valor unitario unit value
valor venal market value
valores a entregar por reporto repurchase agreements [*on the liabilities side of the balance sheet*]
valores a recibir por reporto repurchase agreements [*on the asset side of the balance sheet*]
valores al portador bearer securities
valores de capital equity securities
valores de compraventa trading account securities
valores de inversión investment securities
valores de mayor contratación bursátil most actively traded shares
valores en depósito securities on deposit
valores en garantía pledged securities
valores muebles e inmuebles adjudicados (netos) assets acquired through judicial proceedings (net)
valores negociables marketable securities
valores realizables marketable securities
valoración assessment, evaluation, appraisal
valoración de la prueba weighing of the evidence
valoración de las ofertas evaluation of the bid [*in a public tender*]
valorar to assess
valuar to appraise
vecino resident
veda política (Arg) moratorium on campaigning just prior to an election [*cf. "jornada de reflexión" in Spain*]
velador guard, watchman
vencido y pagadero due and payable
vencimiento 1. maturity 2. expiration
vendedor seller, vendor
vendedor mayorista wholesaler
vendedor minorista retailer

vender con pérdida to sell at a loss
venia de la sala by leave of the court
venta
> **venta con reserva de dominio** conditional sale [*reserves
> ownership until purchase price is paid in full*]
> **venta contra documentos** sale against documents
ventaja unfair advantage, undue advantage
ventanilla única (Mex) special filing window
venta sale
> **venta al gusto** sale subject to buyer's approval
> **venta con pacto de retracto** sale with the option to repurchase
> the thing sold
> **venta de liquidación** clearance sale, close-out sale
> **ventas brutas** gross sales
> **ventas nacionales** domestic sales
> **ventas netas** net services billed
ventilar to bring to trial, to litigate
ver una causa to hear a case
verbi gratia (Lat) for example
veredicto verdict
verificación
> **verificación de créditos** proof of claims in bankruptcy
> **verificación por sondeo** spot check
verificar la diligencia posesoria to make delivery of possession
verificarse to take place, to be held
> **el lugar en que se verificará el remate** the place where the
> auction will be held
> **se verificará la sesión** the session will be held
vía proceedings
> **vía constitucional, esta (Mex)** this amparo proceeding
> **vía de apremio** foreclosure proceedings
> **vía ordinaria** ordinary proceedings
> **vía rápida** fast track
> **vía sumaria** summary proceedings
viáticos traveling expenses, travel allowance
vicio defect
> **vicio del consentimiento** defect in consent [*such as fraud,
> coercion or duress—These are referred to as "defenses to
> contract formation" in English.*]
> **vicio de fondo** substantive defect
> **vicio de forma** procedural defect
> **vicio de la voluntad** defect in consent
> **vicio formal** procedural defect
> **vicio oculto** latent defect, hidden defect
> **vicio redhibitorio** hidden defect that may annul the sale of the
> item
vigilancia supervision, oversight

vinculación aduanera inter-company pricing
vínculo link
    vínculo matrimonial bonds of matrimony
violación 1. violation, breach 2. rape 3. trespass
    violación de contrato breach of contract
    violación de domicilio burglary, breaking and entering
    violación de las reglas infraction of the rules
    violación de patente patent infringement
    violación presunta statutory rape
violar la ley to break the law
violentar to break a lock
visita
    visita conyugal conjugal visit
    visita domiciliaria (Mex) search of premises pursuant to a
      warrant for investigating compliance with tax laws
vista 1. [*la vista*] hearing 2. [*el vista*] customs inspector
    vista a puerta cerrada in camera hearing
    vista abierta hearing in open court
    vista preliminar preliminary hearing
Vistador General de la PGR (Mex) Inspector General
Vistaduría General (Mex) Office of the Inspector General
visto, para resolver having reviewed and considered X, for
    purposes of issuing this decision
visto bueno ("vo.bo.") approval
    dar el visto bueno to sign off on something
vocal member of the board
    Vocal Superior (Per) appellate court judge
    vocal suplente alternate member of the board
    Vocal Supremo (Per) Supreme Court Justice
    vocal titular regular member of the board
volenti non fit iniuria (Lat) He who consents cannot receive an
    injury. [*similar to the common law doctrine of "assumption of the
    risk"*]
volumen de contratación volume of trading
voluntad intent, will
    **La voluntad de las partes fue la de someterse al Código
    Civil.** The parties' intent was to be governed by the Civil
    Code.
    por hechos ajenos a su voluntad because of events beyond
      one's control
    por motivos ajenos a su voluntad for reasons beyond one's
      control
volverse insolvente en fraude de acreedores to become insolvent
    committing fraud against creditors
votación voting
    votación a mano alzada voting by show of hands
    votación económica voting by show of hands

votación nominal voting by roll call
votación oral voice vote
votación ordinaria voting by show of hands
votación por lista voice vote, yea-or-nay vote
votación por poder voting by proxy
votación secreta voting by secret ballot
voto vote
    voto acumulativo cumulative voting
    voto de calidad deciding vote, casting vote
    voto discrepante dissenting vote
    voto en disidencia dissenting vote
    voto favorable affirmative vote
    voto particular dissenting vote
    voto pasivo right to speak but not to vote
    voto reservado (Spa) dissenting vote
    voto salvado (Col, Ven) dissenting vote
Vuestra Excelencia (Arg) Your Honor [*appellate court judge*]
Vuestra Señoría (Arg) Your Honor [*trial court judge*]
zanjar to settle, to resolve
zona
    zona catastrófica disaster area
    zona de ensanche (Spa) area of new development
    zona de guerra war zone
    zona de libre comercio free-trade zone
    zona federal marítimo terrestre (Mex) federal maritime land zone [*beachfront property is owned by the government of Mexico*]
    zona franca foreign trade zone, duty-free area, free trade zone (FTZ)
    zona parachoque buffer zone

CORTE SUPREMA

ENGLISH
SPANISH-

Abreviaturas

adj	adjetivo
Arg	Argentina
Bol	Bolivia
Chi	Chile
Col	Colombia
Cos	Costa Rica
Cub	Cuba
Dom	República Dominicana
Ecu	Ecuador
Esp	España
Gua	Guatemala
Hon	Honduras
Méx	México
Nic	Nicaragua
Pan	Panamá
Per	Perú
Pue	Puerto Rico
s	sustantivo
Sal	El Salvador
Uru	Uruguay
v	verbo
Ven	Venezuela

abandoned property bienes abandonados
abduction secuestro
abettor instigador
above par por encima del valor nominal
above-captioned case el juicio señalado al rubro (Méx)
above-styled case el juicio señalado al rubro (Méx)
abrogation of a law derogación de una ley
absentee ballot voto por correo [*de una persona ausente*]
absolute divorce divorcio vincular [*también llamado "divorce a vinculo matrimonii" en inglés*]
abstract of title antecedentes catastrales de un inmueble
abuse
    abuse of discretion abuso de poder
    abuse of process abuso de derecho
accede to a treaty v adherir a un tratado
accelerate a loan v exigir el reembolso anticipado de un préstamo
accelerated depreciation amortización acelerada
acceleration of a loan vencimiento anticipado de un préstamo
accept service of process v recibir emplazamiento
accession to a treaty adherencia a un tratado
accessory
    accessory after the fact cómplice encubridor
    accessory before the fact cómplice instigador
    accessory during the fact cómplice por omisión
accomplice cómplice
accord and satisfaction dación en pago
accounting contabilidad
    accounting entry asiento contable
    accounting method método de contabilidad
    accounting period periodo contable
account cuenta
    account activity movimiento de cuenta
    accounts payable cuentas por pagar
    accounts payable ledger auxiliar de cuentas por pagar
    accounts receivable cuentas por cobrar
    accounts receivable ledger auxiliar de cuentas por cobrar
accrual basis base acumulativa, base de acumulación
accrued
    accrued expenses gastos devengados
    accrued interest intereses devengados
    accrued right derecho adquirido
acid test ratio índice ácido, índice de solvencia inmediata
acknowledge v reconocer
    acknowledge receipt v acusar recibo
    acknowledges and agrees that he is an independent contractor reconoce y acepta ser contratista independiente
acquisition adquisición

acquisition cost precio de compra
acquit v absolver
acquittal absolución
act s 1. acto 2. ley
    act of Congress ley del Congreso
    act of God caso fortuito
    act of state acto soberano
    act or omission acto u omisión
act v
    act in bad faith v actuar de mala fe, obrar de mala fe
    act in good faith v actuar de buena fe, obrar de buena fe
action at law acción en justicia
    action for breach of contract acción por responsabilidad
        contractual
    action for damages acción por daños y perjuicios
    action in tort acción por responsabilidad extracontractual
actionable accionable, procesable
actual
    actual notice notificación efectiva [*en contraposición a
        "constructive notice"*]
    actual value valor real
ad hoc committee comité especial
ad valorem tax impuesto al valor
additional paid-in capital prima de emisión (Esp)
additur facultad del tribunal para incrementar la cantidad concedida
    al demandante por el jurado
adhesion contract contrato de adhesión
adjourn a meeting v 1. levantar una sesión 2. aplazar una sesión
adjournment aplazamiento
adjustable-rate mortgage (ARM) hipoteca con tasa de interés
    variable
adjustment for currency devaluation corrección monetaria
administrative
    administrative expenses gastos de administración
    administrative law derecho administrativo
    administrative law judge juez de lo contencioso-administrativo
    administrative offense infracción
    Administrative Procedure Act Ley de Procedimiento
        Administrativo
    administrative remedy recurso administrativo
administrator of an estate albacea judicial, albacea dativo
admiralty
    admiralty case caso de derecho marítimo
    admiralty law derecho marítimo
admission of guilt confesión de culpabilidad
admit v
    admit a partner v incorporar un socio

admit liability v reconocer responsabilidad
admit to the bar v incorporar al colegio de abogados
admitted into evidence aceptado como prueba
adopted child hijo adoptivo
adoptee adoptado
adoption adopción
adoptive parent padre adoptivo, adoptante
advance
    advance parole libertad condicional anticipada
    advance payment pago anticipado
    advance sheet copia preliminar de la sentencia [*antes de su publicación en un repertorio*]
adversary proceedings procedimiento contencioso
adverse
    adverse balance of payments balanza de pagos negativa
    adverse interest interés contrario al de otra persona
    adverse party parte contraria
    adverse possession usucapión
    adverse witness testigo desfavorable
advice of counsel asesoría de abogados
adviser consejero
advisory opinion opinión consultativa
affiant declarante
affidavit declaración jurada
affiliation proceeding juicio de filiación
affirmative
    affirmative covenant obligación de hacer
    affirmative defense defensa de fondo
    affirmative easement servidumbre activa, servidumbre afirmativa, servidumbre positiva
    affirmative vote voto favorable, voto positivo
affix a seal v estampar un sello
affordability accesibilidad financiera
affordable housing vivienda al alcance de su bolsillo
aforementioned antes mencionado, susodicho
agency 1. mandato [*relación entre mandante y mandatario*] 2. organismo [*del gobierno*]
agent mandatario
aggravated
    aggravated assault amenaza de acometimiento grave
    aggravated offense delito calificado
    aggravating circumstances circunstancias agravantes
aging schedule lista de cuentas a cobrar vencidas, clasificadas según su antigüedad
agree unanimously v acordar por unanimidad de votos
agreement contrato, acuerdo, pacto
aid and abet v auxiliar e instigar

aider and abetter cómplice
airbill guía aérea
alderman regidor
aleatory contract contrato aleatorio
alibi coartada
    alibi witness testigo de coartada
alien extranjero
    alien certification unit unidad de certificación de extranjeros
    alien employment authorization autorización para emplear
        extranjeros
    alien registration number número de registro de extranjero
alienable enajenable
alimony pensión alimenticia
all my worldly goods el total de mis bienes reales y personales
allocate v asignar
alternate juror jurado suplente
alternative
    alternative dispute resolution procedimientos extrajudiciales
        para la resolución de controversias [*tales como arbitraje y*
        conciliación]
    alternative minimum tax impuesto mínimo alternativo
alternatively subsidiariamente
ambulance chaser picapleitos [*abogado sin pleitos que anda*
    buscándolos]
amend reformar, modificar, enmendar
    shall be amended to read as follows se reformará para
        quedar como sigue
    amended return declaración enmendada, planilla enmendada
        (Pue)
amendment modificación, reforma
American Depositary Receipt (ADR) recibo de depósito americano
amiable compositeur amigable componedor
amicable settlement transacción amigable
amicus curiae persona ajena al litigio quien, por propia voluntad,
    asesora al tribunal en relación con aspectos del derecho o
    hechos que hacen al litigio
amnesty amnistía
amortization amortización
amount monto, cantidad, cuantía
    amount in controversy cuantía del litigio
ancestor ascendiente
anchor tenant arrendatario principal [*negocios muy conocidos,*
    como ser grandes tiendas, que generan circulación de clientes
    en centros comerciales]
Andean Pact Pacto Andino
annotated statute ley comentada

annual meeting asamblea anual de accionistas, junta anual de accionistas

annualize v elevar al año

antitrust law derecho antimonopolio

any person or entity cualquier persona natural o jurídica, cualquier persona física o moral (Méx), cualquier persona física o jurídica (Arg)

apostille apostilla

apparent easement servidumbre aparente

appeal s apelación, recurso

    appeal bond fianza exigible para que se dé curso a una apelación

appeals court tribunal de apelaciones

appeal v apelar

appear v comparecer

appearance comparecencia

appellant apelante

appellate court tribunal de apelaciones, tribunal de alzada

appellation of origin denominación de origen

appellee apelado

applicant solicitante

application solicitud

    application for adjustment of status solicitud de cambio de clasificación [*en la inmigración*]

appraisal avalúo, tasación

    appraisal contingency contingencia relacionada con la tasación

    appraisal report informe de tasación

appraised value valor tasado

appraiser tasador, evaluador

approach the bench v acercarse al estrado

approval aprobación

appurtenances affixed to the land anexidades fijas del terreno

arbitrage arbitraje

arbitrageur arbitrajista

arbitral

    arbitral award laudo arbitral

    arbitral tribunal tribunal de arbitraje

arbitration arbitraje, arbitramento (Col, Ven)

    arbitration clause cláusula de arbitraje, cláusula compromisoria

arbitrator árbitro

arm's length transaction operación normal entre empresas no relacionadas

armed robbery robo a mano armada

arraignment lectura de cargos

arrest s detención

    arrest and pretrial detention detención y prisión preventiva

arrest of judgment suspensión temporal de los efectos de una sentencia

arrest warrant auto de detención, orden de aprehensión (Méx)

arrest v detener

arrestee detenido

arson incendio intencional

arsonist incendiario

article artículo

articles of amendment acta modificatoria del contrato social

articles of impeachment artículos de incriminación

articles of incorporation acta constitutiva, escritura constitutiva, escritura de constitución

artificial person persona jurídica, persona moral (Méx)

as a court of first and last resort en única instancia

as a matter of law de pleno derecho

as amended y sus reformas

as amended from time to time y sus reformas periódicas

as it appears según se desprende

as of now desde ahora, a partir de ahora

as the case may be según sea el caso

as you know como es de su conocimiento

as-built drawing plano conforme a obra

asking price precio demandado

assault and battery amenazas y agresión violenta

assessment determinación del impuesto

asset

asset purchase agreement contrato de compraventa de fondo de comercio

assets activo

assets of an estate caudal hereditario

assignee 1. cesionario [*persona natural o jurídica en cuyo favor se hace la cesión de deudas o de derechos*] 2. causahabiente [*persona que sucede o subroga a otra en una cosa o un derecho*]

assignment cesión

assignor cedente

associate abogado que todavía no es socio del despacho jurídico

associate judge conjuez, juez que no preside el tribunal

assumable mortgage hipoteca asumible

assume v

assume a loan v asumir un préstamo

assume a mortgage v asumir una hipoteca

assume facts not in evidence v suponer hechos no comprobados

assumption of risk asunción del riesgo [*es el principio al que alude el aforismo latino "volenti non fit injuria"*]

asylee asilado

asylee status condición de asilado
asylum asilo
    asylum hearing audiencia sobre asilo
at all times en todo momento
at bar ante el tribunal
at issue en tela de juicio
at its option a su elección
at its own expense por su propia cuenta
at the close of business al final del día hábil
at the request of a petición de, a requerimiento de, a instancia de
at warehouse prices a precios reducidos
at-will employee empleado a quien se puede despedir sin causa justificada
at year end al finalizar el año
attach v embargar
attachment embargo
attempt tentativa
    attempt on someone's life atentado contra la vida de alguien
attendance by conference telephone asistencia mediante comunicación telefónica en conferencia
attorney abogado, letrado
    attorney-at-law abogado
    attorney general fiscal, procurador, abogado fiscal
    attorney's fees honorarios del abogado
    attorney-in-fact apoderado
auction s subasta, remate, almoneda
auctioneer rematador, martillero (Arg), martillador (Ecu), rematista (Per)
audit auditoría
    audit committee comité de auditoría
    audit trail referencia de auditoría
audited accounts cuentas dictaminadas/auditadas
auditor auditor
authenticated copy copia legalizada
authorized capital capital autorizado
auto
    auto stripping desmantelamiento de vehículo
    auto tampering desmantelamiento de vehículo
    auto theft robo de vehículo
automated teller machine (ATM) cajero automático, caja permanente
autopsy autopsia
award v
    award a contract v adjudicar un contrato
    award a diploma v otorgar un diploma
    award custody v otorgar la tenencia
award s laudo

back

> **backbond** reafianzamiento
> **back-end ratio** proporción de la deuda total mensual al ingreso bruto mensual
> **backlog of orders** cartera de pedidos atrasados
> **back order** pedido pendiente [*pedido a surtirse cuando haya en existencia*]
> **backpay** salarios caídos
> **back taxes** impuestos atrasados
> **backup withholding** retención adicional de impuesto sobre intereses y ciertos dividendos

bad check cheque en descubierto, cheque sin fondos
bad debt deuda incobrable
bad faith mala fe
bag-and-baggage letter notificación de que en 30 días la persona debe salir del país
bail fianza

> **bail bond** documento de fianza

bailiff alguacil
bait and switch práctica de venta fraudulenta en la cual el vendedor atrae al cliente utilizando mercadería de menor valor para ofrecerle mercadería de mayor valor
balance s 1. saldo 2. balanza

> **balance brought forward** saldo arrastrado
> **balance carried forward** saldo traspasado
> **balance of payments** balanza de pagos
> **balance of trade** balanza comercial
> **balance owed** saldo en contra
> **balance sheet** balance general
> **balance sheet date** fecha de cierre del balance
> **balance an account v** cuadrar una cuenta

balancing entry contrapartida
balloon

> **balloon loan** préstamo con pago global final
> **balloon mortgage** hipoteca con pago global final
> **balloon payment** pago global final

ballot boleta, papeleta

> **ballot box** urna electoral

ballpark figure cifra aproximada
bank

> **bank account** cuenta bancaria
> **bank bonds** bonos bancarios
> **bank draft** giro bancario, letra bancaria
> **bank fee** comisión bancaria
> **bank holding company** sociedad controladora de bancos
> **bank holiday** día inhábil bancario
> **banknote** billete de banco

bank secrecy secreto bancario
bank statement estado de cuenta bancario
bank syndicate consorcio de bancos, consorcio bancario
bank vault caja fuerte
banker banquero
bankers' acceptance aceptación bancaria
banking banca
banking day día bancario
banking law derecho bancario
bankrupt adj en quiebra
bankrupt estate masa de la quiebra
bankruptcy quiebra, bancarrota
bankruptcy court tribunal en materia de quiebras
bankruptcy proceedings juicio de insolvencia
banns of matrimony amonestaciones matrimoniales
baptismal certificate certificado de bautismo, fe de bautismo
bar s
bar association colegio de abogados
bar examination examen de ingreso al colegio de abogados
barred by the statute of limitations prescrito
barter trueque, canje
bartering income ingreso resultante de trueque
basis point centésimo de punto porcentual
batter v golpear
battered child niño golpeado
battered spouse esposa golpeada
be in the public interest v ser de conveniencia pública
be under arrest v estar detenido
bear market mercado a la baja, mercado bajista
bearer al portador
bearer bond bono al portador, obligación al portador
bearer instrument documento al portador
bearer shares acciones al portador
become effective v surtir efecto
being duly sworn habiendo prestado debido juramento
bench 1. estrado 2. juez 3. judicatura, magistratura
bench trial juicio sin jurado
bench warrant orden judicial de detención
come on the bench v llegar a la judicatura
serve on the bench v ejercer la judicatura
benchmark bond bono referencial
beneficial
beneficial interest derecho del beneficiario sobre los bienes de
    un fideicomiso
beneficial use usufructo, uso provechoso, derecho de uso y
    disfrute
beneficiary beneficiario, fideicomisario

bequeath v legar bienes muebles
bequest asignación testamentaria
Berne Convention for the Protection of Literary and Artistic Works Convenio de Berna para la protección de las obras literarias y artísticas
best efforts obligation obligación de medios [*implica hacer los mejores y más fieles esfuerzos que corresponden para obtener el fin del contrato*]
best evidence prueba original
 best evidence rule regla que prohíbe el ofrecimiento de pruebas secundarias a menos que las originales se hayan perdido o destruido
best interests of the child lo que más conviene al niño [*criterio para la adjudicación de la custodia del niño*]
beyond a reasonable doubt sin lugar a duda razonable, fuera de toda duda razonable
beyond the scope fuera del alcance
bid oferta
 bid bond fianza de licitación, fianza de validez de oferta
 bid documents bases de la licitación, pliego de condiciones
bidder postor, oferente
bilateral contract contrato sinalagmático
bill proyecto de ley, iniciativa de ley (Méx)
 bill of costs planilla de costas, pliego de costas
 bill of exchange letra de cambio
 bill of indictment auto de acusación
 bill of lading conocimiento de embarque, guía de embarque (Cos)
 bill of rights declaración de derechos y garantías
 bill of sale contrato de compraventa de bienes muebles
binding
 binding arbitration arbitraje obligatorio
 binding force obligatoriedad
 binding on the parties obligatorio para las partes
 binding precedents decisiones que sientan jurisprudencia
birth
 birth certificate partida de nacimiento, acta de nacimiento, certificado de nacimiento
 birth mother madre de nacimiento
 birth parents padres de nacimiento
black letter law los principios legales básicos y explícitos, libres de ambigüedad
black market mercado negro
Blackacre bien inmueble ficticio
blackmail chantaje
blank check cheque en blanco

blanket mortgage hipoteca colectiva [*una sola hipoteca que comprende varias propiedades en garantía*]
block of shares paquete de acciones, paquete accionario
blood relative pariente consanguíneo
blue
    blue book compendio de abreviaciones jurídicas
    blue chip stocks acciones de excelente cotización
    blue law ley de descanso dominical
    blue sky laws leyes estatales que rigen los valores [*Tienen por miras proteger a los inversionistas de la compra de un "pedazo del cielo azul" (i.e. bienes sin valor alguno).*]
board of directors consejo de administración (Esp, Gua, Hon, Méx); directorio (Arg, Bol, Chi, Par, Per, Uru); junta directiva (Col, Cos, Dom, Gua, Nic)
bodily injury daños corporales, daños a terceros en sus personas
boilerplate clauses cláusulas de cajón (Méx)
bond bono, obligación, fianza
    bondholder obligacionista
    bond indenture acta de emisión de bonos
    bond rating calificación crediticia
bonded warehouse almacén general de depósito, recinto aduanal (Méx)
bonding company afianzadora
bonus gratificación, prima
book value valor en libros, valor contable
bookbuilding creación de una cartera de clientes potenciales
book-entry securities acciones escriturales
bootstrap sale utilización de los bienes de una compañía adquirida para financiar parte del costo de la adquisición misma
border
    border crossing station garita de la frontera
    border patrol patrulla fronteriza
    border patrol officer agente de la patrulla fronteriza
borderline case caso dudoso
borrower prestatario, mutuatario, acreditado
borrowing
    borrowing facility línea de crédito
    borrowing power capacidad crediticia
    borrowing rate tasa pasiva
branch sucursal
    branch banking banca de sucursales
    branch office sucursal
brand
    brand loyalty fidelidad a una marca
    brand name marca de fábrica
    brand you can trust marca de confianza

Brandeis brief escrito que incluye estudios sociológicos y económicos además de argumentos legales

breach

breach of contract incumplimiento contractual, violación de contrato

breach of copyright violación de los derechos de autor

breach of the peace alteración del orden público

breach of trust abuso de confianza

breaching party parte que incurre en incumplimiento

break

break curfew v infringir el toque de queda

break even v salir sin ganancias ni pérdidas

break the law v violar la ley

break even analysis análisis del punto de equilibrio

break even point punto de equilibrio

breaking and entering allanamiento de morada, allanamiento de domicilio

bribe mordida (Méx)

bribery cohecho [*de un funcionario*] soborno [*de un testigo*]

bridge loan crédito puente

brief escrito, memorial

bring a proceeding before a court v entablar una acción ante el tribunal

bring an action v entablar juicio

bring in a verdict dictar un veredicto, pronunciar un veredicto [*se dice de un jurado*]

bring suit v promover juicio, acudir a la vía judicial

bring to trial v procesar

bring-down search actualización de la verificación de dominio [*continuación de la verificación del dominio de una propiedad para corroborar que ningún embargo haya sido presentado contra el inmueble desde la búsqueda inicial. También se denomina "continuation" o "take-down search".*]

broad powers of management amplias facultades administrativas

broker corredor

brokerage corretaje

brokerage fees comisiones de corretaje

brokerage firm casa de bolsa

budget presupuesto

budget deficit déficit presupuestario

buffer stock existencia reguladora

bulk sale venta a granel

bulk sales act ley que impide la venta en masa de los bienes del deudor realizada en fraude de los acreedores

bull market mercado al alza, mercado alcista

bullet

bullet loan préstamo reembolsable en un pago

bullet payment amortización única
bundle of rights conjunto de derechos
burden of proof carga de la prueba
burglary robo con allanamiento de morada
business negocio, empresa
    business community el mundo de los negocios
    business corporation sociedad mercantil
    business cycle coyuntura
    business day día hábil
    business district zona comercial
    business expense gastos del negocio
    business hours horas hábiles
    business interruption insurance seguro de lucro cesante
    business judgment rule regla eximente de responsabilidad en la toma de decisión de los administradores cuando actúan como buenos hombres de negocio
    business law derecho mercantil
    business license patente de comercio
    business outlook perspectivas del negocio
    business premises locales comerciales
    Thank you for your business. Gracias por su preferencia.
    We appreciate your business. Gracias por su preferencia.
buy out v adquirir el control
buyer comprador
    buyer's agent agente del comprador
    buyer's market mercado favorable al comprador
buying power poder de adquisición, poder de compra
buy down s pago inicial para obtener reducción de la tasa de interés
buy-sell agreement contrato de compraventa
by and between entre
by consensus por consenso
by the authority vested in me en uso de mis facultades
by the close of business antes que se termine el día hábil
by unanimous vote por unanimidad de votos
bylaws estatutos
cafeteria plan plan que le permite al trabajador seleccionar uno de varios beneficios ofrecidos por el patrón/empleador
calendar year año civil, año calendario, año natural
call v
    call a loan v exigir el reembolso anticipado de un préstamo
    call a meeting to order v abrir una sesión, declarar abierta una sesión
    call a meeting v convocar a una asamblea
call option opción de compra
callable bond bono redimible [*bono que puede ser amortizado antes de su vencimiento*]

cap límite máximo
capacity 1. capacidad 2. carácter, condición
capital capital
    capital assets bienes de capital
    capital contribution aporte de capital
    capital felony delito punible con la pena de muerte
    capital flight fuga de capitales
    capital gain plusvalía, ganancia de capital
    capital indebtedness endeudamiento de capital
    capital inflow afluencia de capital
    capital intake entrada de capital
    capital investment inversión de capital
    capital lease arrendamiento financiero [*un arrendamiento que de acuerdo con los principios de contabilidad generalmente aceptados, debe figurar en el balance general del arrendatario como un activo y también como un pasivo, porque el arrendatario recibe la mayoría de los beneficios de la propiedad*]
    capital loss minusvalía, pérdida de capital
    capital market mercado de capitales
    capital offense delito punible con la pena de muerte
    capital outflow salida de capital
    capital punishment pena de muerte
    capital stock capital social
    capital structure capitalización
    capital surplus excedente de capital
    capital turnover rotación de capital
capitalization capitalización
captive market mercado cautivo
carjacking robo de vehículo con violencia
carriage
    carriage and insurance paid to (CIP) transporte y seguros pagados hasta [*Incoterm*]
    carriage paid to (CPT) transporte pagado hasta [*Incoterm*]
carryover loss pérdida trasladada al año siguiente
Cartagena Agreement Acuerdo de Cartagena
    Cartagena Agreement Board Junta del Acuerdo de Cartagena
case caso, causa
    case of first impression caso respecto del cual no existen precedentes
casebook libro de precedentes judiciales que se usa en las facultades de derecho norteamericanas
caselaw jurisprudencia
cash dinero en efectivo
    cash advance anticipo en efectivo, disposición en efectivo
    cash and cash equivalents caja y equivalentes de caja

Chancery Court - Tribunal de Equidad

cash contribution aportación dineraria, aportación en efectivo, aportación en numerario

cash flow flujo de fondos

cash on delivery (COD) pago contra entrega

cash on shipment (COS) pago contra embarque

cash price valor efectivo

cash reserve reserva de dinero en efectivo

cash surrender value valor de rescate en efectivo

cash value valor en efectivo

cash voucher vale de caja

cashier's check talón bancario (Esp), cheque de gerencia, cheque de caja

cast a vote v emitir un voto

casting vote voto de calidad

catch a market window v aprovechar una oportunidad de mercado

cause of action 1. pretensión objeto de la causa 2. derecho de iniciar acción

caveat emptor (Lat) a riesgo del comprador

central securities depository central de depósito de valores

certificate certificado

   certificate of good standing certificado de cumplimiento de obligaciones

   certificate of incorporation 1. [*en la mayoría de los estados*] constancia de registro de una sociedad 2. [*en el estado de Delaware*] acta constitutiva [*en Delaware es sinónimo de "articles of incorporation"*]

   certificate of incumbency lista certificada de directivos de una empresa y sus funciones

   certificate of origin certificado de origen

   certificate of withdrawal certificado de suspensión de actividades [*en cierto estado*]

certified check cheque certificado, talón conformado (Esp)

chairman of the board presidente del consejo de administración (Esp, Gua, Hon, Méx), presidente del directorio (Arg, Bol, Chi, Par, Per, Uru)

chambers despacho del juez

change of venue traslado de jurisdicción

character

   character evidence testimonio sobre la solvencia moral de una persona

   character witness testigo de solvencia moral

charitable trust fideicomiso con fines benéficos

chartered life underwriter agente de seguros colegiado

chattel mortgage hipoteca prendaria, hipoteca mueble (Bol), hipoteca mobiliaria (Ven)

check cheque, talón (Esp)

   check clearing compensación de cheques, canje de cheques

city council - concejo municipal

check kiting giro doloso de cheques
checkbook chequera, talonario (Esp)
    checking account cuenta de cheque, cuenta chequera, cuenta corriente
chief
    chief justice presidente de la corte suprema
    chief of staff oficial mayor
child
    child abuse abuso de menores, malos tratos a menores
    child born out of wedlock hijo natural
    child by a previous marriage hijo de un matrimonio anterior
    child molestation abuso sexual de menores
    child support pensión para el sustento de hijo(s)
chilling effect efecto disuasivo [*desalienta el ejercicio de derechos constitucionales*]
choice of law clause cláusula de derecho aplicable
Christmas bonus aguinaldo, regalía pascual
circuit court tribunal de primera instancia [*en los estados de Alabama, Arkansas, Florida, Hawai, Illinois, Indiana, Kentucky, Maryland, Michigan, Misisipí, Misuri, Oregon, Carolina del Sur, Dakota del Sur, Tennesee, Virginia, Virginia Occidental y Wisconsin*]
    circuit court of appeals tribunal federal de apelaciones de circuito
circumstantial evidence prueba indiciaria, prueba de indicio
civil
    civil action acción civil
    civil court juzgado de lo civil
    civil division of a court sala de lo civil
    civil procedure derecho procesal civil
    Civil Rights Act Ley de Derechos Civiles
    civil servant funcionario
    civil service función pública
    civil trial juicio civil
claim reclamo, reclamación
class action acción colectiva
clear
    clear and convincing evidence prueba clara y convincente
    clear and present danger peligro claro y actual
    clear title título sano
clearance sale venta de liquidación
clearing house cámara de compensación
clerical error error administrativo
clerk
    clerk of a judge pasante
    clerk of the court secretario judicial, actuario
clerkship pasantía

close corporation sociedad cerrada [*controlada por un grupo reducido de personas, cuyas acciones no cotizan en bolsa y sobre cuya transferencia existen restricciones*]

closed session sesión a puerta cerrada

closely-held corporation sociedad de pocos accionistas

close-out sale venta de liquidación

cloud on title defecto de un título de propiedad

codicil codicilo

coercive coactivo

collateral bienes afectados en garantía

collective bargaining contratación colectiva

    collective bargaining agreement contrato colectivo

collusive price fixing nivelación convencional de precios

color of title título aparente

combined offense delito complejo

comfort letter carta de patrocinio, carta de alivio (Arg)

commercial comercial, mercantil

    commercial bank banco comercial

    Commercial Code Código de Comercio

    commercial invoice factura comercial

    commercial law derecho comercial, derecho mercantil (Gua, Méx, Ven)

    commercial paper papel comercial

    commercial slogan aviso comercial

    commercial transactions actos de comercio

commingling of assets confusión de patrimonios

commission comisión, mandato

    My commission expires Mi mandato cesa, mis funciones cesan

commit v

    commit a crime v incurrir en un delito

    commit perjury v jurar en falso

commitment letter carta de compromiso

commodity productos básicos

    commodities exchange bolsa de contratación

common

    common law el common law, derecho angloamericano

    common law country país de derecho angloamericano

    common law marriage matrimonio de hecho *unión libre*

    common stock acciones ordinarias

commonwealth

    Commonwealth of Pennsylvania Estado de Pensilvania

    Commonwealth of Puerto Rico Estado Libre Asociado de Puerto Rico

    Commonwealth of Virginia Estado de Virginia

community

    community property bienes gananciales

compliance in letter + spirit –cumplimiento de la letr[a]
cumplir con la ley en letra y de espíritu de la ley.

Community Reinvestment Act Ley de Reinversión en la Comunidad [*ley federal que en Estados Unidos obliga a las instituciones crediticias regidas por el sistema federal, a informar sobre el área geográfica que sirven, para que los depósitos que provengan de la misma sean reinvertidos en la medida de lo posible en ella*]

community service trabajo en favor de la comunidad

comparative law derecho comparado

compensation remuneración

competent witness testigo hábil

complainant querellante

complaint 1. demanda 2. denuncia penal

complex litigation litigios complejos

compos mentis en su sano juicio

composite picture retrato hablado (Méx, Ven), retrato robot (Esp)

compound interest interés compuesto

compulsory joinder litisconsorcio obligatorio

conclusive presumption presunción juris et de jure

condition condición

    condition precedent condición suspensiva

    condition subsequent condición resolutoria

conflict of interests conflicto de intereses

conflict of laws conflicto de leyes, derecho internacional privado

conform one's conduct to v ajustar su conducta a

confusingly similar trademark marca semejante en grado de confusión

conjugal rights derechos conyugales

conscientious objector objetor de conciencia (Esp)

consent consentimiento

    consent judgment sentencia acordada por las partes

consequential damages daños emergentes

consideration contraprestación, contrapartida

    for other good and valuable consideration por otra contrapartida valiosa

consignee consignatario

consolidated balance sheet balance consolidado

consolidation of cases acumulación de autos

conspiracy asociación ilícita

constant dollar accounting contabilidad en dólares constantes

Constitution Constitución, ley de leyes, texto fundamental, carta magna

constitutional

    constitutional convention asamblea constituyente

    constitutional law derecho constitucional

    constitutional rights garantías constitucionales

construction [of a treaty, contract, law] interpretación

constructive
> **constructive eviction** desalojo virtual [*como consecuencia de la inhabitabilidad del inmueble*]
> **constructive fraud** fraude implícito
> **constructive notice** notificación implícita
> **constructive trust** fideicomiso impuesto por ministerio de la ley
> **constructive trustee** fideicomisario por ministerio de la ley

consular
> **consular fees** derechos consulares
> **consular invoice** factura consular

consumer consumidor
> **consumer goods** bienes de consumo
> **consumer price index** índice de precios al consumidor, índice de precios de consumo (Esp, Uru)

contempt of court rebeldía, desacato al tribunal, contumacia
contest a will v impugnar un testamento
contingency contingencia
> **contingency fee** cuota litis
> **contingency fee agreement** pacto de cuota litis

contingent reserve reserva para eventualidades, reserva para contingencias
continuance aplazamiento, postergación
continuing legal education (CLE) formación jurídica permanente
continuous easement servidumbre continua
contract contrato
contractor contratista
contractual obligation obligación contractual
contributory negligence culpa concurrente
controlled substance sustancia regulada
controlling interest participación mayoritaria
conversion apropiación ilícita
convertible bond bono convertible
conviction condena
cop a plea v realizar un pacto sobre la declaración de culpabilidad
copy copia, ejemplar, tanto
copyright derechos de autor
> **copyright holder** titular de los derechos de autor
> **copyright infringement** violación a los derechos de autor
> **copyright notice** mención de los derechos de autor
> **copyrightable** susceptible de ser registrado como propiedad intelectual
> **copyrighted work** obra registrada como propiedad intelectual

core capital capital primario, capital básico [*se denomina también "Tier I Capital"*]
corporate
> **corporate assets** bienes sociales
> **corporate issuer** emisor corporativo

corporate law derecho corporativo, derecho societario
corporate lawyer abogado corporativista
corporate planning planificación corporativa
corporate policy política corporativa
corporate purpose objeto social
corporation sociedad anónima, compañía anónima (Ecu, Ven)
corpus delicti cuerpo del delito
correspondent bank banco corresponsal
co-sign v avalar
cosigner avalista
cost
    cost accounting contabilidad de costos
    cost and freight (CFR) costo y flete [*Incoterm*]
    cost of living costo de vida
    cost of living adjustment ajuste por aumento del costo de la vida
    cost of living allowance asignación por costo de vida
    cost, insurance and freight (CIF) costo, seguro y flete [*Incoterm*]
counter check talón de ventanilla (Esp), cheque de ventanilla
counterfeit v falsificar
counteroffer contraoferta
counterpart of a contract ejemplar
countervailing duty cuotas compensatorias
country of last residence país de domicilio más reciente
coupon cupón
    coupon bond bono con cupón
court tribunal, juzgado, corte
    Court adjourned. Se levanta la sesión.
    court clerk secretario de actas */secret. de ACUERDOS*
    court costs costas judiciales
    court interpreter intérprete judicial
    court of common pleas tribunal de primera instancia [*en los estados de Pensilvania y Ohio*]
    court of competent jurisdiction tribunal competente
    court of first instance tribunal de primera instancia, juzgado de primera instancia
    court of last resort tribunal de última instancia
    court of law tribunal de justicia
    court of original jurisdiction tribunal de primera instancia
    court order auto, resolución judicial
    court reporter taquígrafo
    court sitting en banc tribunal plenario, tribunal en pleno
courtroom sala del juzgado
covenant convenio
    covenant not to compete convenio de no competir, pacto de no competencia

covenant of quiet enjoyment convenio de goce pacífico
cover letter carta remesa
coverage cobertura
coworker compañero de trabajo
credit crédito
   credit analysis análisis de crédito
   credit balance saldo acreedor, saldo a favor
   credit bureau sociedad de información crediticia
   credit entry asiento de abono
   credit history antecedentes crediticios
   credit rating calificación de crédito
   credit record antecedentes crediticios
   credit report informe de crédito
   credit union cooperativa de crédito, unión de crédito (Méx)
creditor acreedor
creditworthiness solvencia crediticia
creeping inflation inflación reptante, inflación furtiva
crime delincuencia
   crime of passion delito pasional
   crime prevention prevención de la delincuencia
criminal delincuente
   criminal action acción penal
   criminal court juzgado de lo penal
   criminal division of a court sala de lo penal
   criminal forfeiture confiscación por el estado de un bien usado
     en un delito
   criminal law derecho penal
   criminal lawyer abogado penalista
   criminal offense delito penal
   criminal procedure derecho procesal penal
   criminal record antecedentes penales
cross
   cross-bill letra de resaca
   cross claim demanda contra coparte
   cross trade operación cruzada, cruce (Méx)
cruel and unusual punishment pena cruel e insólita [*son penas abolidas por ser excesivas y en contra de la moral*]
cumulative
   cumulative sentences condenas acumulativas
   cumulative voting voto acumulativo
cure a breach of contract v subsanar el incumplimiento del
   contrato
curfew toque de queda
current
   current account surplus superávit en cuenta corriente
   current assets activo circulante, activo corriente
   current liabilities pasivo circulante, pasivo corriente

current monthly expenses gastos mensuales actuales
current ratio índice de solvencia
custodial parent el titular del derecho de guarda y custodia
custody custodia de menores, tenencia de menores (Arg)
customary law derecho consuetudinario
customs aduana
    customs clearance despacho aduanero
    customs duties derechos aduaneros, aranceles de aduana
    customs examiner dictaminador aduanero
    customs inspection reconocimiento aduanero
    customs officer agente de aduana, inspector de aduana,
      aduanero
    customs seizure decomiso aduanal
date
    date of maturity fecha de vencimiento
    date stamp sello fechador
day
    day in court derecho a ser oído
    day shift jornada diurna
de minimis insignificante
deadline fecha límite
deal negocio, trato
death
    death certificate certificado de defunción, acta de defunción,
      partida de defunción
    death penalty pena de muerte
    death row corredor de la muerte
    death sentence condena a la pena de muerte
debit
    debit balance saldo deudor, saldo en contra
    debit entry asiento de cargo
    debit memorandum nota de cargo
debt deuda, obligación
    debt financing financiación mediante endeudamiento
    debt ratio porcentaje de deudas
    debt service pago de la deuda
debtor deudor
deceased fallecido, difunto, finado
decedent fallecido, difunto, finado
deciding vote voto de calidad
decision on the merits decisión sobre el fondo
declaratory judgment sentencia declarativa
decriminalization despenalización
deductible adj deducible
deductible s franquicia [*en una póliza de seguros*]
deduction deducción

deed escritura

deed in lieu of foreclosure escritura en lugar de ejecución de la hipoteca por resolución judicial

deed of trust escritura de fideicomiso

deep pockets capacidad de abonar grandes sumas de dinero

defamatory difamante

default incumplimiento

default interest intereses moratorios

default judgment sentencia en rebeldía

defaulting party parte incumplidora

defeasance condición resolutoria, anulación

defeasible anulable, revocable

defendant 1. [*en lo civil*] demandado, parte demandada 2. [*en lo penal*] acusado, reo

defendant's standing legitimación pasiva

defense counsel abogado defensor

degree of kinship grado de parentesco

Delaware corporation sociedad constituida conforme a leyes del Estado de Delaware [*no necesariamente una sociedad en Delaware*]

delectus personae la selección de la persona

delinquency 1. morosidad 2. delincuencia

delivered

delivered at frontier (DAF) entregada en frontera [*Incoterm*]

delivered duty paid (DDP) entregada derechos pagados [*Incoterm*]

delivered duty unpaid (DDU) entregada derechos no pagados [*Incoterm*]

delivered ex quay (DEQ) entregada en muelle [*Incoterm*]

delivered ex ship (DES) entregada sobre buque [*Incoterm*]

delivery note albarán (Esp), remito (Arg)

demand requerimiento de pago

demand deposit depósito a la vista

demonstrative evidence prueba gráfica

department

Department of Justice Ministerio de Justicia

Department of Labor Ministerio de Trabajo

Department of Social Services Ministerio de Servicios Sociales

Department of State Ministerio de Relaciones Exteriores

deponent declarante

deportability validez de los cargos de deportación

Deportability has been established. Se han comprobado los cargos de deportación.

deportable quien puede ser deportado

deportation deportación [*se refiere a las personas detenidas después de entrar en los Estados Unidos, mientras que* *"exclusión" se refiere a las personas detenidas en los puertos de entrada a los Estados Unidos*]

deportation proceedings trámites de deportación

depose someone v tomar la declaración a alguien

deposit slip planilla de ingreso (Esp), ficha de depósito (Méx), boleta de depósito (Arg, Chi)

deposit v 1. depósito [*en el banco*] 2. arras, enganche (Méx), seña (Arg), pie (Chi)

deposition declaración jurada extrajudicial

depositor depositante

depreciation amortización, depreciación

deregulation liberalización

derivative
> **derivative action** acción entablada por los accionistas en base a un derecho de la sociedad
> **derivative instruments** instrumentos derivados
> **derivatives market** mercados de derivados

desertion abandono

determinate obligation obligación de dar cosa cierta

developed land terreno edificado

developing country país en vías de desarrollo

die without issue v morir sin descendencia

diplomatic immunity inmunidad diplomática

directed verdict veredicto por instrucción judicial

disability
> **disability insurance** seguro de incapacidad, seguro de invalidez
> **disability payments** pagos por incapacidad

disabled incapacitado

disaster area zona catastrófica/de catástrofe

disbarment exclusión del foro

discharge a debt v liquidar, cancelar una deuda

discharge in bankruptcy s extinción de la quiebra

disclaimer of warranty s exclusión de garantías

disclosure declaración

discount to present value v descontar al valor presente

discounted cash flow analysis análisis de flujo de fondos descontado

disintermediation desintermediación financiera

dismiss an appeal v desestimar un recurso

disposable income ingreso disponible

dispose of v enajenar

dissent v votar en contra

dissenting opinion opinión en contra

dissenting vote voto discrepante, voto en disidencia, voto reservado (Esp), voto salvado (Col, Ven)

dissociation disociación

dissolve an attachment v levantar un embargo
district court tribunal de primera instancia
districting distribución de distritos
disturbing the peace perturbación del orden público
diversity case conflicto entre ciudadanos de diferentes estados
dividend
    dividend in kind dividendo en especie
    dividend per share of common stock dividendo por acción
      ordinaria
division of a court sala
divorce
    divorce a mensa et thoro separación de cuerpos
    divorce a vinculo matrimonii divorcio vincular
    divorce by mutual consent divorcio por mutuo consentimiento
    divorce decree sentencia de divorcio
docket lista de causas
doctor-patient privilege secreto profesional médico
documentary evidence prueba documental
domestic
    domestic law derecho interno, derecho nacional
    domestic market mercado interno, mercado nacional
    domestic policy política interior, política nacional
    domestic relations relaciones familiares
    domestic relations court juzgado de familia
    domestic sales ventas nacionales
    domestic violence violencia en el hogar
domiciled draft letra de cambio domiciliada
dominant estate predio dominante
donation donación
donee donatario
donor donante
double taxation doble imposición
dower usufructo vitalicio de la esposa
down payment pago inicial, arras, enganche (Méx), seña (Arg), pie
    (Chi)
downsizing reducción de personal
draft card libreta militar (Ecu, Per)
draftsman of a contract redactor de un contrato
drag-along rights derechos de arrastre [*derechos de los*
    accionistas mayoritarios (establecidos en un pacto entre
    accionistas) de forzar a los accionistas minoritarios a vender sus
    acciones cuando se presenta una oferta de adquisición
    interesante]
drainage easement servidumbre de desagüe
Dram Shop Act Ley de Tabernas
draw funds v girar fondos
draw on an account v girar contra una cuenta

drawdown disposición de un crédito
  drawdown date fecha de disposición del crédito
  drawdown period periodo de disponibilidad del crédito
drawee girado, librado
drawer girador, librador
driver's license licencia de conducir, registro de conductor (Arg), brevete (Per), pase (Col)
drunk driving delito de conducir bajo la influencia del alcohol
dual citizenship doble ciudadanía
dual status alien extranjero con doble residencia
due
  due and payable vencido y pagadero
  due date fecha de vencimiento
  due diligence revisión de aspectos importantes de un negocio para descubrir posibles contingencias
  due process of law debido proceso legal
dumped price precio vil
durable
  durable goods bienes duraderos
  durable power of attorney poder no caducable por incapacidad superviniente del mandante
duress coacción
Dutch auction subasta a la baja
dutiable value valor en aduanas
duty
  duty free exento de derechos
  duty of care deber de cuidado
  duty to mitigate obligación de atenuar los daños y perjuicios
each and every year todos y cada año
early
  early retirement jubilación anticipada
  early termination terminación anticipada
earned income ingresos provenientes del trabajo, rentas del trabajo
earnest money arras, seña (Arg), enganche (Méx), pie (Chi)
  earnest money deposit depósito de buena fe
earning capacity capacidad de producir ingreso
easement servidumbre
  easement appurtenant servidumbre real
economic
  economic cutback reajuste económico
  economic hardship dificultades económicas
economies of scale economías de escala
effective
  effective as to third parties oponible a terceros, que puede oponerse a terceros
  effective date fecha de entrada en vigencia
  effective rate tasa de interés efectiva

elevation sheet plano de alzada
embezzle v desfalcar, escalfar (Méx)
embezzlement desfalco, malversación, peculado
embezzler desfalcador, malversador
emerging market mercado emergente
eminent domain dominio eminente
emotional distress daño moral
employee empleado, trabajador
employer patrón (Méx), patrono (Esp), empleador (Arg)
employment
    employment agreement contrato de trabajo
    employment at will relación laboral que se puede rescindir sin
      causa justificada
    employment authorization autorización para trabajar
    employment relationship relación laboral
en banc en pleno
enabling
    enabling act ley de autorización
    enabling legislation legislación de autorización
enact legislation v promulgar legislación
encumber v gravar
encumbrance gravamen
endowment dotación
    endowment insurance seguro de vida dotal, seguro dotal
enforceable exigible, que puede hacerse valer judicialmente
    enforceable against third parties oponible a terceros, que
      puede oponerse a terceros
enforcement of a law aplicación de una ley
engage in an act v realizar un acto
engagement letter carta de contratación, carta compromiso (Arg)
enter
    enter an appearance v apersonarse al proceso
    enter in the books v asentar en los libros
    enter in the record v hacer constar en las actas
    enter into a contract v celebrar un contrato
entertainment expenses gastos de representación
entire agreement integridad del contrato
equal protection igual protección ante la ley
equilibrium exchange rate tipo de cambio de equilibrio
equity
    equity financing financiación mediante la emisión de acciones
    equity kicker cláusula de participación en las ganancias
      [*disposición en un préstamo o contrato de arrendamiento*
      que le permite al prestamista o al arrendatario principal
      participar en el flujo de fondos o en los ingresos de reventa
      de un proyecto inmobiliario]

equity method of accounting método de puesta en equivalencia

— **escheat s** reversión al estado

— **escrow** depósito de confianza, plica (Pue)
    escrow agent depositario
    escrow company compañía de custodia
    escrow deposit account cuenta de fondos en custodia, en depósito, en plica (Pue)
    escrow funds fondos en custodia, fondos en depósito, fondos en plica (Pue)

establishment clause cláusula constitucional que prohibe el establecimiento de una religión del Estado

estate masa hereditaria, sucesión, caudal hereditario
    estate tax impuesto sucesorio

estimate s estimación de costos

estimate v calcular

estopped impedido

— **estoppel** preclusión, impedimento
    estoppel by conduct impedimento por razón de conducta
    estoppel by deed impedimento por escritura
    — **estoppel by laches** impedimento por negligencia
    estoppel by silence impedimento por falta de declaración

et seq. y siguientes

— **et ux** y su esposa

— **ethnic cleansing** homicidio eugenésico

euthanasia homicidio consentido, homicidio piadoso, homicidio por piedad

evict v desalojar, desahuciar

eviction desalojo, desahucio
    eviction notice notificación de desalojo
    eviction proceedings juicio de desalojo

— **ex parte proceedings** juicio no contencioso

ex works (EXW) en fábrica [*Incoterm*]

exchange rate tipo de cambio, tasa de cambio
    exchange rate hedge seguro de cambio

excise tax impuesto sobre artículos de uso y consumo

excludable excluible, que puede ser excluido

exclusionary rule principio de exclusión de pruebas obtenidas ilegalmente

excusable homicide homicidio casual, homicidio por caso fortuito, homicidio excusable

execute v
    execute a contract v firmar un contrato, otorgar un contrato
    execute a judgment v ejecutar una sentencia

executive branch poder ejecutivo

— **executor** albacea testamentario

executors and administrators albaceas testamentarios y
dativos

exemplary damages daños y perjuicios punitorios

exhaustion

exhaustion of administrative remedies agotamiento de la vía
administrativa

exhaustion of remedies agotamiento de recursos

exhibit 1. documento de prueba [*en un juicio*] 2. anexo [*de un
contrato, una demanda, etc.*]

Exhibit A to the Agreement Anexo A del Contrato

exit poll encuesta a pie de urna, encuesta en boca de urna

expert perito

expert appraisal tasación pericial

expert opinion dictamen pericial

expert testimony prueba pericial

expiration vencimiento

export

export license permiso de exportación

export subsidy subvención a la exportación

express waiver renuncia expresa

extended voluntary departure aplazamiento general de la salida
voluntaria [*política general de no deportar a personas de cierta
nacionalidad hasta estar segura la situación en su país*]

extenuating circumstances circunstancias atenuantes

external

external audit auditoría externa

external auditor auditor externo

extort v extorsionar, boletear (Col)

extortion extorsión, boleteo (Col)

extraordinary item partida extraordinaria

extreme hardship situación crítica

eyewitness testigo ocular, testigo de vista

facsimile signature firma facsímil

factoring factoraje

failure

failure to appear incomparecencia, contumacia

failure to attend a meeting inasistencia a una reunión

fair

fair market value valor de mercado justo

fair trial juicio imparcial

false arrest detención injustificada

family familia

family allowance asignación familiar

family court juzgado de familia

family court judge juez de lo familiar (Méx)

family law derecho de familia

family lawyer abogado de familia

Fannie Mae apodo de la Federal National Mortgage Association
fast track vía rápida
fax cover sheet portada de fax
federal common law precedentes establecidos por los tribunales
 federales
Federal Register Gaceta Oficial de los Estados Unidos
fee simple pleno dominio, riguroso dominio
 fee simple defeasible dominio sujeto a una condición
  resolutoria
fellow employee compañero de trabajo
fellow servant rule norma según la cual el empleador no es
 responsable por lesiones causadas a un empleado por otro
felony delito grave, delito mayor
felony murder homicidio cometido en el curso de un delito mayor
file s expediente
 files archivos
file v
 file a complaint with the court v entablar una demanda ante el
  tribunal
 file a police report v hacer una denuncia, entablar denuncia
 file a tax return v presentar una declaración de impuestos
 file an appeal v interponer recurso
 file for bankruptcy v presentar una solicitud de declaración de
  quiebra
 file for divorce v entablar una demanda de divorcio
filing
 filing desk mesa de entradas (Arg), oficina de partes (Chi),
  mesa de partes (Per), oficialía de partes (Méx)
 filing fee tasa judicial
 filing of the articles of incorporation registro de la escritura
  constitutiva
 filing status estado civil para los efectos de la declaración de
  impuestos
fill a vacancy v cubrir una vacante
fill or kill order orden de ejecución inmediata [*en la bolsa*]
final
 final acceptance recepción definitiva
 final adjudication resolución definitiva dictada por un tribunal
 final decision resolución definitiva
 final judgment sentencia definitiva
financial
 financial advisor asesor financiero
 financial institution institución financiera
 financial position situación financiera
 financial statement estado financiero
financing financiamiento, financiación (Esp)
 financing terms términos del financiamiento

find v
    find for the plaintiff v decidir en favor del demandante
    find guilty v declarar culpable
findings of fact and conclusions of law conclusiones de hecho y derecho
finished goods productos terminados
fire marshal jefe de bomberos
firm offer oferta en firme
first
    first deed of trust primera escritura de fideicomiso
    first degree murder asesinato premeditado
    first in, first out (FIFO) primeras entradas, primeras salidas
    first instance primera instancia
    first mortgage hipoteca en primer lugar, hipoteca de primer grado
    first offender delincuente primario
    first to occur of según lo que suceda en primer término
    first-time offender delincuente primario, delincuente sin antecedentes penales
fiscal year ejercicio, año fiscal
fixed
    fixed assets activo fijo, bienes de uso (Arg), activo inmovilizado (Esp)
    fixed expenses gastos fijos
    fixed income renta fija
    fixed income securities valores de renta fija
    fixed interest rate tasa de interés fija
    fixed investment inversión en capital fijo
    fixed-rate mortgage hipoteca con tasa de interés fija
fixtures muebles adheridos
flat
    flat amount importe fijo
    flat increase aumento uniforme
    flat lease arrendamiento sin interés [*acuerdo que exige que se efectúen pagos de alquiler iguales por el período completo del arrendamiento*]
    flat market mercado inactivo
    flat rate tarifa fija, tarifa única, tasa uniforme
floating
    floating exchange rate tipo de cambio flotante
    floating lien gravamen continuado
    floating rate bond bono con interés variable
flood insurance seguro contra inundación
floor trader corredor de bolsa por cuenta propia
FOIA request petición en base a la Ley de Libre Acceso a la Información [*FOIA se refiere a la Freedom of Information Act*]
for future reference para consultas en el futuro

for purposes of para los efectos de, a los efectos de
for reasons beyond his control por motivos ajenos a su voluntad
for the record para que conste
for valuable consideration a título oneroso
forbearance acuerdo de diferir demanda de la ejecución hipotecaria
force majeure fuerza mayor
forced
    forced heir heredero forzoso
    forced sale venta forzada
foreclose on a mortgage v entablar juicio hipotecario
foreclosure ejecución hipotecaria
foregoing (the) lo anterior
foreign
    foreign corporation sociedad constituida conforme a las leyes
        de otra jurisdicción
    Foreign Corrupt Practices Act Ley contra Prácticas Corruptas
        en el Extranjero
    foreign exchange market mercado de cambios, mercado
        cambiario
    foreign exchange position posición de cambio
    foreign exchange risk riesgo cambiario
    foreign indebtedness endeudamiento externo, endeudamiento
        con el exterior
    foreign policy política exterior
    foreign source income ingreso de fuente del extranjero
    foreign trade zone zona franca
foreman of the jury presidente del jurado
foreseeability previsibilidad
forfeiture of a right pérdida de un derecho
forged signature firma falsificada
forgive a debt v perdonar una deuda
form will formulario para testamentos
forum
    forum non conveniens jurisdicción inadecuada
    forum selection clause cláusula de selección de jurisdicción
    forum shopping búsqueda de tribunal conveniente
forward
    forward rate tipo de cambio a futuro
    forward thinking perspicacia
    forward transaction operación a plazo
forwarding agent agente de despacho
foster
    foster child hijo de crianza
    foster home hogar tutelar
    foster parent padre tutelar, padre de crianza
founders' shares acciones de fundador

fractional
    fractional currency moneda fraccionaria
    fractional shares acciones fraccionadas
franchise franquicia
franchisee franquiciado
franchisor franquiciador
fraud fraude, dolo
    Fraud vitiates a contract. El fraude invalida un contrato.
fraudulent misrepresentation manifestación dolosa
free 1. libre 2. gratuito
    free alongside ship (FAS) franco al costado del buque
      [*Incoterm*]
    free and clear of all liens and encumbrances libre de todo
      gravamen
    free carrier (FCA) franco transportista [*Incoterm*]
    free exercise clause cláusula constitucional sobre libertad de
      culto
    free market economy economía de mercado libre
    free on board (FOB) franco a bordo [*Incoterm*]
    free on rail franco vagón [*Incoterm*]
    free trade zone zona franca
freedom libertad
    freedom of assembly libertad de reunión
    Freedom of Information Act (FOIA) Ley de Libre Acceso a la
      Información
    freedom of religion libertad de cultos
    freedom of speech libertad de palabra
    freedom of the press libertad de prensa
freight forwarder agente expedidor
fringe benefits beneficios adicionales
from time to time periódicamente
front-end ratio proporción del pago mensual de la hipoteca en
    relación con el ingreso bruto mensual
fruit
    fruit of an unlawful arrest consecuencia de una detención
      ilegal
    fruit of the poisonous tree doctrine doctrina de la
      inadmisibilidad de prueba obtenida ilegalmente
frustration of contract frustración del contrato
fugitive prófugo
    fugitive warrant orden de detención de un prófugo
full
    full consolidation integración global (Esp), consolidación global
    full faith and credit entera fe y crédito
    full faith and credit clause cláusula constitucional según la
      cual cada estado tiene que reconocer las leyes y
      resoluciones judiciales de los demás estados

fundamental analysis análisis fundamental
futures futuros financieros
gag order imposición de silencio perpetuo al litigante
gainful
    gainful employee empleado retribuido
    gainful employment empleo provechoso, ocupación lucrativa
garnishee embargado
garnishment proceedings proceso de embargo
gearing adjustment ajuste por apalancamiento (Arg), ajuste por endeudamiento (Esp)
general
    general partner socio comanditado
    general partnership sociedad colectiva, sociedad en nombre colectivo
    generally accepted accounting principles principios contables generalmente aceptados
    generally accepted auditing standards normas de auditoría generalmente aceptadas
generic brand marca blanca
gerrymander v dividir los distritos electorales en forma arbitraria con el objeto de otorgar ventajas a un partido político
give v
    give judgment for the plaintiff v dictar sentencia a favor del demandante
    give someone a fair trial v juzgar a alguien con imparcialidad
global bond bono global
go on strike v hacer huelga
going concern empresa en funcionamiento
going public salida a bolsa
gold standard patrón oro
good
    good faith buena fe
    good law norma de jurisprudencia que no ha sido revocada en un fallo posterior
    good moral character solvencia moral
    good offices buenos oficios
    good till canceled válido hasta su revocación
    good title título válido
goodwill fondo de comercio (Esp), llave de un negocio (Arg), plusvalía (Ecu), crédito mercantil (Méx)
governing law derecho aplicable
government
    government agency organismo público
    government bonds deuda pública
graduated-payment mortgage (GPM) hipoteca de amortización gradual

grand
> **grand jury** jurado de acusación
> **grand larceny** hurto de cuantía mayor
> **grand total** total general

grandfather clause cláusula de una ley nueva que excluye de su aplicación a aquellos comprendidos en el sistema anterior

grant v
> **grant amnesty v** indultar
> **grant relief v** otorgar reparación

grantee otorgado

grantor otorgante

grievance queja

gross
> **gross domestic product** producto bruto interno (PBI) (Arg), producto interno bruto (PIB) (Cos, Méx, Ven), producto interior bruto (PIB) (Esp)
> **gross income** ingreso bruto
> **gross national product** producto bruto nacional
> **gross negligence** culpa lata, falta grave, negligencia manifiesta

ground lease arrendamiento del terreno solamente

grounds for divorce causal de divorcio

group
> **group insurance** seguro colectivo
> **group life insurance** seguro de vida colectivo

growth stock acciones de crecimiento

guarantor fiador

guardian curador, tutor
> **guardian ad litem** curador ad litem

guardianship curatela, tutela

guideline lineamiento

gunrunner contrabandista de armas

gunrunning contrabando de armas

habeas corpus hábeas corpus

hand down a judgment v dictar una sentencia

hand
> **I have hereunto set my hand and seal this 25th day of August.** Firmo y estampo mi sello a los 25 días de agosto.

harassment acoso, hostigamiento

hard
> **hard case** caso en el cual la estricta aplicación del derecho genera una injusticia
> **hard currency** moneda fuerte
> **hard labor** trabajos forzados

hardship dificultades

hate
> **hate crime** delito motivado por prejuicios
> **hate mail** cartas llenas de insultos y amenazas

have
 have the floor v tener la palabra
 to have and to hold para ser poseído en propiedad
hazard insurance seguro contra riesgos
head
 head of household cabeza de familia, jefe de familia (Pue)
 head of state jefe de estado
 head teller cajero principal
headhunter cazatalentos
health insurance seguro de enfermedad, seguro médico
hear a case v conocer de una causa, entender en una causa, ver
 una causa
hearing audiencia, vista
 hearing in open court audiencia pública
 hearing officer funcionario a cargo de la audiencia
hearsay evidence prueba de oídas, prueba por referencia
hedging transaction operación de cobertura
heir
 heir at law heredero legal
 heir of the body heredero en línea recta
 heir testamentary heredero testamentario
hereby por el presente, por la presente
herein en el presente, en la presente
hereinabove más arriba
hereinafter referred to as X en lo sucesivo denominado X, en
 adelante denominado X
hereto al presente, del presente
heretofore hasta ahora
hereunder conforme al presente, en virtud del presente
herewith adjunto al presente
hidden reserve reserva oculta
highest
 highest and best use uso máximo y óptimo
 highest bidder mejor postor
hijacking secuestro de un avión
hired assassin sicario, asesino a sueldo
hitman sicario, asesino a sueldo
hold v
 hold a shareholders' meeting v celebrar una asamblea de
  accionistas, celebrar una junta de accionistas
 hold harmless v mantener indemne, liberar de responsabilidad,
  sacar a paz y en salvo (Méx)
 hold office v ejercer su cargo, ejercer su mandato
  He shall hold office until his successor is elected and
  qualified ejercerá su mandato hasta que su sucesor haya
  sido elegido y habilitado
hold harmless agreement acuerdo de indemnidad

holder tenedor
> **holder in due course** tenedor legítimo
> **holder in good faith** tenedor de buena fe
holding company sociedad controladora
holdover tenant locatario/arrendatario que no desocupa el bien locado al terminarse el contrato de locación/arrendamiento
holographic will testamento ológrafo
home equity loan préstamo garantizado con el valor residual de una vivienda
homeowner propietario de vivienda
> **homeowner's insurance** seguro del propietario
> **homeowner's warranty** garantía del propietario
homestead bien de familia (Arg), patrimonio de familia (Méx)
honor a check v aceptar un cheque
hornbook texto que contiene un sumario de los principios legales de una rama o área de derecho
hostile witness testigo que declara en contra de la parte que lo presenta
hotchpot colación
house arrest arresto domiciliario
household unidad familiar
housing shortage crisis de la vivienda
human rights violation violación a los derechos humanos
hung jury jurado estancado por desacuerdo
illegal alien inmigrante ilegal
illegitimate child hijo natural
immaterial no esencial, no importante, que carece de importancia
immediate
> **immediate family** familia directa
> **immediate relative** pariente directo
> **immediate supervisor** supervisor directo
immigrant inmigrante
immigration
> **Immigration and Naturalization Service** Dirección General de Inmigración y Naturalización
> **immigration court** tribunal de inmigración
> **immigration judge** juez de inmigración
> **immigration officer** agente de inmigración
impact fees derechos por impacto sobre la infraestructura [*pagos impuestos por un organismo público local por un nuevo emprendimiento, para cubrir costos adicionales de servicios públicos*]
impeach v hacer juicio político a alguien
impeachment juicio político
implead v llamar en garantía, citar en garantía
impleader llamamiento en garantía, citación en garantía

implied
    implied waiver renuncia implícita
    implied warranty garantía implícita
    implied warranty of habitability garantía implícita de habitabilidad
import tariff arancel de importación
importantly cabe destacar que, cabe señalar que
imprison v aprisionar, encarcelar
improvements mejoras
in arrears en mora
in camera hearing audiencia a puerta cerrada
in consideration of the rights a título de contraprestación por los derechos
in contemplation of death previendo la muerte
in default en rebeldía
in full force and effect en plena vigencia
in its sole discretion a su entero juicio
in kind en especie
in re en el proceso de, en la causa de
in reliance on al amparo de
in the aggregate en su conjunto
in the case at hand en el caso de autos, en la especie
in the matter of en el asunto de
in the ordinary course of business en el giro habitual del comercio
in view of the foregoing en base a lo expuesto anteriormente
in whole or in part total o parcialmente, en todo o en parte
in witness whereof en fe de lo cual, en testimonio de lo cual
inchoate incompleto
    inchoate interest interés incompleto
    inchoate lien gravamen sujeto a revocación
    inchoate right derecho en expectativa
including but not limited to a título indicativo y no limitativo; de manera enunciativa y no taxativa; de manera enunciativa y no limitativa; inclusive, entre otros; que incluyen, pero no taxativamente
income ingreso
    income bracket grupo de ingresos
    income statement estado de pérdidas y ganancias, estado de resultados
    income tax impuesto sobre la renta (Col, Esp, Méx, Ven), impuesto a la renta (Ecu, Per, Uru), impuesto a las ganancias (Arg)
    income tax return declaración de impuestos sobre la renta
incompetent witness testigo inhábil
incorporate
    incorporate a company v constituir una sociedad

incorporate by reference v tenerse por reproducido tal como se insertara a la letra (Méx)

incorporator fundador

incumbency ejercicio del cargo

incumbent ocupante de un cargo, titular

incur liability v incurrir en responsabilidad

indebtedness endeudamiento

indecent behavior atentado contra las buenas costumbres

indecent exposure exhibicionismo

indemnify and hold harmless v liberar de responsabilidad

independent contractor contratista independiente

indeterminate obligation obligación de dar cosa incierta

indigent sin recursos económicos

individual
>**individual income** ingreso personal
>**Individual Retirement Account (IRA)** cuenta personal de jubilación

inflation accounting contabilidad ajustada por inflación

inflationary inflacionario, inflacionista

informant 1. declarante 2. soplón

information return declaración informativa

inheritance tax impuesto sobre herencia, impuesto sucesorio

in-house lawyer abogado interno, abogado de empresa

initial public offering (IPO) oferta pública inicial (OPI)

injunctive relief medidas cautelares

inland bill of lading conocimiento de embarque terrestre

in-law pariente por afinidad, pariente político

innocent until proven guilty presumido inocente mientras no se establezca legalmente la culpabilidad

insanity enajenación mental, demencia

inside information información privilegiada

insider trading delito del iniciado (Esp), utilización abusiva de información privilegiada, aprovechamiento de información confidencial

inspect v revisar

inspection revisión
>**inspection point** garita de revisión

inspector of elections escrutador

installment
>**installment debt** deuda abonada en cuotas
>**installment loan** préstamo reembolsable a plazos

instrumentality dependencia de un gobierno

insufficient funds fondos insuficientes

insurance seguro
>**insurance agent** agente de seguros
>**insurance carrier** empresa aseguradora
>**insurance coverage** cobertura de seguro

insurance policy póliza de seguro
insurance premium prima de seguro
intangible assets inmovilizado inmaterial, activo inmaterial
integral part parte integrante
intellectual property propiedad intelectual
intent-to-deny letter aviso de intención de negar el asilo político
intentional tort acto ilícito civil doloso
interbank market mercado interbancario
interchangeably indistintamente
inter-company pricing vinculación aduanera
interest 1. interés 2. participación
    interest expense gastos financieros, gastos por intereses
    interest income ingresos financieros, ingresos por intereses
    interest method of accounting método de acumulación a base de intereses
    interest rate tasa de interés, tipo de interés (Esp)
    interest-free loan préstamo sin interés
interim
    interim dividend dividendo provisional
    interim financial statements estados financieros provisionales
international
    International Chamber of Commerce (ICC) Cámara de Comercio Internacional (CCI)
    international law derecho internacional, derecho de gentes
    International Monetary Fund (IMF) Fondo Monetario Internacional (FMI)
interspousal entre cónyuges
introduction of evidence ofrecimiento de pruebas, promoción de pruebas
inure to the benefit v redundar en favor de, redundar en beneficio de
inventory existencias
investment
    investment grade bonds bonos calificados aptos para la inversión
    investment property propiedad de inversión
investment value valor de inversión
investor inversionista, inversor (Arg)
invitation to bid invitación a licitar, convocatoria a licitación
involuntary involuntario
    involuntary bankruptcy quiebra involuntaria [*es la solicitada por los acreedores*]
    involuntary manslaughter homicidio culposo
IRA (Individual Retirement Account) cuenta individual para jubilación
irresistible force fuerza irresistible
issue of law cuestión de derecho

issued and outstanding shares acciones emitidas y en circulación
issuer emisor
item on the agenda punto del orden del día
itemized deductions deducciones detalladas
Jane Doe Fulana de Tal
Job Training Partnership Act Ley del Pacto Federal-Estatal sobre
    la Capacitación Laboral
John Doe Fulano de Tal
join in the holy bonds of matrimony v unir en los sagrados lazos
    del matrimonio
joinder acumulación de acciones
joint
    joint account cuenta conjunta
    joint and several liability responsabilidad solidaria
    joint custody tenencia compartida (Arg)
— **joint tenants** condóminos
— **joint tortfeasor** coresponsable en un acto ilícito civil
journal entry asiento de diario
judgment
    judgment creditor acreedor por fallo, acreedor por sentencia
    judgment debtor deudor por fallo, deudor por sentencia
    judgment-proof sin recursos suficientes para liquidar una
        sentencia
judicial
    judicial notice reconocimiento de un hecho notorio
    judicial review revisión judicial
    judicial sale remate judicial
Judiciary Act of 1789 Ley Orgánica del Poder Judicial de 1789
jump bail v fugarse bajo fianza
junior
    junior debt deuda subordinada
    junior lien gravamen subordinado
junk bond bono basura [*bono especulativo de elevado riesgo*]
jurisdiction jurisdicción, competencia
    jurisdiction in personam competencia en razón de la persona
jurisprudence filosofía del derecho
juror jurado
jury
    jury box tribuna del jurado
    jury duty juraduría, servicio en un jurado
    jury tampering influencia en la deliberación del jurado
justice 1. justicia 2. Magistrado de la Corte Suprema
    justice of the peace juez de paz
    justice of the peace court juzgado de paz
justifiable homicide homicidio legítimo, homicidio inculpable,
    homicidio justificado

juvenile
  juvenile court tribunal de menores
  juvenile delinquency delincuencia de menores
  juvenile delinquent delincuente juvenil
  juvenile offender delincuente juvenil
kidnap v secuestrar
kidnapper secuestrador
kidnapping secuestro, rapto, plagio
Know all men by these presents Sépase por el presente, Conste por el presente
knowingly a sabiendas
known to me de mi conocimiento
labor
  labor certification certificación por el tipo de empleo
  labor dispute conflicto laboral
  labor law derecho del trabajo
  labor lawyer abogado laboralista
lame-duck president presidente cesante
landlocked
  landlocked country país mediterráneo
  — **landlocked property** predio enclavado
landlord locador, arrendador
— **landmark decision** sentencia de antología
last will and testament testamento
late charge intereses moratorios
latent defect vicio oculto
— **laughing heir statute** ley que establece un límite de parentesco mínimo para la sucesión intestada
launder money v blanquear dinero
law ley, derecho
  law and the regulations thereunder la ley y su reglamento
  law dictionary diccionario jurídico
  law enforcement officer agente de policía / *funcionario policial*
  law of diminishing returns ley de rendimientos decrecientes
  law of supply and demand ley de la oferta y la demanda
  — **law of the land** derecho de aplicación general en un país
  law offices estudio de abogados, bufete
  law reform reforma legislativa
  law review revista jurídica
  law school facultad de derecho
lawful
  lawful act hecho lícito
  lawful owner propietario legítimo
lawlessness 1. conductas al margen de la ley 2. anarquía
lead manager director de emisión, líder de emisión, jefe de fila (Esp)
— **leading question** pregunta sugestiva, pregunta tendenciosa

lean manufacturing manufactura esbelta (Méx)
lease contrato de arrendamiento, contrato de locación
    lease with purchase option contrato de arrendamiento con
        opción a compra
leased premises locales arrendados
leasehold improvement mejora al local arrendado
ledger libro mayor
    ledger account cuenta del mayor
    ledger balance saldo del mayor
    ledger entry asiento en el libro mayor
legacy legado
legal
    legal advice asesoría legal
    legal age mayoría de edad
    legal custody patria potestad
    legal dispute controversia judicial
    legal entity persona jurídica, persona moral (Méx)
    legal fees honorarios de abogados
    legal fiction ficción jurídica
    legal holiday feriado oficial
    legal instrument instrumento jurídico
    legal recruiting contratación de personal jurídico
    legal resident residente legal
    legal resident card tarjeta de residente legal
    legal secretary secretaria de abogado
    legal separation separación de cuerpos
    legal system ordenamiento jurídico
    legal tender moneda de curso legal
legalese lenguaje jurídico innecesariamente difícil de entender
legality legalidad
legatee legatario
legislator legislador
legitimate descent filiación legítima
lemon law ley sobre automóviles defectuosos
lender prestamista
less developed country país en vías de desarrollo
lessee arrendatario
lessor arrendador, arrendante
letter
    letter of credit carta de crédito
    letter of intent carta de intención
    letter of the law la letra de la ley
    letters rogatory carta rogatoria, exhorto
leverage apalancamiento
leveraged buyout adquisición forzada apalancada

lex
    lex loci contractus la ley del lugar en el que se celebró el contrato
    lex loci delictus la ley del lugar en el se cometió el delito civil
    lex loci rei sitae la ley de la situación
    lex non cogit ad impossibilia la ley no obliga a nadie a hacer cosas imposibles
liability responsabilidad
    liability insurance seguro de responsabilidad civil
libel difamación escrita
license licencia
lien gravamen
life
    life estate dominio vitalicio
    life imprisonment cadena perpetua
    life insurance seguro de vida
    life sentence pena de cadena perpetua, pena de reclusión mayor, pena de reclusión perpetua
limited
    limited liability company sociedad de responsabilidad limitada
    limited partner socio comanditario
    limited partnership sociedad comanditaria, sociedad en comandita
lineup confrontación, rueda de presos
link vínculo
liquidated damages penas convencionales
liquidator liquidador
liquidity liquidez
liquidity ratio razón de liquidez, coeficiente de liquidez
list a security on the exchange v admitir un valor a cotización
litigant litigante
litigate v litigar
litigation litigios
litigator abogado litigante
live birth nacimiento con vida
living will testamento vital (Pue), instrucciones de no prolongar la vida
load fund fondo de inversión que cobra comisión
loan préstamo
    loan loss reserve reserva para pérdidas sobre préstamos
    loan officer agente de préstamo
    loan origination fee comisión por tramitación de préstamo
    loan portfolio cartera de créditos, cartera crediticia
    loan proceeds recursos del préstamo
    loan processing tramitación del préstamo
    loan repayment devolución de préstamo

local
>**local counsel** asesores jurídicos locales
>**local currency** moneda nacional

lock-in rate tasa de interés garantizada, tasa de interés asegurada
lock-out cierre patronal
long arm statute ley de prórroga de competencia en razón de la persona
long-term largo plazo
>**long-term debt** deuda a largo plazo

loss of consortium pérdida del consorcio conyugal
lost profits lucro cesante
lower of cost and market costo o precio de mercado, el que resulte menor
lucid interval periodo de lucidez temporal [*durante el que una persona demente puede testar*]
lump sum precio alzado, suma global
luxury tax impuesto sobre el lujo, impuesto suntuario
lying in wait al acecho
magistrate juez de tribunal inferior
mailbox rule principio legal según el cual una oferta se considera aceptada en el momento de ponerse la aceptación en el buzón
maintenance costs costos de mantenimiento
make v
>**make partner v** incorporarse como socio de una firma
>**make someone whole v** resarcir plenamente a alguien

malice aforethought intención dolosa, malicia deliberada
malicious prosecution denuncia falsa, dolo procesal
malpractice mala praxis (Arg)
managerial position cargo administrativo
mandatory retirement jubilación forzosa
manhours horas hombre
manpower mano de obra
manslaughter homicidio
Mapp rule principio constitucional que establece que la prueba obtenida ilegalmente no puede usarse en un proceso penal [*se denomina también "exclusionary rule"*]
marital status estado civil
maritime law derecho marítimo
market mercado
>**market access** acceso al mercado
>**market disruption** perturbación del mercado
>**market maker** creador de mercado
>**market niche** nicho de mercado
>**market price** precio de mercado, precio de plaza
>**market value** valor en el mercado

marriage certificate acta de matrimonio, partida de matrimonio
marshal s alguacil

marshal the evidence v reunir las pruebas
massage the figures v maquillar los números
master agreement contrato marco
mastermind behind a crime autor intelectual de un delito
material esencial
>   **material error** error significativo
>   **material witness** testigo cuyo testimonio es esencial

materiality importancia relativa
materialman's lien gravamen del proveedor de materiales
maternity leave baja por maternidad (Esp), licencia por maternidad
matter on the agenda punto del orden del día
maturity vencimiento
may it please the court con la venia de la sala
mean v significar
>   **X shall mean** Por X se entiende

mechanic's lien gravamen de constructor
mediation mediación
medical
>   **medical examiner** médico forense
>   **medical hardship** dificultades de salud
>   **medical jurisprudence** medicina legal

meeting
>   **meeting of creditors** junta de acreedores
>   **meeting of minds** acuerdo de voluntades
>   **meeting of the board of directors** reunión/sesión del consejo
>   de administración/de la junta directiva/del directorio

member bank banco miembro de la Reserva Federal
memorandum
>   **memorandum decision** sentencia inmotivada
>   **memorandum of understanding** acuerdo preliminar

mens rea intención criminal, dolo penal
mental
>   **mental anguish** sufrimiento psíquico
>   **mental cruelty** crueldad psicológica

merge v fusionar
merger fusión
>   **merger clause** cláusula de integridad del contrato
>   **merger of rights** confusión de derechos

metes and bounds medidas y colindancias
military attaché agregado militar
minimum wage salario mínimo
minor menor de edad
minority interest participación minoritaria
minute book libro de actas
mirandize v informar al acusado de sus derechos constitucionales
miscarriage of justice error judicial que causa gravamen
>   irreparable

missing person persona desaparecida
mistrial juicio nulo
mitigating circumstances hechos extintivos, hechos impeditivos
mitigation of damages atenuación de daños y perjuicios
model
    model contract contrato tipo
    Model Penal Code Código Penal Tipo
modification modificación
monetary
    monetary damage daño pecuniario
    monetary standard patrón monetario
money
    money damages indemnización pecuniaria, resarcimiento
        pecuniario
    money desk mesa de dinero
    money laundering blanqueo de dinero
    money order giro postal
    money supply masa monetaria, oferta monetaria
monthly installment mensualidad
monthly payment mensualidad
moot court proceso simulado
moral turpitude vileza moral
mortgage hipoteca
    mortgage bank banco hipotecario
    mortgage broker corredor de hipotecas, corredor hipotecario
    mortgage company compañía hipotecaria
    mortgage financing financiamiento hipotecario
    mortgage insurance seguro hipotecario
    mortgage loan préstamo hipotecario
    mortgage loan application solicitud de préstamo hipotecario
    mortgage note pagaré hipotecario
    mortgage shopping búsqueda del mejor préstamo hipotecario
    mortgage underwriting evaluación de la solicitud de un
        préstamo hipotecario
mortgagee acreedor hipotecario
mortgagor deudor hipotecario
motion 1. petición 2. moción [*únicamente en la práctica
    parlamentaria*]
    motion for a directed verdict petición de veredicto mandado
        por el juez
    motion for a judgment notwithstanding the verdict (JNOV)
        petición de fallo contrario al veredicto
    motion for a more definite statement excepción de oscuridad
    motion for a new trial petición de nuevo juicio
    motion for change of venue petición de prórroga de
        jurisdicción

motion in limine solicitud in limine litis [*solicitud para excluir cierta prueba mientras se determine su admisibilidad*]

motion to extend time petición de prórroga de plazo

motion to suppress petición para que se excluya prueba obtenida ilegalmente

motive for the crime móvil del crimen

mug shot foto (de archivo policial), fotografía de delincuente

multi-step income statement estado de resultados de pasos múltiples [*muestra subtotales que se consideran útiles para evaluar la gestión del ente (resultado bruto de ventas, resultado de la actividad principal, etc.)*]

murder asesinato, homicidio calificado (Méx), homicidio agravado (Per)

murder for hire asesinato por recompensa

murder weapon arma asesina

murderer asesino

mutatis mutandis con los cambios que correspondan

mutual fund fondo mutual de inversiones (Ven), fondo común de inversión (Arg), fondo mutuo de inversión (Col), sociedad de inversión (Méx)

mutual mistake error mutuo

national s súbdito [*ciudadano de un país que está sujeto a las autoridades políticas de éste*]

a Mexican national un súbdito mexicano

natural person persona natural, persona física (Arg, Méx)

naturalization naturalización

negative

negative covenant obligación de no hacer

negative easement servidumbre negativa, servidumbre pasiva

negative goodwill fondo de comercio negativo, plusvalía negativa

negligence per se negligencia en sí misma

neighborhood vecindario

net

net book value valor contable neto

net income beneficio neto

net interest income margen financiero

net profit ganancia líquida

net rent multiplier multiplicador de ingresos netos

next of kin pariente más cercano, pariente más próximo

night depository buzón nocturno, caja nocturno

night shift jornada nocturna

no action letter recomendación de no procesar [*carta elaborada por un abogado de la Comisión de Valores recomendando a dicha Comisión no procesar en relación con un posible incumplimiento de sus normas*]

No littering. Prohibido arrojar basura.

notary public (en US.) sólo un Certificado de firmas

no load fund fondo de inversión que no cobra comisión
No loitering. Se prohibe permanecer en este lugar. Se prohibe la
estancia en este lugar a personas que no tengan negocios con
este establecimiento.
no-par value stock acciones sin valor nominal, acciones sin valor a
la par
No trespassing. Prohibido el paso.
nominal
    nominal damages daños nominales
    nominal value 1. valor nominal 2. valor reducido [*v.gr. "gifts of a
       nominal value"*]
nonappearance no comparecencia
nonassessable shares acciones liberadas (Méx)
non-bank bank sociedad financiera de objeto limitado (Méx)
nonmember bank banco fuera del Sistema Federal de Reserva
nonprofit organization organización sin fines de lucro
non-recognition transaction operación no sujeta a los impuestos
note pagaré, letra
    notes payable documentos por pagar, efectos a pagar (Esp)
    notes receivable documentos por cobrar, efectos a cobrar
       (Esp)
nothing contained in this agreement ninguna disposición del
    presente contrato
notice
    notice by publication notificación por edicto
    notice of default notificación de incumplimiento de pago
    notice of protest aviso de protesto
    notice to quit aviso de desocupación de un bien inmueble
       locado
notwithstanding no obstante, sin perjuicio de
    notwithstanding any provision to the contrary no obstante
       cualquier disposición en contrario
    notwithstanding the foregoing no obstante lo anterior
novation novación
null and void nulo y sin efecto
nunc pro tunc que tiene efecto retroactivo
nuncupative will testamento oral
oath of allegiance juramento de lealtad al país
obiter dictum lo dicho de paso en una sentencia
object v protestar
objection, your Honor! ¡protesto, su Señoría! (Esp)
obligee obligante, a quien se le debe la obligación
obligor obligado, quien debe la obligación
obliteration tachadura
obstruction of justice delito contra la administración de justicia
ocean bill of lading conocimiento de embarque marítimo
of age mayor de edad

of even date herewith con la misma fecha del presente
of legal age mayor de edad
of sound mind sano de juicio, en su sano juicio
off-balance-sheet items cuentas de orden
offense delito
offer oferta
office
>   **Office of Thrift Supervision** Dirección General de Cajas de
>   Ahorro
>   **office of vital statistics** registro civil
officer 1. funcionario 2. directivo
>   **The officers shall serve at the pleasure of the Board.** Los
>   directivos desempeñarán su cargo hasta tanto no sean
>   removidos por el consejo de administración/directorio/junta
>   directiva.
offsetting entry asiento compensatorio
offshore bank banco extraterritorial, banco offshore
on a quarterly basis trimestralmente
on a timely basis oportunamente
on duty de turno
on or about [date] con fecha X aproximadamente
on or before a más tardar el día X
one-sided agreement pacto leonino
ongoing costs costos continuos, gastos continuos
onus probandi carga de la prueba
open a judgment v reconsiderar una sentencia
opening statement declaración inicial
operating
>   **operating expenses** gastos de operación (Méx, Per), gastos de
>   explotación (Esp), gastos operativos (Arg)
>   **operating income** ingresos de operación (Méx, Per), beneficio
>   de operaciones, ingresos de explotación (Esp), ingreso
>   operativo (Arg)
operative part parte dispositiva
option opción
oral evidence prueba testimonial
order bill of lading conocimiento de embarque a la orden
ordinance ordenanza
organizational
>   **organizational chart** organigrama
>   **organizational meeting** asamblea constitutiva
organized crime delincuencia organizada
out-of-court settlement arreglo extrajudicial
out-of-wedlock ilegítimo, natural
outside directors directores externos [*no forman parte del personal
de la empresa*]
outsourcing externalización (Esp), tercerización (Arg)

outward bill of lading conocimiento de embarque a la salida
overbreadth doctrina según la cual una ley que atenta contra los derechos constitucionales es nula
overdraft sobregiro, giro en descubierto
    overdraft protection protección de sobregiro
overdraw v sobregirar, girar en descubierto
overdue vencido, retrasado
overhead gastos generales
    overhead expenses gastos generales
overpayment pago en exceso
overrule v denegar, anular
overseas market mercado exterior
overt act acto manifiesto
over-the-counter market mercado extrabursátil
overtime horas extraordinarias, horas extras
    overtime pay pago por horas extras
overview descripción general
owner dueño
    owner financing financiamiento por parte del dueño
    owner-occupied propiedad ocupada por el dueño
paid-in capital capital desembolsado, capital integrado, capital exhibido (Méx)
pain and suffering daño moral
Paperwork Reduction Act Ley de Reducción de Papeleo
par value valor a la par, valor nominal
paralegal asistente legal
paramount title título superior
parent company empresa matriz
parish court tribunal de parroquia [*en Luisiana*]
parliamentary procedure prácticas parlamentarias
parol evidence prueba verbal
    parol evidence rule principio según el cual un contrato por escrito no puede ser modificado por prueba verbal
parole libertad condicional
    parole board junta encargada de otorgar la libertad condicional
    parole revocation revocación de la libertad condicional
    parole violation incumplimiento con las condiciones de la libertad condicional
    parole violator quien no cumple con las condiciones de la libertad condicional
partial consolidation integración parcial (Esp), consolidación parcial
partner socio
partnership sociedad de personas
part-time job trabajo de tiempo parcial
party
    party in interest parte interesada

party to a contract parte de un contrato, parte contratante
party wall muro medianero, medianería
pass
    pass a law v aprobar una ley
    pass constitutional muster v ser compatible con la
        Constitución
    pass judgment v dictar sentencia
pass-through taxation transparencia fiscal
patent patente de invención
    patent application solicitud de patente
    patent claim reivindicación de patente
    patent defect defecto manifiesto, falla evidente [*en
        contraposición a un "latent defect"*]
    patent holder titular de una patente
    patent infringement violación de patente, infracción de patente
    patent rights derechos de patente
patentee titular de una patente
paternity suit juicio de filiación
pawn shop monte de piedad, montepío, casa de empeños
pawn v empeñar
pay
    payday día de cobro, día de raya (Méx)
    pay for itself v amortizarse
    pay stub talón de salario, recibo de sueldo, boleta de pago
        (Per)
    pay to the order of páguese a la orden de
payable
    payable in advance pagadero por adelantado
    payable in installments pagadero a plazos
    payable on demand pagadero a la vista
    payable upon delivery pagadero a la entrega
payment
    payment cap límite máximo de pago de hipoteca
    payment change date fecha de cambio de pago de hipoteca
    payment in full pago total
penalty penalidad
pendent jurisdiction poder de atracción
peppercorn rent alquiler nominal
per annum anual, por año
per capita por cabeza, por persona
per stirpes por estirpes
peremptory challenge recusación sin causa
perfection of a security interest perfeccionamiento de un derecho
    de garantía, de forma de hacerlo plenamente oponible a terceros
perform a contract v ejecutar un contrato
performance
    performance bond fianza de cumplimiento

performance indicators indicadores de rentabilidad
performance of a contract ejecución de un contrato
periodic alimony alimentos periódicos
perishable goods mercancías perecederas
perjury juramento falso
perpetrator of a crime autor material de un delito
person of age persona mayor de edad
personal
    personal jurisdiction competencia en razón de la persona
    personal property bienes muebles
    personal service notificación personal
personalty bienes muebles
petty
    petty cash caja chica
    petty cash voucher vale de caja chica
    petty larceny hurto de cuantía menor
phone tapping escuchas telefónicas
physical
    physical abuse malos tratos de obra [*causal de divorcio*]
    physical asylum asilo físico
    physical delivery entrega material
    physical property bienes materiales
picket line cordón huelguista
piece work trabajo a destajo
piercing the corporate veil desestimación de la personalidad
    jurídica, corrimiento del velo societario (Arg), levantamiento del
    velo corporativo (Esp)
piracy piratería
PITI (principal, interest, taxes, and insurance) capital, interés,
    impuestos, y seguros
place an order v hacer un pedido
placement colocación
plagiarism plagio
plagiarist plagiario
plagiarize v plagiar
plaintiff demandante, actor, parte demandante, parte actora
    plaintiff's standing legitimación activa
plat map plano catastrado
plea
    plea bargaining pacto sobre declaración de culpabilidad
    plea in abatement excepción de defecto legal
    plea of double jeopardy excepción de non bis in idem
plead guilty v declararse culpable
pleadings alegaciones
please take notice that por el presente le hago saber que
pledge of allegiance juramento de fidelidad
plot plan plano de trazado

poisoned fruit prueba inadmisible por vicio de producción
police
    police lineup rueda de presos (Esp), confrontación (Méx)
    police officer agente de policía
    police report atestado policial
    police station comisaría
political asylum asilo político
poll a jury v escrutar los votos del jurado
pooling of interests combinación de los balances de dos empresas
    que se fusionan
    pooling of interests method of accounting método de la
        fusión de intereses
portfolio management gestión de cartera
pose a issue v plantear un asunto
post a bond v prestar fianza
post office box apartado (Col, Dom, Gua, Hon, Méx, Nic, Pan, Sal),
    casilla (Arg, Bol, Chi, Ecu, Par, Uru)
power coupled with an interest poder vinculado a derechos que
    sean legalmente suficientes para sustentar su carácter
    irrevocable
practice law v ejercer la abogacía
practice of law s la abogacía
preference
    preference alien extranjero con preferencia para inmigrar
    preference category clasificación en el sistema de preferencias
preferred stock acciones preferentes
prejudicial error error perjudicial
preliminary
    preliminary hearing audiencia preliminar
    preliminary injunction mandamiento judicial preliminar
premium prima
prepaid expenses gastos anticipados
prepayment pago por adelantado
    prepayment clause cláusula de pago por adelantado
    prepayment penalty penalidad por pagos adelantados
preside over a meeting v presidir una asamblea/reunión/sesión
presumption of innocence presunción de inocencia
pretermitted heir heredero preterido
price escalation escalamiento de precios
price oneself out of the market v perder clientela por poner
    precios muy altos
price range nivel de precio
prima facie evidence pruebas suficientes a primera vista
principal 1. capital 2. mandante
    principal and interest (P&I) capital e interés
    principal place of business domicilio comercial
    principal residence residencia principal

prior inconsistent statement previa declaración contradictoria
priority date fecha de preferencia
private
    private enterprise iniciativa privada
    private placement colocación privada
pro forma invoice factura pro forma
probable cause causa probable
probate a will v convalidar un testamento, homologar un
    testamento
probate
    probate court tribunal sucesorio
    probate proceeding juicio testamentario
probation libertad vigilada
probative value valor probatorio
procedural law derecho procesal, derecho adjetivo
process server emplazador
procurement contract contrato de suministro
product liability responsabilidad civil del fabricante
    product liability insurance seguro de responsabilidad civil de
        fabricantes
professional partnership sociedad civil
profit and loss ganancias y pérdidas
profit-sharing plan plan de participación en las utilidades
promissory estoppel impedimento promisorio [*La institución que
    más se le aproxima en el derecho civil, sin ser lo mismo, es la
    llamada defensa de "nemo audiendus propriam turpitudinem
    allegans".*]
promissory note pagaré, vale
property propiedad
    property damage daño material, daño patrimonial
    property developer promotor inmobiliario
    property insurance seguro sobre la propiedad
    property owner propietario, dueño
    property tax impuesto sobre bienes
proprietary de propiedad exclusiva
prorate v prorratear
prospectus prospecto, folleto bursátil (Esp)
protective tariff arancel proteccionista
provider proveedor
provision disposición
provisional acceptance recepción provisoria
public
    public assistance funds fondos de asistencia pública
    public auction almoneda pública, subasta pública
    public defender defensor de pobres, defensor de oficio
    public holiday fiesta oficial
    public official funcionario público

public policy orden público
public prosecutor agente del ministerio público, agente fiscal
public servant funcionario
public utilities empresas de servicios públicos
purchase s compra, adquisición
    purchase method of accounting método de la compra
    purchase money security interest garantía real que se
        constituye para asegurar el pago del precio de venta
    purchase order orden de compra
    purchase price precio de compra
purchase v comprar, adquirir
purchaser comprador, adquirente
    purchaser for value adquirente a título oneroso
purchasing power poder adquisitivo
purpose
    for purposes of para los efectos de, a los efectos de
    The purpose of this Agreement is ... El presente Contrato
        tiene por objeto
qualified
    qualified endorsement endoso con reservas
    qualified opinion dictamen con salvedades, dictamen con
        reservas
qualify for v reunir las condiciones necesarias para
quarter trimestre
quarterly trimestral
quasicontract cuasicontrato
quick ratio índice de solvencia inmediata, coeficiente de
    disponibilidades
quiet enjoyment uso y goce pacífico
quitclaim deed escritura de finiquito
quorum quórum
    a quorum was present and voting throughout siempre hubo
        quórum cuando se votó
    although less than a quorum aunque no haya quórum
quote s cotización
quote v cotizar
race discrimination discriminación racial
raider persona natural o jurídica que intenta tomar control de una
    sociedad mediante la adquisición de la mayoría de sus acciones
rainmaker abogado que atrae a clientes para su bufete
raise s aumento de sueldo
rank pari passu v tener igual prelación
rap sheet antecedentes penales
rape violación
rapist violador
rate cap límite de la tasa de interés
raw materials materias primas

reach
>   **reach a verdict v** dictar un veredicto, pronunciar un veredicto
>   **reach the age of majority v** alcanzar la mayoría de edad

read
>   **it reads as follows** es del tenor siguiente
>   **it shall be amended to read as follows** se reformará para quedar como sigue

real estate bienes raíces
>   **real estate agent** agente inmobiliario
>   **real estate taxes** impuestos inmobiliarios

real property bienes inmuebles
realtor agente inmobiliario
realty bienes raíces, bienes inmuebles
reasonable man buen padre de familia
reasons beyond their control motivos ajenos a su voluntad
rebuttable presumption presunción juris tantum
receivables financing descuento de créditos en libros
recidivist reincidente
recitals antecedentes
reckless endangerment imprudencia temeraria
recklessness temeridad
record date fecha en el registro
recording fees costos de inscripción
recover damages v obtener reparación judicial, obtener indemnización por daños y perjuicios
recurring expenses gastos periódicos
reduce to writing v hacer constar por escrito
refinance v refinanciar
refinancing refinanciamiento
refugee refugiado
>   **Refugee Act of 1980** Ley de Refugiados de 1980
>   **refugee status** condición de refugiado

refund reembolso
registered
>   **registered security** título nominativo
>   **registered trademark** marca registrada

registrar of vital records oficial del registro civil
registration statement declaración de venta de valores
regulations el reglamento [*singular en castellano*]
regulatory framework marco regulatorio
relative
>   **relative by affinity** pariente por afinidad
>   **relative by marriage** pariente por afinidad, pariente político

release from prison s excarcelación
release v
>   **release a mortgage v** cancelar una hipoteca
>   **release from an obligation v** relevar de una obligación

release on his own recognizance v poner en libertad bajo promesa

relevant evidence prueba pertinente

reluctant witness testigo renuente

remainderman nudo propietario

remand a case v devolver una causa

removal

    removal of a director remoción de un consejero/director

    removal of an immigrant repatriación de un inmigrante

render an opinion as to the financial statements v dictaminar los estados financieros

rent alquiler, renta (Méx)

rent v alquilar, rentar

renter arrendatario; inquilino

repayment of principal reembolso del capital

repayment period plazo de pago

repeal of a law derogación de una ley

repeat offender delincuente reincidente

replevin reivindicación

repo reporto (Méx, Gua), pase (Arg), operación de doble (Esp)

report a crime v denunciar un delito

reportable income ingreso que se debe declarar

represent and warrant v declarar y garantizar

representations and warranties declaraciones y garantías

res judicata cosa juzgada

resident vecino

resolutions adopted without a meeting resoluciones tomadas fuera de asamblea

responsible for enforcing a law responsable de la aplicación de una ley

rest a case v terminar la presentación de pruebas

restitution restitución

restraint of trade atentado contra la libertad de comercio

retail

    retail banking banca de menudeo, banca minorista

    retail price precio al detal, precio de venta al público, precio al por menor

retailer vendedor minorista, detallista

retain counsel v contratar abogado

retainer anticipo de honorarios, iguala

retire a debt v saldar una deuda

return a verdict v pronunciar un veredicto

return receipt requested se solicita acuse de recibo

returned check cheque rechazado

revenue ingresos

reversal revocación

reverse
    reverse discrimination discriminación inversa
    reverse mortgage hipoteca revertida
reversionary interest nuda propiedad
revolving line of credit línea revolvente de crédito (Méx)
rider cláusula adicional, anexo
right
    right of way servidumbre de paso
    right to bear arms derecho a portar armas
    right to counsel derecho a recibir asesoría jurídica
    right to privacy derecho a la intimidad, derecho a la vida
        privada
    right to proceed in forma pauperis beneficio de pobreza (Méx,
        Per), beneficio de justicia gratuita (Esp), privilegio de
        pobreza (Chi)
    right to sue notice aviso de derecho a demandar
    right to work state estado cuyas leyes garantizan el derecho
        de trabajo sin afiliarse a un sindicato
riparian rights derechos ribereños
ripe for decision autos en estado de dictar sentencia
risk-based capital capital ajustado por el nivel de riesgo
roadshow gira promocional
robbery robo
robe (of a judge) toga
robing room sala contigua a la sala de vistas
rule against double jeopardy non bis in idem
rule
    a rule of law un principio de derecho
    the rule of law la supremacía del derecho
    **Rules of Conciliation and Arbitration of the International
        Chamber of Commerce** Reglamento de Conciliación y
        Arbitraje de la Cámara de Comercio Internacional
run on a currency movimiento especulativo (contra una moneda)
safe deposit box caja de seguridad
safe harbor estipulación en las leyes tributarias que ampara a una
    persona que ha tratado de cumplir con la ley
salary sueldo
sale
    sale buyback venta con readquisición
    sale in lieu of foreclosure venta en lugar de ejecución
        hipotecaria
    sale-leaseback venta con compromiso de arrendamiento
        [*operación en la que el dueño de un inmueble vende el
        mismo a un inversionista, y luego se lo arrienda al
        comprador bajo términos previamente acordados*]
    sale price precio de liquidación
    sales commission comisión de venta

sales contract contrato de compraventa
sales price precio de venta
sales tax impuesto a las ventas
salvage value valor residual
savings ahorros
    savings account cuenta de ahorros
    savings and loan association caja de ahorros [*Se denomina también "thrift" en inglés.*]
    savings bank caja de ahorros
scene of the crime lugar de los hechos
scienter s dolo [*literalmente quiere decir "a sabiendas", pero se usa en inglés como sustantivo*]
scope of employment esfera del trabajo, ámbito del trabajo
scrap value valor de desecho
sealed bid oferta en sobre cerrado
search warrant orden de registro
seasonal
    seasonal employment trabajo por temporada
    seasonal income ingreso por trabajo temporal
seasoned loans créditos muy cotizados [*créditos en los cuales se han hecho pagos en término durante un lapso de tiempo suficiente como para evidenciar la intención de pago del prestatario*]
second a motion v apoyar una moción [*en la práctica parlamentaria*]
second
    second mortgage segunda hipoteca
    second-degree murder asesinato sin premeditación
    second-tier bank banco de segundo categoría, banco de importancia secundaria
secondary
    secondary liability responsabilidad secundaria
    secondary mortgage mercado secundario de hipotecas
    secondary mortgage lender prestamista del mercado secundario
    secondary public offering oferta pública en el mercado secundario
secret ballot votación secreta
section of a law or contract artículo
secure a loan v 1. garantizar un préstamo 2. obtener un préstamo
secured loan préstamo garantizado
securities títulos valores
    Securities and Exchange Commission Comisión de Valores y Bolsas
    Securities Exchange Act of 1934 Ley de Bolsas de Valores de 1934
    securities portfolio cartera de valores

security 1. título valor 2. garantía
    security interest garantía real; una prenda sobre X
sedition sedición
seed capital capital inicial, capital generador
self
    self defense defensa legítima
    self-dealing negocios en beneficio propio
    self-employed quien trabaja por cuenta propia
    self-help autotutela
sell v
    sell at a loss v vender con pérdida
    sell short v vender en descubierto
sell-by date fecha límite de venta
seller
    seller take-back mortgage hipoteca financiada por el vendedor
    seller's market mercado favorable al vendedor
selling agent agente de ventas
semi-annual semestral
senior
    senior debt deuda prioritaria
    senior judge juez decano
seniority antigüedad
sentence pena, condena
sentence v imponer una pena
sentencing imposición de la pena
separation of powers división de poderes
sequester v aislar
sequestration aislamiento
serial killer asesino en serie, asesino múltiple
serve a sentence v cumplir una condena
service
    service by publication citación por edictos
    service mark marca de servicio
    service of process emplazamiento
    service of the complaint traslado de la demanda
set for trial v fijar fecha para juicio
settlement 1. liquidación 2. arreglo extrajudicial
severability divisibilidad
severance pay indemnización por despido
sex discrimination discriminación sexual
sexual harassment hostigamiento sexual, acoso sexual
share
    shares issued and outstanding acciones emitidas y en
        circulación
shareholder accionista
    shareholder agreement pacto entre accionistas

shareholders' equity patrimonio neto, capital contable (Méx), fondos propios

shareholders' meeting junta de accionistas (Bol, Chi, Ecu, Esp, Nic, Per), asamblea de accionistas (Arg, Col, Cos, Gua, Hon, Méx, Par, Uru, Ven)

Shepardize a case v utilizar el libro de citas de Shepard para seguir la suerte que cada precedente haya corrido a través de todas las nuevas ejecutorias que se hayan dictado, para enterar al investigador jurídico de cuáles son las últimas decisiones judiciales en la materia

shoplifter ratero de tiendas, hurto de tienda

shoplifting raterismo en tiendas

short-term a corto plazo

shrink wrap license agreement acuerdo implícito según el cual se aceptan las condiciones de licencia de un paquete de software una vez abierto el envoltorio plástico

sick leave baja por enfermedad (Esp), licencia por enfermedad

sight draft giro a la vista, letra a la vista

sign off on something v dar el visto bueno

signatory to an agreement parte firmante de un contrato

sinking fund fondo de amortización

sit v

> **Judges sit on courts of various types** Los jueces ejercen sus funciones en tribunales de diversos tipos.
>
> **sit on a committee** formar parte de una comisión
> **sit on a jury** ser miembro de un jurado
> **The Court sits in Washington** La Corte tiene su sede en Washington.

sit-down strike huelga de brazos caídos, huelga con ocupación

slander difamación verbal

> **slander of title** jactancia

slip opinion sentencia publicada individualmente inmediatamente después de su dictamen

slush fund fondo para sobornos políticos

small businessman dueño de negocio pequeño

So ordered. Cúmplase.

social security benefits beneficios de seguro social

soft

> **soft currency** moneda débil
> **soft loan** préstamo subvencionado [*préstamo a una tasa de interés inferior al de mercado, que se concede con el fin de fomentar alguna actividad determinada*]
> **soft market** mercado débil

sole proprietor empresario por cuenta propia

> **sole proprietorship** empresa unipersonal

solicitor general abogado que representa al gobierno ante la Corte Suprema de los Estados Unidos

Son of Sam law ley que impide a los delincuentes lucrar con la difusión de sus delitos en los medios
Speaker of the House Presidente de la Cámara de Representantes en el Congreso estadounidense
special
    special drawing rights derechos especiales de giro
    special meeting asamblea extraordinaria, junta extraordinaria [*de accionistas*]; reunión extraordinaria, sesión extraordinaria [*del directorio/consejo de administración*]
    special use permit permiso especial que autoriza a variar el tipo de uso previamente planificado para una zona urbana
specific performance ejecución forzosa
speedy trial juicio sin demora
spendthrift trust fideicomiso para pródigos
split shift jornada partida
spot
    spot market mercado de contado
    spot price precio al contado
    spot transaction operación al contado
spousal support manutención del cónyuge
spread sobretasa, diferencial (Esp)
spreadsheet hoja de cálculo
staff s personal, plantilla
staff v dotar de personal
stagflation estanflación [*una situación donde coexisten inflación y estancamiento económico*]
staggered terms plazos escalonados
stale bill of lading conocimiento de embarque con fecha vencida
stand trial v ser procesado
standard of living nivel de vida
standing legitimación
    standing committee comité permanente
start-up expenses gastos de primer establecimiento
state
    state of emergency estado de emergencia
    state of siege estado de sitio
    state of war estado de guerra
    state-of-the art technology tecnología de vanguardia
statute ley
    statute of frauds requisito de hacer constar un acto jurídico por escrito
    statute of limitations prescripción
    statutes at large compilación de leyes
statutory legal, establecido por ley [*no es lo mismo que "estatutario"*]
    statutory crime delito tipificado [*en contraposición a los creados por el common law*]

statutory lien gravamen establecido por ley [*gravamen creado por ley en lugar de por contrato, como por ejemplo un gravamen por impuestos no pagados*]

statutory offense delito tipificado

statutory rape estupro

stay s

    stay of deportation suspensión del auto de deportación (mientras dure el litigio)

    stay of enforcement suspensión de ejecución

stay a trial v suspender un juicio

steal v hurtar

stipulation estipulación

stock

    stock broker agente de bolsa, comisionista de bolsa

    stock dividend dividendo en acciones

    stock market analysis análisis bursátil

    stock option plan plan de opción de compra de acciones

    stock purchase agreement contrato de compraventa de acciones

    stock split división de una acción en varias

    stock swap oferta pública de intercambio (OPI)

stockholders' equity patrimonio neto, capital contable (Méx)

stop-gap loan crédito de emergencia

strict

    strict liability responsabilidad objetiva

    strict scrutiny examen riguroso de la constitucionalidad de una ley

strike from the record v eliminar de los autos

strike price precio de ejercicio de una opción

sua sponte de oficio

subject matter jurisdiction competencia en razón de la materia

sublease subarriendo

sublessee subarrendatario

sublessor subarrendador

sublet v subarrendar

submit v ofrecer para la consideración

subornation of perjury

subpoena citación, citatorio (Méx)

    subpoena duces tecum citación para aportar pruebas

subsequent ulterior, posterior, subsiguiente

subsidiary ledger libro mayor auxiliar

subsidize v subvencionar

subsidy subvención

substantive law derecho sustantivo, derecho de fondo

substituted service notificación por cédula

successful bidder adjudicatario

sue for damages v entablar acción de indemnización por daños y perjuicios

suffer emotional distress v sufrir daños morales

summon v emplazar

summons cédula de emplazamiento

sum-of-the-years-digits method método de la suma de los dígitos de los años

sunset law ley que requiere que una dependencia gubernamental pruebe periódicamente al poder legislativo la necesidad de su existencia

sunshine law ley que requiere que las reuniones de dependencias gubernamentales sean abiertas al público

superior court tribunal de primera instancia [*en los estados de Alaska, Arizona, California, Connecticut, Delaware, Distrito de Columbia, Georgia, Maine, Nueva Hampshire, Nueva Jersey, Carolina del Norte, Rhode Island, Vermont y Washington*]

supermajority mayoría reforzada

supervening cause causa sobreviniente

supporting documentation comprobantes

suppression motion solicitud de exclusión de pruebas

supremacy clause cláusula de la Constitución estadounidense según la cual las leyes federales prevalecen sobre las leyes estatales que son contrarias a aquellas

Supreme Court Tribunal Supremo (Cub, Esp, Pue), Suprema Corte (Dom, Méx), Corte Suprema (Arg)

    Supreme Court of Appeals Corte Suprema de Virginia Occidental

surcharge recargo

surety bond fianza de caución

surplus productivity superávit de productividad

surrender value valor de rescate

surrogate mother madre portadora

suspended sentence condena condicional

swap intercambio

swear in v tomar juramento a

swindler estafador

swing shift jornada mixta

sympathy strike huelga de solidaridad

syndicated loan préstamo sindicado [*crédito otorgado en forma conjunta por varias instituciones financieras*]

tag-along rights derechos de adhesión [*derecho de los accionistas minoritarios (establecidos en un pacto entre accionistas) de adherirse a la venta de las acciones de los accionistas mayoritarios*]

take v

    take an oath v prestar juramento

    take effect v entrar en vigor, entrar en vigencia

take judicial notice v tomar nota de un hecho notorio
take office v entrar en funciones
take out insurance v contratar un seguro
take someone's deposition v tomar declaración a alguien
take the Fifth v ejercer el derecho a no declarar contra sí mismo
take the floor v hacer uso de la palabra
take the stand v atestiguar, sentarse en el estrado de testigos, subirse al estrado
take under advisement v tomar en estudio
take or pay contract contrato firme de compraventa
takehome pay salario neto
takeover
    takeover bid oferta pública de adquisición (OPA)
    takeover of a bank by the regulators intervención en un banco
tangible
    tangible assets bienes corporales
    tangible evidence prueba real
tax impuesto, contribución
    tax advisor asesor fiscal
    tax assessment estimación de la base imponible
    tax audit auditoría fiscal
    tax avoidance evasión lícita de impuestos
    tax benefit beneficio impositivo, beneficio tributario
    tax bracket categoría impositiva
    tax break exoneración fiscal, alivio fiscal
    tax burden carga tributaria, carga fiscal
    tax collector recaudador de impuestos
    tax consultant asesor fiscal
    tax credit crédito fiscal
    tax cut reducción en los impuestos
    tax deductible deducible de impuestos, desgravable
    tax deduction gasto deducible
    tax evasion fraude fiscal, evasión fiscal, evasión de impuestos
    tax exempt libre de impuestos
    tax exemption franquicia impositiva, franquicia tributaria
    tax expenditures gastos fiscales
    tax exposure riesgo fiscal
    tax haven paraíso fiscal
    tax holiday exoneración temporal de impuestos
    tax incentive incentivo tributario
    tax law derecho tributario
    tax lawyer abogado tributarista
    tax lien gravamen por impuestos no pagados
    tax loophole escapatoria tributaria
    tax penalty multa fiscal
    tax rate tasa impositiva

tax refund reembolso fiscal, reembolso tributario
tax relief desgravación impositiva
tax return declaración de impuestos
tax shelter refugio fiscal
tax withholding retención de impuestos
tax write-off amortización fiscal, deducción tributaria por
    pérdida
tax year año gravable
taxable
    taxable event hecho imponible
    taxable income renta gravable, renta imponible
taxpayer contribuyente, sujeto pasivo
teller 1. cajero [*en un banco*] 2. escrutador [*persona que cuenta los
    votos en una elección*]
temporary restraining order (TRO) orden inhibitoria temporaria
tenant arrendatario, inquilino
    tenant at sufferance precarista
tender offer oferta pública de adquisición (OPA)
term 1. plazo, término [*de un contrato*] 2. periodo de sesiones [*de un
    tribunal*]
    term of art término de jerga jurídica
    term of office mandato
    terms of reference (TOR) términos de referencia, pliego de
        condiciones, bases de la licitación
testamentary capacity capacidad para testar
testify v testificar
theft hurto
theory of the case criterio jurídico, base jurídica
thereafter de allí en adelante
thereof del mismo, de la misma, de los mismo, de las mismas
thereupon acto seguido
third party tercera
    third party defendant litisconsorte
three strikes law ley sobre la reincidencia de delincuentes
thrift caja de ahorros [*también llamado "S&L"*]
through bill of lading conocimiento de embarque directo
ticker symbol clave de pizarra (Méx)
Tier I capital capital primario, capital básico
Tier II capital capital secundario, capital suplementario
time
    time-barred prescrito
    time deposit depósito a plazo
    time draft letra de cambio a plazo
    Time is of the essence. Los plazos deben cumplirse
        estrictamente.
    time value of money valor del dinero a través del tiempo
timeliness oportunidad

to the best of my knowledge and belief a mi leal saber y entender
to the full extent of the law como mejor proceda en derecho
to whom it may concern a quien pueda interesar, a quien corresponda
toll the statute of limitations v interrumpir la prescripción
tolling of the statute of limitations interrupción de la prescripción
tort acto ilícito civil
    tort liability responsabilidad civil extracontractual
tortfeasor autor de un acto ilícito civil
trade comercio
    trade barrier barrera comercial
    trade creditor acreedor comercial
    trade deficit déficit de balanza comercial, déficit externo
    trade dress imagen comercial
    trade name nombre comercial
    trade secret secreto industrial
    trade surplus superávit de la balanza comercial
    trade-in value valor de cambio
trade v
    trade in v entregar como parte del pago
trademark marca de comercio, marca de fábrica
    trademark fee derechos de marca registrada
trading comercio, intercambio mercantil
    trading floor piso de remates, parquet (Esp), corro (Méx, Ven)
    trading session rueda de bolsa
transfer tax impuesto de transferencia
transfer v transferir
transferee adquirente, cesionario
transferor enajenante
travel allowance asignación para gastos de viaje, asignación para viáticos
treasury stock acciones propias en tesorería
treble damages daños triplicados
trespass s entrada sin autorización en propiedad ajena
trespass v entrar sin autorización en propiedad ajena
trespasser intruso
trial juicio, proceso
    trial balance balance de comprobación
    trial by jury juicio por jurados
    trial court tribunal de primera instancia
    trial de novo nuevo juicio
    trial lawyer abogado litigante
trier of fact juzgador de hecho [*En un juicio con jurado, el jurado es el juzgador de hecho. En un juicio sin jurado, el juez mismo es el juzgador de hecho.*]
trover acción de recuperación de un bien mueble
true copy copia fiel

trust fideicomiso
    trust fund fondo fiduciario
    trust indenture escritura de fideicomiso
trustee fiduciario
trusteeship cargo fiduciario
trustor fideicomitente
truth in lending divulgación de todos los términos de un préstamo
turnkey contract contrato llave en mano
ultra vires acts extralimitación de funciones
unappealable inapelable, irrecurrible
uncertificated security título escritural
under age menor de edad
under arrest detenido
under duress bajo coacción
under oath bajo juramento
under penalty of perjury bajo pena de perjurio
undercapitalized con capital insuficiente
underdeveloped property suburbanizada
underinsured motorist coverage cobertura de conductor no
    suficientemente asegurado
underpayment pago insuficiente
undersigned (the) infrascrito, quien suscribe, el abajo firmante
undertake v obligarse
undisclosed no revelado, oculto
    undisclosed principal mandante no revelado
undue influence influencia indebida
unearned income ingreo no derivado del trabajo
unemployment desempleo
    unemployment insurance seguro de desempleo
    unemployment rate tasa de desempleo
unencumbered libre de gravámenes
unfair
    unfair business practices prácticas desleales de comercio
    unfair competition competencia desleal
uniform
    Uniform Commercial Code (UCC) Código Uniforme de
        Comercio
    Uniform Simultaneous Death Act Ley Uniforme sobre la
        Conmoriencia
unincorporated sin personalidad jurídica
uninsured motorist coverage cobertura de conductor no
    asegurado
unintentional tort cuasidelito
union
    union dues cuotas sindicales
    union label marca sindical
    union worker agremiado

unit
 unit price precio unitario
 unit value valor unitario
United Nations Naciones Unidas
 United Nations Commission on International Trade Law
  (UNCITRAL) Comisión de las Naciones Unidas para el
  Derecho Mercantil Internacional
 United Nations Convention on Contracts for the
  International Sale of Goods Convención de las Naciones
  Unidas sobre los Contratos de Compraventa Internacional de
  Mercaderías
United States Estados Unidos
 U.S.-based bank banco con sede en los Estados Unidos
 U.S. mainland los Estados Unidos continentales
 U.S. national ciudadano de los Estados Unidos
unjust enrichment enriquecimiento ilícito, enriquecimiento ilegítimo,
 enriquecimiento injusto
unlawful
 It shall be unlawful queda prohibido
 unlawful act hecho ilícito
unless otherwise agreed to in writing a menos que se especifique
 lo contrario por escrito/salvo disposición en contrario por escrito
unless otherwise provided salvo disposición en contrario, a menos
 que se disponga lo contrario
unless otherwise specified herein a menos que aquí se
 especifique lo contrario
unqualified opinion dictamen sin reservas, dictamen sin
 salvedades
unreasonable search and seizure registro y embargo arbitrario
unsecured
 unsecured creditor acreedor quirografario
 unsecured debt deuda no garantizada
 unsecured loan préstamo sin garantía
untapped market mercado no explotado
until further notice hasta nuevo aviso
until their successors have been elected and qualified hasta que
 sus sucesores hayan sido elegidos y habilitados
untimely extemporáneo
upfront costs costos iniciales
upkeep expenses gastos para el mantenimiento de la propiedad
upon acceptance en el momento de ser aceptado
upon demand a solicitud
upon information and belief a mi leal saber y entender
upon notice previa notificación
upon request previa solicitud
upon submittal a la presentación
upon the earlier of lo que ocurra antes

upon the first to occur of lo primero que ocurra
use one's best efforts v hacer sus mejores esfuerzos para
utilities servicios públicos
utility patent modelo de utilidad
vacate
   vacate a judgment v anular una sentencia
   vacate the premises v desocupar el local
value-added tax impuesto al valor añadido, impuesto al valor
   agregado
variance permiso de desviación de la política edilicia vigente
vehicular manslaughter homicidio causado con un vehículo
venture capital capital de riesgo
   venture capitalist inversionista arriesgado
venue jurisdicción
verbal abuse malos tratos de palabra [*es una causal de divorcio*]
verbatim al pie de la letra
verdict veredicto
versus contra [*En castellano 'versus' significa 'hacia'. Es un
   anglicismo usarlo con el significado de 'contra'.*]
vest v
   **The executive power shall be vested in the President of the
   United States of America.** El poder ejecutivo recae en el
   Presidente de los Estados Unidos de América.
   vested interest interés adquirido
   vested rights derechos adquiridos
veto a bill v anular un proyecto de ley
vicarious liability responsabilidad por los actos de otro
violation of a law violación a una ley
violent crime delito de sangre
visitation schedule régimen de visitas
vital records actas del registro civil
voice vote votación por lista
void for vagueness nulo por imprecisión en la tipificación [*se dice
   de una ley penal*]
voir dire interrogatorio preliminar de un jurado o testigo
voluntary voluntario
   voluntary bankruptcy quiebra voluntaria [*es la solicitada por el
   deudor*]
   voluntary departure salida voluntaria [*de los Estados Unidos*]
   voluntary lien gravamen voluntario
   voluntary manslaughter homicidio intencional, homicidio
   doloso
voter registration inscripción electoral
voting
   voting by proxy votación por poder
   voting by roll call votación nominal
   voting by secret ballot votación secreta

voting by show of hands votación a mano alzada, votación económica
voting stock acciones con derecho a voto
voucher comprobante, vale
wage and hour laws leyes sobre salarios mínimos y jornadas máximas
waive v renunciar a
waiver renuncia
    waiver of immunity renuncia a la inmunidad
    waiver of notice of a meeting renuncia al derecho de ser notificado de la convocatoria
    waiver of premium renuncia a la prima
want of jurisdiction falta de jurisdicción
warehouse almacén, depósito, bodega (Chi, Col, Cos, Méx)
warehouse receipt certificado de depósito
warrant v garantizar
warranty garantía
    warranty of merchantability and fitness for a particular purposes garantía de que el producto puede ser objeto de comercio y de que es adecuado para el fin al que está destinado
watered stock acciones emitidas por menos de su valor nominal
waybill hoja de ruta
wear and tear desgaste natural, uso natural
welfare previsión social
    welfare state estado benefactor, estado de bienestar
well-known mark marca notoria
whereabouts paradero
whereas por cuanto, considerando que
whichever comes first lo que suceda primero; sea cual fuere la fecha que se cumpla primero
whichever is greater el que sea mayor
whip diputado responsable de la disciplina de su grupo parlamentario
whistleblower soplón, denunciante [*empleado que informa sobre actividades ilícitas en su empresa*]
white
    white collar crime delito de guante blanco
    white goods línea blanca
    white knight caballero blanco [*persona física o jurídica que adquiere una empresa para evitar que la adquieran otros*]
whole life insurance seguro de vida entera
wholesale venta al por mayor
    wholesale bank banco de segundo piso
    wholesale price precio mayorista
wholesaler mayorista, comerciante al por mayor
wholly-owned subsidiary filial enteramente controlada

wildcat strike huelga salvaje
will testamento
willful intencional
window dressing maquillaje
wire transfer giro telegráfico
with the caveat that con la salvedad de que
withdraw v
    withdraw a bid v rescindir una oferta
    withdraw a motion v rescindir un pedimento
    withdraw a suit v desistir de la demanda
    withdraw funds v retirar fondos
within
    the within letter la carta adjunta
    within or without the United States dentro o fuera de los
        Estados Unidos
    within the meaning of en los términos de
witness testigo
    witness for the defense testigo de descargo
    witness for the prosecution testigo de cargo
    witness stand estrado de testigos, banquillo de los testigos
    witness to a will testigo testamentario
witness v 1. atestiguar, testificar 2. presenciar, ser testigo de
    This Agreement witnesseth Por el presente contrato se hace
        constar; Conste por el presente contrato
    witness my hand and seal Doy fe con mi firma y sello.
workers' compensation indemnización por accidentes de trabajo
working capital capital de trabajo
worksheet hoja de trabajo
World Bank Banco Mundial
writ auto
    writ of habeas corpus auto de hábeas corpus
    writ of mandamus despacho [*diligencia judicial cuya ejecución*
        se ordena a un juez o tribunal subordinado]
written agreement acuerdo por escrito
wrongful death muerte por negligencia de otro
wrongfully indebidamente, injustamente
Y2K compliance cumplimiento con los requisitos del año 2000
yield rentabilidad
Your Honor su Señoría (Esp), vuestra Señoría (Arg), C. Juez (Méx,
    Ven)

APPENDIX 1
SPANISH ABBREVIATIONS AND ACRONYMS

AEIE	Spa	Agrupación Europea de Interés Económico
AFJP	Arg	Administradoras de Fondos de Jubilaciones y Pensiones
AFORE	Mex	Administradores de Fondos para el Retiro
AJA	Spa	Actualidad Jurídica Aranzadi
ALDF	Mex	Asamblea Legislativa del Distrito Federal
ANSSAL	Arg	Administración Nacional del Seguro de Salud
ApNDL	Spa	Apéndice al Nuevo Diccionario de Legislación
AVB	Spa	agencia de valores y bolsa
BCBA	Arg	Bolsa de Comercio de Buenos Aires
BCRA	Arg	Banco Central de la República Argentina
BCRP	Per	Banco Central de Reserva del Perú
BOE	Spa	Boletín Oficial del Estado
BUL	Per	boleta única de litigante
BVL	Per	Bolsa de Valores de Lima
CC	Col	cédula de ciudadanía
CCA	Col	Código Contencioso-Administrativo
CCSS	Cos	Caja Costarricense de Seguro Social
CGPJ	Spa	Consejo General del Poder Judicial
CI	Chi	cédula de identidad
CIF	Spa	código de identificación fiscal
CNAE	Spa	Código Nacional de Actividades Económicas
CNBV	Mex	Comisión Nacional Bancaria y de Valores
CNMV	Spa	Comisión Nacional del Mercado de Valores
CONASEV	Per	Comisión Nacional Supervisora de Valores
CPA	Arg	Colegio Público de Abogados
CPCC	Arg	Código Procesal Civil y Comercial
CPCCN	Arg	Código Procesal Civil y Comercial de la Nación
CPCE	Arg	Consejo Profesional de Ciencias Económicas
CSJ	Col	Corte Suprema de Justicia
CTS	Per	compensación por tiempo de servicios
CUFIN	Mex	cuenta de utilidad fiscal neta
CUIL	Arg	Clave Única de Identificación Laboral
CUIT	Arg	Clave Única de Identificación Tributaria
DGI	Arg	Dirección General Impositiva
DGR	Ecu	Dirección General de Rentas
DIEX	Ven	Dirección Nacional de Identificación y Extranjería
DNI	Spa	documento nacional de identidad
DOF	Mex	Diario Oficial de la Federación
DS	Bol, Chi	Decreto Supremo
EIRL	Cos	empresa individual de responsabilidad limitada
FCI	Arg	fondo común de inversión
FIAMM	Spa	fondo de inversión en activos del mercado monetario
FICORCA	Mex	Fideicomiso para la Cobertura de Riesgos Cambiarios
FII	Spa	fondo de inversión inmobiliaria

FIM	Spa	fondo de inversión mobiliaria
FOGADE	Ven	Fondo de Garantía de Depósitos y Protección Bancaria
IAE	Spa	impuesto sobre actividades económicas
IBI	Spa	impuesto sobre bienes inmuebles
ICAC	Spa	Instituto de Contabilidad y Auditoría de Cuentas
ICONA	Spa	Instituto para la Conservación de la Naturaleza
IFE	Mex	Instituto Federal Electoral
IGJ	Arg	Inspección General de Justicia
IGV	Per	impuesto general a las ventas
IMAGRO	Uru	impuesto a las actividades agropecuarias
IMCP	Mex	Instituto Mexicano de Contadores Públicos
IMPI	Mex	Instituto Mexicano de la Propiedad Industrial
IMSS	Mex	Instituto Mexicano del Seguro Social
INCE	Ven	Instituto Nacional de Cooperación Educativa
INDEC	Arg	Instituto Nacional de Estadística y Censos
INDET	Mex	Indicadores Estadísticos en Tiempo Real
INMEX	Mex	Índice México
INOS	Arg	Instituto Nacional de Obras Sociales
IPC	Mex	Índice de Precios y Cotizaciones
IPSA	Ven	Instituto de Previsión Social del Abogado
IPSS	Per	Instituto Peruano de Seguridad Social
IRIC	Uru	impuesto a la renta de industria y comercio
IRPF	Spa	impuesto sobre la renta de las personas físicas
ISLR	Ven	impuesto sobre la renta
ISPT	Mex	impuesto sobre productos del trabajo
ITCP	Arg	Instituto Técnico de Contadores Públicos
IUSI	Gua	impuesto único sobre inmuebles
IVMC	Ven	Instituto Venezolano del Mercado de Capitales
J y D	Col	Jurisprudencia y Doctrina
LCOJ	Gua	Ley Constitutiva del Organismo Judicial
LE	Per	libreta electoral
LGS	Per	Ley General de Sociedades
LMV	Mex	Ley del Mercado de Valores
LMZAA	Mex	Ley Federal sobre Monumentos y Zonas Arqueológicas, Artísticas e Históricas
LN	Mex	Ley del Notariado del Distrito Federal
LNCM	Mex	Ley de Navegación y Comercio Marítimo
LNN	Mex	Ley de Nacionalidad y Naturalización
LO	Cos	Ley de Ocupantes
LOAPF	Mex	Ley Orgánica de la Administración Pública Federal
LOBC	Cos	Ley Orgánica del Banco Central
LODE	Spa	Ley Orgánica del Derecho a la Educación
LOPA	Ven	Ley Orgánica de Procedimientos Administrativos
LOPJF	Mex	Ley Orgánica del Poder Judicial Federal
LORM	Ven	Ley Orgánica de Régimen Municipal
LOTFF	Mex	Ley Orgánica del Tribunal Fiscal de la Federación
LPC	Mex	Ley Federal de Protección al Consumidor

LQ	Mex	Ley de Quiebras y Suspensión de Pagos
LR	Mex	Ley de Responsabilidades
LSI	Mex	Ley de Sociedades de Inversión
LT	Mex	Ley sobre la Celebración de Tratados
LVGC	Mex	Ley de Vías Generales de Comunicación Federal
M/Cte.	Col	moneda corriente
MEFF	Spa	Mercado Español de Futuros Financieros
MGJ	Pan	Ministerio de Gobierno y Justicia
MMEX	Mex	Mercado para la Mediana Empresa Mexicana
NDL	Spa	Nuevo Diccionario de Legislación Aranzadi
NIF	Spa	número de identificación fiscal
NIT	Col, Ven	número de identificación tributaria
OPA	Spa	oferta pública de adquisición
OPAH	Spa	oferta pública de adquisición hostil
OPV	Spa	oferta pública de venta
OTAC	Ven	Oficina Técnica de Administración Cambiaria
PAAG	Col	porcentaje de ajuste sobre el año gravable
PAMI	Arg	Protección y Asistencia Médica Integral
PGC	Spa	Plan General de Contabilidad
PIP	Per	Policía de Investigaciones del Perú
PTU	Mex	participación de los trabajadores en las utilidades
RAPU	Arg	Registro de Asociaciones de Profesionales Universitarios
RCL	Spa	Repertorio Cronológico de Legislación
REI	Per	resultado por exposición a la inflación
RFC	Mex	Registro Federal de Causantes
RFT	Mex	Registro Federal de Trámites
RIF	Ven	Registro de Información Fiscal
RJ	Spa	Repertorio de Jurisprudencia
RJN	Arg	Reglamento para la Justicia Nacional
RMV	Per	remuneración mínima vital
RO	Ecu	Registro Oficial
RT	Arg	Resolución Técnica
RTC	Spa	Repertorio del Tribunal Constitucional
RTCT	Spa	Repertorio del Tribunal Central de Trabajo
RUC	Bol, Ecu	Registro Único de Contribuyentes
RUT	Chi	Rol Único Tributario
RVP	Arg	renta vitalicia previsional
SACA	Ven	sociedad anónima de capital autorizado
SAICA	Ven	sociedad anónima inscrita de capital abierto
SAEel	Arg	sociedad anónima editora e impresora
SCLV	Spa	Servicio de Compensación y Liquidación de Valores
SDIB	Spa	Sociedad de Difusión de Información Bursátil
SENIAT	Ven	Servicio Nacional Integrado de Administración Tributaria
SENTRA	Mex	Sistema Electrónico de Negociación, Transacción, Registro y Asignación
SERPAJ	Uru	Servicio de Paz y Justicia
SIBE	Spa	Sistema de Interconexión Bursátil Español

SIEX	Ven	Superintendencia de Inversiones Extranjeras
SII	Chi	Servicio de Impuestos Internos
SIM	Spa	sociedad de inversión mobiliaria
SIMAV	Spa	sociedad de inversión de capital variable
SIVA	Mex	Sistema Integral de Valores Automatizado
SJF	Mex	Semanario Judicial de la Federación
SMV	Per	sueldo mínimo vital
SNC	Mex	sociedad nacional de crédito
SUNAT	Per	Superintendencia Nacional de Administración Tributaria
TEM	Ven	títulos de estabilización monetaria
TIIE	Mex	tasa de interés interbancaria de equilibrio
TJCE	Spa	Tribunal de Justicia de las Comunidades Europeas
TP	Col	tarjeta profesional
TSJDF	Mex	Tribunal Superior de Justicia del Distrito Federal
UF	Chi	unidad de fomento
UIT	Per	unidad impositiva tributaria
UPAC	Col	unidad de poder adquisitivo constante
URP	Per	unidad de referencia procesal
UT	Ven	unidad tributaria
UTE	Arg	unión transitoria de empresas
VECA	Uru	valor estimado de contratación anual

AAA	American Arbitration Association
	American Automobile Association
	Agricultural Adjustment Act
ABA	American Bar Association; American Bankers Association
ADA	Americans with Disabilities Act
ADEA	Age Discrimination in Employment Act
ADR	American depositary receipt
	alternative dispute resolution
AFDC	Aid to Families with Dependent Children
AFL-CIO	American Federation of Labor and Congress of Industrial Organizations
AIME	Average Indexed Monthly Earnings
aka	also known as
AMA	American Medical Association
ANSI	American National Standards Institute
APA	Administrative Procedure Act
APR	annual percentage rate
ASE	American Stock Exchange
ATA	American Translators Association
BIA	Board of Immigration Appeals
C&D	cease and desist
CAB	Civil Aeronautics Board
CBD	central business district
CBOE	Chicago Board of Options Exchange
CC&R	covenants, conditions and restrictions
CDC	Centers for Disease Control
CEO	chief executive officer
CFO	chief financial officer
CFR	Code of Federal Regulations
CIA	Central Intelligence Agency
CLE	continuing legal education
CLS	Critical Legal Studies
CLU	Chartered Life Underwriter
CMO	collateralized mortgage obligation
COB	close of business
COO	chief operating officer
CPI	Consumer Price Index
CPSA	Consumer Product Safety Act
CPSC	Consumer Product Safety Commission
CUSIP	Committee on Uniform Securities Identification Procedures
D&B	Dun & Bradstreet
dba	doing business as
DEA	Drug Enforcement Administration
DIDMCA	Depository Institutions and Monetary Control Act

DMV	Department of Motor Vehicles
DOJ	Department of Justice
DOL	Department of Labor
DOT	Department of Transportation
DUI	driving under the influence (of alcohol or drugs)
DWI	driving while intoxicated
EBIT	earnings before interest and taxes
ECPA	Electronic Communications Privacy Act
EEOC	Equal Employment Opportunity Commission
EFT	electronic funds transfer
EPA	Environmental Protection Agency
ERISA	Employee Retirement Income Security Act
ERTA	Economic Recovery Tax Act
ESA	Endangered Species Act
ESOP	Employee Stock Ownership Plan
EST	Eastern Standard Time
F.2d	Federal Reporter, Second Series
F.3d	Federal Reporter, Third Series
F. Supp.	Federal Supplement
FAA	Federal Aviation Administration
FASB	Financial Accounting Standards Board
FBI	Federal Bureau of Investigation
FCC	Federal Communications Commission
FCPA	Foreign Corrupt Practices Act
FCRA	Fair Credit Reporting Act
FDA	Food and Drug Administration
FDCA	Food, Drug and Cosmetic Act
FDIC	Federal Deposit Insurance Corporation
FECA	Federal Elections Campaign Act
FERC	Federal Energy Regulatory Commission
FHA	Federal Housing Administration
FHLMC	Federal Home Loan Mortgage Corporation
FICA	Federal Insurance Contributions Act
FIRREA	Financial Institutions Reform, Recovery and Enforcement Act
fka	formerly known as
FLSA	Fair Labor Standards Act
FNMA	Federal National Mortgage Association
FOIA	Freedom of Information Act
FRB	Federal Reserve Board
FRCP	Federal Rules of Civil Procedure
FRE	Federal Rules of Evidence
FRM	fixed rate mortgage
FTC	Federal Trade Commission
FTCA	Federal Tort Claims Act
GAAP	generally accepted accounting principles
GAO	General Accounting Office
GATT	General Agreement on Tariffs and Trade

GDP	gross domestic product
GEM	growing equity mortgage
GIC	guaranteed investment contract
GNMA	Government National Mortgage Association
GNP	gross national product
HMO	health maintenance organization
HUD	Housing and Urban Development
HVAC	heating, ventilation and air conditioning
ICC	International Chamber of Commerce
IDB	Industrial Development Bond
ILSA	Interstate Land Sales Disclosure Act
IMF	International Monetary Fund
INS	Immigration and Naturalization Service
IRA	individual retirement account
IRR	internal rate of return
IRS	Internal Revenue Service
JD	juris doctor
L/C	letter of credit
LBO	leveraged buyout
LHA	Local Housing Authority
LIFO	last in, first out
LLC	limited liability company
LLLP	limited liability limited partnership
LLP	limited liability partnership
LSAT	Law School Admission Test
LUI	land use intensity
M&A	mergers and acquisitions
MBA	master of business administration
MD&A	management's discussion and analysis
MLP	master limited partnership
MOE	merger of equals
MOU	memorandum of understanding
mpg	miles per gallon
mph	miles per hour
MSA	metropolitan statistical area
MSPB	Merit Systems Protection Board
N/A	not applicable
NAFTA	North American Free Trade Agreement
NASA	National Aeronautics and Space Administration
NASDAQ	National Association of Securities Dealers Automated Quotations
NEPA	National Environmental Policy Act
NIRA	National Industrial Recovery Act
NLRB	National Labor Relations Board
NYSE	New York Stock Exchange
OBRA	Omnibus Budget Reconciliation Act of 1990
OCC	Office of the Comptroller of the Currency

OID	original issue discount
OPIC	Overseas Private Investment Corporation
OSHA	Occupational Safety and Health Administration
OTC	over the counter
OTS	Office of Thrift Supervision
P&L	profit and loss
PEBES	Personal Earnings and Benefit Estimate Statement
POS	point of sale
PTO	Patent and Trademark Office
PUHCA	Public Utility Holding Company Act
QDRO	qualified domestic relations order
QMB	Qualified Medicare Beneficiary
R&D	research and development
RCRA	Resource Conservation and Recovery Act
REIT	real estate investment trust
REMIC	real estate mortgage investment conduit
RESPA	Real Estate Settlement Procedures Act
RFP	request for proposals
RICO	Racketeer Influenced and Corrupt Organizations Act
RLA	Railway Labor Act
RRM	renegotiable rate mortgage
SBA	Small Business Administration
SEC	Securities and Exchange Commission
SEP	simplified employee pension
SWIFT	Society for Worldwide Interbank Financial Telecommunications
TOR	terms of reference
TVA	Tennessee Valley Authority
UCC	Uniform Commercial Code
UFTA	Uniform Fraudulent Transfer Act
UK	United Kingdom
UNCITRAL	United Nations Commission on International Trade Law
UPA	Uniform Partnership Act
UPC	Uniform Probate Code
USCA	United States Code Annotated
USDA	United States Department of Agriculture
USLW	United States Law Week
USPS	United States Postal Service
VA	Veterans Administration
VOA	Voice of America
VRM	variable rate mortgage
WATS	Wide Area Telecommunications Service
WHO	World Health Organization

APPENDIX 3
BIBLIOGRAPHY

Argentina   Cabanellas de Torres, Guillermo. Diccionario jurídico elemental. Buenos Aires: Editorial Heliasta, 1994.
DeSanto, Víctor. Diccionario de derecho procesal. Buenos Aires: Editorial Universidad, 1995.
Fowler Newton, Enrique. Diccionario de contabilidad y auditoría. Buenos Aires: Ediciones Macchi, 1994.
Greco, O. and A. Godoy. Diccionario contable y comercial. Buenos Aires: Valletta Ediciones, 1996.   .
Ossorio, Manuel. Diccionario de ciencias jurídicas, políticas y sociales. Buenos Aires: Editorial Helista, 1994.

Chile   Diéguez, M. Isabel and Rosa María Lazo. Textos legales: terminología básica. Santiago: Ediciones Universidad Católica de Chile, 1995.

Ecuador   Biblioteca Edino. Diccionario de definiciones legales. Quito: Edino, 1991.

Mexico   Barandiarán, Rafael. Diccionario de términos financieros. Mexico City: Trillas, 1996.
Cortina Ortega, Gonzalo. Prontuario bursátil y financiero. Mexico City: Trillas, 1995.
DePina, Rafael and Rafael DePina Vara. Diccionario de derecho. Mexico City: Editorial Porrúa, 1996.
Enríquez Palomec, Raúl. Léxico básico del contador. Mexico City: Trillas, 1994.
Instituto de Investigaciones Jurídicas. Diccionario jurídico mexicano. 4 volumes. Mexico City: Porrúa, 1997.
Palomar de Miguel, Juan. Diccionario para juristas. Mexico City: Mayo Ediciones, 1981.
Reyes, Rigoberto Reyes. Diccionario de términos fiscales. Mexico City: Tax Editores Unidos, 1997.

Peru   Chanamé Orbe, Raúl. Diccionario jurídico moderno. Lima: Editorial San Marcos, 1995.
Chanamé Orbe, Raúl. Diccionario de derecho constitucional. Lima: Editorial San Marcos, 1993.
Pérez Caballo, Aurelio. Diccionario jurídico peruano. Lima: Centro de Documentación Andina, 1987.

Spain   Fundación Tomás Moro. Diccionario jurídico Espasa. Madrid: Editorial Espasa Calpe, 1991.
Infante Lope, Julia. Diccionario jurídico. Barcelona: Editorial De Vecchi, 1984.
Ribó Durán, Luis. Diccionario de derecho. Barcelona: Bosch, 1995.

Uruguay   Couture, Eduardo J. Vocabulario jurídico. Buenos Aires: Ediciones Depalma, 1993.

Venezuela   Banco Provincial. Manual de términos bancarios. Caracas: Banco Provincial, 1992.
Nieschulz de Stockhausen, Elke and Gisela Bosque Pax. Léxico normalizado de terminología legal. Caracas: Biblioteca Nacional, 1993.

APPENDIX 4
NUMBERS IN SPANISH-SPEAKING COUNTRIES

In the following countries, the <u>period</u> is used as the decimal point, and the <u>comma</u> is used to separate thousands. Thus, in these countries, 1,000 = one thousand, and 1.00 = one.

Dominican Republic
El Salvador
Guatemala
Honduras
Mexico
Nicaragua
Panama
Peru
Puerto Rico
United States

In the following countries, the <u>comma</u> is used as the decimal point, and the <u>period</u> is used to separate thousands. Thus, in these countries, 1.000 = one thousand, and 1,00 = one.

Argentina
Bolivia
Chile
Colombia
Costa Rica
Cuba
Ecuador
Paraguay
Spain
Uruguay
Venezuela